Practical Legal Aid

Fourth Edition

Ian Pollard

Partner in Pollard Coutts & Heseltine, in Wakefield

© Longman Group UK Ltd 1990
First published 1969
Second edition 1976
Third edition 1982
Fourth edition 1990

ISBN 0 85121 6773

Published by
Longman Law, Tax and Finance
Longman Group UK Ltd
21–27 Lamb's Conduit Street, London WC1N 3NJ

Associated offices
Australia, Hong Kong, Malaysia, Singapore, USA

Phototypeset by Input Typesetting Ltd, London SW19 8DR
Printed in Great Britain by
Biddles of Guildford Ltd, Surrey

Contents

Part II: Criminal Legal Aid

Part III: Civil Legal Aid

Table of Statutes

Table of Statutory Instruments

XX TABLE OF STATUTORY INSTRUMENTS

Part I

General

Chapter 1

Introduction

A democracy does not rest solely on free elections held every few years. Elections cannot guarantee the rights and freedoms of any people, only the choice as to which band of politicians should be entrusted with power. If that trust is broken, if power is abused, as all too often it is, even in a democracy, the courts with its judges acting without fear or favour are the only place to which people can turn for justice and protection. A strong and accessible legal system is therefore one of the pillars of a true democracy, without which it will crumble and fall.

1 The importance of legal aid

If access to the legal system is not readily available to all classes of society, not only does that system fail, but the laws which have been designed as the shield of the wronged, the abused and the oppressed might as well not exist. Magna Carta, a Bill of Rights, a European Convention on Human Rights are worthless if a large section of the population cannot afford to obtain their protection in the courts.

In England we regard ourselves as being fortunate to live in a country which is regarded worldwide as the bedrock of democracy, but it might be argued that our rights, whether to read a book or to travel the length and breadth of the land without let or hindrance from authority or even simply to challenge authority, have over the past few years been seriously eroded. Who would have thought that in the 1980s it would be in Britain, that a book would be banned which was freely available in the rest of the world, that two or three men making a perfectly lawful journey on a motorway could be prevented from continuing it and forced to return to their towns and villages. For years we

3

in England have been brought up to regard powers such as these as existing only in countries ruled by dictatorships or oppressive and authoritarian regimes. We have not yet woken up to the implications of *Spycatcher*, the miners strike or to the sight of police on horseback chasing fleeing pickets across a field.

The concealing of evidence useful to the defence, the fabrication of evidence even in major cases, appears to have become widespread. More provincial police forces are the subject of major investigations, than would have been thought credible even only a few years ago. The fatherly Dixon of Dock Green image is dead. No less a person than the Director of Public Prosecutions himself has now been forced to accuse the police of obstructing his department.

Moreover, we are faced with more than just amorphous distant large-scale police forces. The last two decades have also seen the introduction of large-scale local authorities and health authorities and even larger international corporations. The nature of such beasts when challenged is to bring down a veil of secrecy and hope that the nuisance who is trying to assert his rights will eventually tire and withdraw from the unequal combat. Only the lawyers can attempt to tear open that veil for public scrutiny by the courts.

Customs and Excise are given more and more draconian powers, but there is little protection for the tax payer when the VAT man errs or abuses his rights. Then it is only 'a mistake' and many months of correspondence, much of which will be ignored, may eventually produce a half hearted apology but not a penn'orth of compensation.

(a) The limitations of the system

The provision of legal aid for proceedings before tribunals is woefully inadequate. The only tribunal proceedings within the scope of civil legal aid are the Employment Appeal Tribunal and the Lands Tribunal, while with the benefit of ABWOR representation can be obtained for proceedings before Boards of Visitors in HM prisons and before the Mental Health Review Tribunal. Despite the powers which tribunals have to affect people's lives and their finances, and despite the complexities of the law which tribunals often have to apply, there has been stalwart resistance to any increase in the scope of legal aid. A spouse whose marriage has broken down can look for financial support to a plethora of various types of legal aid and a person who has been injured in a car accident or at his place of work is fully entitled to have legal aid to recover damages for his injuries and other losses. A person whose career lies in ruins because he has been unfairly dismissed, perhaps after many years of faithful service and at an age when alternative employment prospects are dim, is left to fight alone without support from the public purse or at best with an unqualified 'friend' from a trade union to assist him. The opportunity was presented with the new Act and a new set of regulations to remedy this gross injustice. Sadly it was an opportunity which was deliberately rejected. The spirit of the Victorian 'poor law' administration appears still to be with us.

The financial limits for the availability of legal aid are extremely low. It is noteworthy that the exemption from the statutory charge of the first £2,500 of property recovered or preserved in matrimonial proceedings has remained the same for many years, despite intervening inflation, especially in property prices. If a similar attitude had been adopted with regard to the financial resources of applicants for legal aid, then many of the criticisms of the present scheme could not be made. As it is millions have, over the past ten years, become ineligible for legal aid, two and half million of those since 1987. In the year to March, 1989 the use of the Green Form Scheme fell by 7.69 per cent and of ABWOR by 5.32 per cent ((1990) *The Lawyer*, 10 October). Legal aid has now virtually become a scheme for the comparatively poor, but many of those whose financial resources are beyond the limits of the schemes, are by no means rich or even well off, and they certainly cannot afford to fund, or perhaps even more importantly defend, litigation on a private basis.

In some respects the Board is largely powerless, save with regard to its administration expenses, for it is the government of the day which holds the purse strings. In the present climate of opinion there can be little hope of any increase in the general availability of legal aid. Thus we shall continue to see, at least over the near future, the continued whittling away of rights and freedoms which English men and women have held dear for many a year. Their inability to gain access to justice may in the end see the crumbling of one of those great pillars of our democracy.

(b) Future developments

The future will see the Legal Aid Board exercising the powers which the Act has given it, to grant franchises and to enter into contracts for the provision of legal aid services by persons or firms who have no professional legal qualifications. But in many respects the profession has brought this on its own head.

Where the Board is wrong, is to equate competence, experience and ability with size. It is often in the larger firms where legal aid work is abandoned by the partners as they grow older and seek more lucrative fields. The Board's initial proposals for franchising with its requirements for at least £40,000 per annum of legal aid fees, would have resulted in the ossification of the profession to the disadvantage of the consumer. The best criminal litigation and matrimonial work is often carried out by the small new firm seeking to build up its practice, and perhaps without, at that stage in its development, much conveyancing or commercial work. Because such a firm is new does not mean that its sole principal or partners are inexperienced. They may have broken away from a larger firm or left public service, perhaps in the prosecution field. To deprive such firms of legal aid work not only reduces competition, it would have killed stone dead the possibility of many new law firms being set up. The established firms would have been laughing, especially in smaller provincial towns, for their work would have been guaranteed. All large firms were small once, and the Board must leave its ivory tower and start examining the effects of its future proposals on the man in the street.

Some firms with large criminal practices are now openly admitting that the bulk of their criminal legal aid work is being carried out by 'para-legals', employees with no professional qualifications or training, and one suspects in some cases, far too little experience. It is claimed that because of the low level of legal aid remuneration, the use of unqualified para-legals is likely to spread rapidly. If the bulk of preparation of criminal or other legal aid work is carried out in this manner, the profession can hardly complain if the Board takes the same view and offers contracts and franchises to professionally unqualified organisations. The profession is also by the same means destroying its own argument that legal aid work is badly paid. There is no reason to pay a professional rate of remuneration for work which does not apparently require professional skill, training and expertise.

The answer of course is that it does require these, and that much of the work carried out by so called para-legals will, depending on the extent to which they are supervised, be neither efficient nor competent. An experienced solicitor can take a reasonably straight forward proof of evidence in thirty to forty minutes. Others may well take over an hour, but the present system is such that there is no method of rewarding competence and efficiency. If it takes an inefficient firm twice as long as an efficient one to perform a particular task, the Board will gladly pay twice as much to the inefficient firm because it has neither the staff nor, one suspects, the skill to make a proper judgement of what is a reasonable time for that particular task. What it certainly will not do is allow the efficient firm an uplift in its remuneration to recognise the savings which it has made to the Board by its efficiency. An extension of the fixed fee system will not provide an answer, for fixed fees can be an encouragement to the indolent and to shoddy work. If fixed too low, they will also encourage still further the use of para-legals. An ambulance-man performs an invaluable task but he would never dream of carrying out the functions of a surgeon.

One of the main tenets of the whole legal aid system is to ensure that wherever possible the Board can recoup its costs where a litigant is successful. Where a legally aided defendant in criminal proceedings is successful however, an order for his costs to be paid out of central funds, as would normally happen with a private client, is specifically prohibited by the Prosecution of Offences Act 1985. The Board has therefore to spend a considerable part of its all too meagre resources in paying the legal fees of people who are acquitted. There is no reason why the Board's resources should be dissipated in this way, and a change in the system could well go a long way to restoring the Board's finances and in making not only criminal but other types of legal aid more widely available.

Chapter 2

The 1988 Legal Aid Scheme

1 The new legislation

The Legal Aid Act 1988 (LAA 1988), repealed, save for a few transitional provisions, the whole of the 1974 Act. All the old regulations were also repealed and replaced with new ones. Despite this wholesale slaughter, much of the former legislation was repeated in the new, albeit with differently numbered regulations and sections.

The major change effected by the Act was the creation of the Legal Aid Board which took over the full responsibility from the Law Society for the administration of the legal aid scheme. Already the Board has set about re-organising and reducing the number of area offices, and it is to be hoped that this effort will prove to be cost-effective.

Another change which is of major practical importance and which affects any assessment of the financial resources of a person who applies, either for legal aid or for advice and assistance, is that the financial resources of a man and woman living together as husband and wife are to be treated as if they were the resources of the applicant. This recognises the growing preference of people for cohabitation, rather than formal marriage. At long last the common law wife and the common law husband have been officially recognised in legislation.

Other changes effected both by the Act and the regulations are given in detail in the relevant chapters, but are summarised below.

(a) Advice and assistance

Subject to certain exceptions, wills and conveyancing services no longer fall within the scope of the Green Form Scheme. A solicitor must require information from a client to enable him to decide whether the making of a particular will does fall within the scope of the scheme.

The old method of ascertaining how much work could be carried out under the Advice and Assistance Scheme, was by reference to a fixed financial limit of £50 or £90 for a green form divorce. These are now replaced with limits based on a time factor, namely two hours work or three in the case of an undefended petition for divorce. Costs are assessed by the Area Director, subject to the right to apply for a review to the Area Committee and for limited appeals from such reviews to a committee appointed by the Board.

The Legal Advice & Assistance (Scope) Regulations 1989 apply Pt III of the Act relating to advice and assistance to Assistance by Way of Representation (ABWOR) for certain proceedings in a magistrates' court or county court and before a Mental Health Review Tribunal and boards of prison visitors.

(b) Civil legal aid

The Civil Legal Aid General Regulations 1989 run to 150 regulations. The new provisions include one which states that an assisted person's solicitor can be required to certify that it is reasonable for a legal aid certificate to continue. There is a duty to report to the Board the non-acceptance of a reasonable offer of a settlement or of a payment into court. New provision is made for payment on account, both of solicitor's costs and disbursements, as well as of counsel's fees. Work done immediately prior to the issue of an emergency certificate can be deemed to be done under the certificate in certain circumstances. Solicitors must notify counsel if their fees are reduced or disallowed so that counsel can require his instructing solicitor to challenge any such reduction or review. Assisted persons who have a financial interest in the taxation of costs, as for example where the statutory charge applies, are given an opportunity to take steps to safeguard their interests.

As from 9 April 1990, there are increased financial eligibility limits which apply only to applications relating to a claim in respect of personal injuries.

(c) Criminal legal aid

Statutory factors for the grant of criminal legal aid in trials in the magistrates' court and Crown Court and also for appeals in the Crown Court are now set out in s 22 of the 1988 Act. A new application form (Form 1) for criminal legal aid is prescribed and the use of this is mandatory. Justices' Clerks are given power to refuse applications for legal aid, whereas formerly their power was limited to determining only applications which they could grant. Counsel must be provided with a copy of a legal aid order by his instructing solicitor. Many of the Legal Aid in Criminal and Care Proceedings (Gen Regulations) 1989 are applied to care proceedings. Remuneration rates for court duty solicitors attending a magistrates' court under a duty solicitor scheme are increased by 25 per cent for work done on a bank holiday or on Saturday or Sunday. The lower limit on fees for advice and assistance given at a police station has been removed.

2 Format of the legislation

The Act is split into seven parts, four of which deal with all aspects of specific types of legal aid. Part III (ss 8 to 13) covers all the various advice and assistance schemes including ABWOR and is supplemented by the following regulations:

Legal Advice and Assistance (Scope) Regulations 1989 (SI 1989 No 550); Legal Advice and Assistance Regulations 1989 (SI 1989 No 340); Legal Advice and Assistance (Amendment) Regulations 1989 (SI 1989 No 560); Legal Advice and Assistance (Duty Solicitor) (Remuneration) Regulations 1989 (SI 1989 No 341); Legal Advice and Assistance at Police Stations (Remuneration) Regulations 1989 (SI 1989 No 342); and the Legal Advice and Assistance (Amendment) Regulations 1990 (SI 1990 No 486).

Part IV (ss 14–18) deals with Civil Legal Aid including emergency certificates and summary jurisdiction certificates for authorised proceedings in the magistrates' courts as well as the statutory charge. The supplementing regulations are:

Civil Legal Aid (General) Regulations 1989 (SI 1989 No 339); Civil Legal Aid (Assessment of Resources) Regulations 1989 (SI 1989 No 338); Civil Legal Aid (Matrimonial Proceedings) Regulations 1989 (SI 1989 No 549); and the Civil Legal Aid (Assessment of Resources) (Amendment) Regulations 1990 (SI 1989 No 338).

Part V (ss 19–26) deals with all aspects of Criminal Legal Aid including a provision as to claims for payment for Advice and

Assistance where a Criminal Legal Aid order is subsequently made. The supplementing regulations are:

Legal Aid in Criminal and Care Proceedings (General) Regulations 1989 (SI 1989 No 344); Legal Aid in Criminal and Care Proceedings (Costs) Regulations 1989 (SI 1989 No 343); and the Legal Aid in Criminal and Care Proceedings (Costs) (Amendment) Regulations 1990 (SI 1990 No 489).

Part VI (ss 27–30) deals with special cases, namely care proceedings and contempt proceedings. The regulations governing the grant of legal aid for and assessment of costs in care proceedings are the same as for Criminal Legal Aid.

3 Definitions

Section 2 of the Act defines the meaning of 'advice', 'assistance', 'representation', 'legally assisted person' and 'person'. These definitions apply to the whole of the legal aid scheme wherever the expressions are used. Further definitions are contained in s 43.

(a) 'Advice'

'Advice' means oral or written advice on the application of English law to any particular circumstances that have arisen in relation to the person seeking the advice, and as to the steps which that person might appropriately take having regard to the application of English law to these circumstances (s 2(2)).

(b) 'Assistance'

'Assistance' means assistance in taking any of the steps which a person might take, including steps with respect to proceedings, having regard to the application of English law to any particular circumstances that have arisen in relation to him, whether by taking such steps on his behalf (including Assistance by Way of Representation) or by assisting him in taking them on his own behalf (s 2(3)).

(c) 'Representation'

'Representation' means representation for the purposes of proceedings and it includes:
   (1) all such assistance as is usually given by a solicitor or counsel in the steps preliminary or incidental to any proceedings;
   (2) all such assistance as is usually given in civil proceedings

in arriving at or giving effect to a compromise to avoid or bring to an end any proceedings; and
(3) in the case of criminal proceedings, advice and assistance as to any appeal (s 2(4)).

(d) 'Person'

'Person' does not include a body of persons corporate or unincorporate which is not concerned in a representative, fiduciary or official capacity so as to authorise advice, assistance or representation to be granted to such a body (s 2(10)).

(e) 'Legally assisted person'

Legally assisted person' means any person who receives, under the Act, advice, assistance or representation and in relation to proceedings, any reference to an assisted party or an unassisted party shall be construed accordingly (s 2(11)).

4 The new forms

From 1 April, 1990 only the new legal aid forms devised by the Board can be used. Those which concern practitioners are:

(a) Advice and assistance:

GF 1	the green form
GF 2	consolidated claims for fees
GF 3	application for extension of green form financial limits
GF 4	advice and assistance for wills
ABWOR 1	application for ABWOR
ABWOR 3	ABWOR Report on case and claim for costs
DSC	report by court duty solicitor and claim for costs
DSPS 1	advice at police stations report and claim for costs
DSPS 2	advice at police stations standby claim by a duty solicitor

(b) Civil legal aid:

CLA 1	application for legal aid non-matrimonial
CLA 2	application for legal aid matrimonial
CLA 3	application for an emergency certificate
CLA 4	statement of applicant's circumstances
L1Rev	statement of applicant's financial circumstances
CLA 4A	assessment of client's resources (from 3 September 1990)

L17A	client's statement of wages (from 3 September 1990)
L1A	statement of financial circumstances of an applicant residing outside England and Wales
L20/21HMF	statement of financial circumstances of an applicant who is a member of HM Forces
17HMF	statement of emoluments of a member of HM Forces
CLA 16	report on case and claim for costs
CLA 17	proforma bill of costs for civil assessment
CLA 28	application for payment on account of costs, disbursements and counsel's fees
CLA 29	undertaking as to costs
SJ 1	application for legal aid for authorised summary proceedings
SJ 3	report on case and claim for costs in respect of authorised summary proceedings Annual Report on care

(c) Criminal Legal Aid:

Form 1	application for Criminal Legal Aid in magistrates' court or Crown Court
Form 5	statement of applicant's means
Form 2	notification of refusal of Criminal Legal Aid
Form 3	application for review by the Area Committee of refusal to grant Criminal Legal Aid
Form 4	notification of Area Committee's decision on a review of a refusal
Form 16	application for legal aid in care proceedings in juvenile court or Crown court

5 Payment for legal aid work

If advice, assistance or representation is provided under the Act, payment for it must be made by the Board or be authorised by the Board or by Regulations made under the Act. No charge can be made to the client for such advice and assistance—save for any contribution which he is liable to pay—nor for representation (s 31(3)). If work is carried out under the Green Form Scheme and the cost exceeds the relevant prescribed limit, the client cannot be charged for the excess over and above that limit, unless an application has first been made to the Area Director for an extension and the application has been refused. The client should be notified of the refusal, and his permission obtained for the work to proceed on a privately paid basis. Similarly, if prior authority is sought for expenditure to be incurred or work to be carried out under a legal aid certificate, or order, and is refused, but the client wishes the work still to be done, he can agree to pay for it privately, because it is not work done under the certificate, or order.

The effect of the revocation of a legal aid certificate is that the assisted person is deemed never to have been legally aided. However, the revocation of a grant of advice, assistance or representation does not affect the right of any legal representative to be paid for work done before the date of the revocation (s 31(4)).

In certain cases, work carried out without a certificate or order may be claimed under a certificate or order which is subsequently granted. This applies where an emergency certificate cannot be applied for because the Area Office is closed, and to certain pre-certificate work carried out prior to the grant of a Criminal Legal Aid Order. In civil proceedings there is a provision, provided the conditions of reg 103 of the General Regulations 1989 are satisfied, enabling a solicitor to obtain payment from the Board for pre-certificate work, provided he has given notice of a lien to the Board.

6 The right to select solicitor and counsel

At present a legally assisted person has, with a few exceptions, complete freedom to choose the solicitor whom he wishes to act for him or to provide advice and assistance (s 32(1)). The main limitation on that basic principle is in criminal cases involving more than one defendant where the court has power to assign a solicitor, but will not assign the same solicitor to more than one defendant, where it is not in the interests of justice to do so. One example would be where there is a conflict of interest. This rule is not however, followed through to its logical conclusion because there is generally no restriction, even in cases involving more than one defendant, on the assisted person's right to select counsel, for there is only a very limited power to assign counsel in criminal cases.

In contempt proceedings s 32(1) does not apply, and the court may assign any counsel or solicitor who is within the precincts of the court (s 32(5)). A county court or magistrates' court may also request a solicitor who is within the precincts of the court to provide ABWOR under regs 7(1)(b) and 8 of the Scope Regs 1989.

Regulation 18 of the Legal Advice and Assistance Regulations 1989 gives a solicitor the right to refuse to accept an application for advice and assistance, as well as to decline to continue to give it, but the refusal must be for a good cause.

As for the future, it appears that the freedom of choice principle which has always been enshrined in our legal aid legislation will be whittled away, although in some cases, not perhaps without benefit to the assisted person. There is power for regulations to be made limiting the right of freedom of choice to solicitors who are members of a particular panel, which hopefully will be consistent with competence, expertise, experience and training in a specialised area of law such as child care. The Board already has power under s 32 with regard to Civil Legal Aid certificates under Pt IV of the Act, to assign a solicitor from among those with whom it has made a contract or to insist that the assisted person selects a solicitor from such solicitors.

7 Professional conduct of solicitors

The fact that a service is given under the Act does not affect the relationship between a client and his solicitor and counsel, nor does it affect the client's rights arising out of such a relationship (s 31(1)(a)). There are now a number of regulations imposing a duty on a solicitor to provide information to the Board and to make reports about legally aided cases. Such disclosure would normally be a breach of privilege if it was made without the client's consent, but reg 71(3) of the General Regulations 1989 provides that no solicitor shall be precluded by reason of privilege from disclosing to the Area Committee or to the Area Director any information or opinion which he is required to disclose, either under the Act or the General Regulations.

A solicitor must observe all the rules of professional conduct in dealing with legally assisted clients. There are additional rules which refer to the duties of a solicitor only with regard to legal aid. For example, a solicitor is under a duty to advise a client as to the availability of legal aid and of advice and assistance. Failure to advise a client of these rights can amount not only to negligence, but also to unbefitting conduct. In civil proceedings a client must be informed at the outset, and at appropriate stages during the case, of the effect of the statutory charge, the court's power to order him to contribute towards his opponent's costs, of the fact that, even if successful, an order for all his costs may not necessarily be made and that any order for costs which is made, may not be enforceable. Furthermore, the client must be told in all cases, both civil and criminal, of his liability to pay a contribution to the cost of his case and of the effect of failing to pay it.

The duty to advise about the availability of legal aid arises not only at the outset, but continues for so long as the solicitor has instructions, so that if he becomes aware of a change in the client's financial circumstances, eligibility to legal aid should be reconsidered.

A solicitor must always warn witnesses in legal aid cases that their fees and disbursements will be taxed or assessed, and that only the amount as taxed or assessed can be paid to them, although if prior authority has been obtained for the expenditure, it cannot be reduced on taxation. Any delay in submitting a bill for taxation can amount to unbefitting conduct if it results in counsel not receiving payment of his fees within a reasonable time.

Solicitors may be excluded from legal aid work under s 47(2) of the Solicitors Act 1974. A solicitor who is so excluded cannot be assigned to, or selected by a legally assisted person under s 31 of the Act.

Comprehensive cover as to the professional conduct of solicitors can be found in *Professional Conduct of Solicitors* published by the Law Society (1990).

8 Professional conduct of barristers

Complaints as to the conduct of barristers in legal aid work are dealt with under the Bar's disciplinary provisions in the same manner as complaints relating to non legal aid work. A Disciplinary Tribunal acting under the disciplinary provisions relating to barristers may order that any fees payable to counsel for services under or in accordance with the Legal Aid Act, or for advice and assistance under Pt III of the Act may be cancelled or reduced. There is a right of appeal against such a decision (s 41 of the Administration of Justice Act 1985 as amended by s 33 LAA 1988).

A Disciplinary Tribunal hearing a charge against a barrister either of professional misconduct or of breach of professional standards may exclude him or her from legal aid work, either temporarily or for a specified period, but an excluded barrister does have the right to apply for an order terminating his exclusion from legal aid work (s 42 of the Administration of Justice Act 1985, as amended).

9 Offences and penalties

Section 38 of the Act prohibits the unauthorised disclosure of any information furnished to the Board, a court, or any other person or body for the purposes of the Act. Section 38(1) lists the disclosure which is authorised and s 38(3) further provides that a disclosure not authorised by s 31(1) may be authorised with the consent of the person furnishing the information. A person who is convicted of making an unauthorised disclosure is liable on summary conviction to a fine not exceeding level 4 on the standard scale (s 38(4)). Proceedings cannot be brought without the written consent of the Attorney General. Information furnished to a counsel or solicitor is not information furnished to the Board or other persons within the meaning of s 38(1).

A person seeking or receiving advice, assistance or representation under the Act is liable under summary conviction to a fine not exceeding level 4 on the standard scale, or to imprisonment for a term not exceeding three months if he:

(1) intentionally fails to comply with regulations as to the information to be furnished by him, or
(2) in furnishing any information required by regulations, knowingly makes any false statement or false representation (s 39(1)).

Proceedings under s 39(1) must be brought within six months of the date on which evidence sufficient in the opinion of the Prosecutor to justify a prosecution came to his knowledge and in any event, must be commenced within two years of the date of the offence (s 39(2) and (3)).

Under s 39(4) of the Act the Board may take civil proceedings in the county court to recover any loss which it has sustained by reason of a person seeking or receiving advice, assistance or representation:

(1) failing to comply with regulations as to the information to be supplied by him; or

(2) making a false statement or false representation in furnishing information for the purposes of the Act.

Civil liability to compensate the Board for its loss arises irrespective as to whether the failure was intentional, or the false statement or representation was made knowingly whereas intention and knowledge are, respectively vital ingredients of the criminal offences created by s 39(1).

If a client fails to comply with the provisions of the Legal Advice and Assistance Regulations 1989 as to the information which he has to furnish, or if in furnishing such information he knowingly makes a false statement or false representation and he thereafter received advice or assistance, the Area Committee may declare that it was not given under the Act and the regulations. The solicitor and the client must be informed if the Area Committee does so decide, and the Board can then recover from the client, any sums paid out of the fund in respect of the advice and assistance which is the subject of the declaration (reg 36 of the Legal Advice and Assistance Regulations 1989).

10 Sanctions against the Board

The Act and the Regulations made under it contain many sanctions against solicitors who fail to carry out their obligations under them, but the reverse does not pertain. Solicitors may be penalised for failing to make claims for costs within the prescribed time limit, but no time limit is imposed on the Board for payment of those costs. No regulations provide that interest shall be payable to the solicitor whose bill is lost by the Board, or payment of which is unduly delayed. There is no recompense in the Act or regulations for a person whose legal aid application may have been dealt with by the Board in dilatory fashion or for the successful litigant who has to wait sometimes months for the Board to account to him for money which has been recovered under his legal aid certificate. In this respect the public can only resort to the protection of the general law.

Undue delays in payment by the Board to legally assisted persons should be countered with a formal letter giving notice of intention to sue the Board if payment is not made within seven days. Clients who have become irate and frustrated by the delays (which, to be fair, are minimal in many areas) should be encouraged to telephone the Board directly, twice a week. Their members of Parliament should be notified about their difficulties and the Board notified of the MP's involvement. The one person who can sting a reluctant bureaucracy into action is the one who has justification for, and knows how to go about, making a nuisance of himself.

11 Legal aid and profitability

(a) Preparation of bills

Basic principles of sound management are essential in any practice where legal aid work is undertaken, and steps must be taken to ensure that all legal aid fee earners adhere to these. Delays in the preparation of legal aid bills is unacceptable for two reasons. Firstly, it is uneconomical and equivalent to giving an interest free loan to the Board. Secondly, it is a sign of an inefficient and badly managed practice. There is no point in doing work, especially at legal aid rates of remuneration and then not bothering to bill it until weeks later.

(b) Time recording

Time recording is essential for all work for which payment is to be claimed by reference to the time spent on it. The recording of time spent need not be computerised, but it must be precise and it must be accurate. It is no good sitting down at the end of the day, or even worse at the end of the week and dictating attendance notes, or making time records for the day or the week. The discipline of recording time as and when work is completed is essential to the ability to charge properly. Nobody, come five o'clock in the afternoon, can remember all the day's telephone calls, never mind how long each one took, or whether each was of sufficient length to justify a separate timed charge. Every fee earner must be supplied with a running sheet to enable him to record the work he has carried out and the appropriate charge rate.

The failure to record only fifteen minutes per day spent on preparation or attendance, plus a few telephone calls, results in a loss of income of approximately £3,500 per annum. Multiplied by three fee earners in a practice, it will produce an annual loss to the practice of some £14,000.

(c) Cash flow

Cash flow is extremely important especially in times of high interest rates. Failure to preserve cash flow results in an overdraft which is expensive to finance, and the cost of which further reduces profits. Cash flow can be improved by taking advantage of the regulations which allow for reimbursement of disbursements, and this is one reason why (when it is necessary), prior authority for expenditure should be applied for to the Area Director. Full advantage should always be taken of the payment on account scheme for Civil Legal Aid cases. Civil cases can take several years to come to trial, without any fault on the part of the solicitors involved. In personal injury cases, damages may not be ascertainable until the client's future disability or rate of recovery is known. In many cases such recovery can be a lengthy process, in addition to which the waiting for a hearing date for a trial in the High Court can involve many months' delay. Each application to the Board for an authority or for an amendment to a legal aid certificate will take at least four weeks to be dealt with and, in some areas, much longer. It is pointless to wait perhaps three years or even longer to claim payment for one hundred per cent of the work done under a legal aid certificate, when the Regulations allow half, or even more to be claimed during the case as payment on account.

Discipline must be applied to the completion and prompt submission of green forms. The temptation to leave them lying in a file until there is time to get round and fill them in is to be avoided, and they should be submitted for payment at least once per month.

(d) Scope of the certificate

The scope of a certificate should always be borne in mind, as should the extent of any limitations on it, for forgetfulness on this point can lead to many hours work being done for which no payment will be able to be obtained, either from the Board or from the client. Criminal clients may have an unfortunate tendency to commit further offences, and where additional charges are brought against a client, application should be made immediately for the legal aid order to be amended to include those additional charges. The Board will have no sympathy for a solicitor who includes in his claim for payment, work undertaken in relation to a robbery charge, where the legal aid order was originally granted for burglary, and it has not been subsequently amended. It is important to avoid doing work for which payment cannot be claimed, when attention to detail and a little forethought will result in payment in full.

Advantage can also be taken of the regulations which in certain circumstances allow payment for pre-certificate work to be claimed under a legal aid certificate or order. Urgent cases do have a habit of refusing to occur during normal office hours. If the Area Office is closed when this happens there is no reason to delay the work until an emergency certificate can be applied for, or worse still, to avoid it altogether in the mistaken belief that it will not be possible to obtain payment for it.

(e) Cases in the Crown Court

It is now possible in Crown Court cases to obtain an enhanced rate of payment for the preparation of a brief which enables counsel to appear alone without a representative of his instructing solicitor. It may well be more profitable to do this than to have a grade 'B' or 'C' fee earner sitting behind counsel, perhaps after waiting over half a day for the case to be called. Obviously the bill for that particular case will be less if a fee earner does not attend Crown Court, but the fee earner is then released for other work, which has to be more profitable than Crown Court waiting and attendance rates.

Until a wider system of fixed fees is introduced, it is more profitable to carry out the preparation of indictable criminal cases before committal, rather than post committal. This is especially true where the work is carried out by a fee earner who is not a solicitor. Completing as much preparation as possible before committal has the added advantage that payment is also received much earlier than if one has to wait until a Crown Court taxation has eventually been carried out.

(f) The statutory charge

Failure to observe the provisions of the regulations relating to the statutory charge is perhaps the largest single cause leading to work having to be done, in effect, for nothing. The regulations themselves are few in number and a close knowledge of them and of the duties imposed on the assisted person's solicitor will help to avoid substantial losses. This must be well worth the effort if one considers that a comparatively simple mistake, such as failure or even delay in notifying the Board of the terms of an order or of property which has been recovered or preserved, can result in the Board losing the benefit of its statutory charge. The immediate result of this for the solicitor will be that he will not be paid for the case, at least to the extent necessary to compensate the Board for its loss. Thus many months and sometimes years of work may in the end produce not a penny in profit costs, and in addition the solicitor will have to stand personally the cost of all the disbursements which he has paid out during the case. If medical and other expert reports are involved, as well as court fees, these can be substantial.

All these simple precautions will help to ensure that payment is not lost for work which has been reasonably undertaken. In the end, however, the economics of legal aid work rests on the level of remuneration. The economics make glum reading, however efficient a particular practice may be. Five hours chargeable work per day, plus twenty letters per day produces annual costs, without any allowance for days lost through illness, of something in the region of £46,000. A recently qualified assistant solicitor will require a salary of between £16,000 and £20,000 and a secretary between £6,000 and £9,000 per annum, dependent on geographical location, thus producing a total wages bill of somewhere between £22,000 and £29,000, leaving at most £24,000 to cover national insurance contributions, rent and other overheads. A rule of thumb is that a fee earner should be able to produce three times his salary in fees earned, one third being needed for overheads and another being profit for the employer. The cheapest, most recently qualified assistant solicitor might therefore cover his expenses or just make a small profit for his employer, if he is fully engaged on legal aid preparation without any waiting time at court.

There is now a substantial argument for supporting the view that experience and efficiency, both of which can be monitored by the Board, are worth paying for and in the long run cheaper to provide. It is perhaps time to consider whether it is not in the interests both of the Board and of the tax payer as well as the public to create a limited grading system for qualified fee earners based on experience and efficiency. This would at least ensure that knowledge and ability built up over years of practice was not lost to the public and was retained to the economic benefit of the Board. The forced loss of many of the best and most experienced of legal aid practitioners could thus be avoided, probably without additional cost to the Board. I do of course declare a certain vested interest, even if only from age, in the adoption of such a scheme!

Admittedly, a system of fixed fees does allow a practice to benefit from its efficiency and experience, provided the fees are not fixed at a level which is too low to justify it.

Chapter 3

Advice and Assistance

1 The Advice and Assistance Schemes

The Advice and Assistance Scheme is generally thought of as the Green Form Scheme which was the first and initially the only form of advice and assistance, but the availability of advice and assistance under Part III of the Act has now extended far beyond those early limitations. The purpose of the Green Form Scheme was to enable advice to be given but (with two comparatively minor exceptions), it did not include any form of representation. Now there are a number of advice and assistance schemes, of which the Green Form Scheme is only one, some of which include limited representation. Court and twenty-four hour duty solicitor schemes provide facilities for a mixture of advice and assistance, as well as of representation, as does the provision for a solicitor to assist his own client at a police station. All forms of ABWOR, as well as of advice and assistance are governed by Pt III of the Act, and by the Legal Advice and Assistance (Scope) Regulations 1989 (The Scope Regulations) and the Legal Advice and Assistance Regulations 1989. In addition the Legal Advice and Assistance (Duty Solicitor) (Remuneration) Regulations 1989 and the Legal Advice and Assistance at Police Stations Regulations 1989 further regulate advice and assistance in criminal matters and in criminal ABWOR.

Despite the fact that the Green Form Scheme is a fundamental part of advice and assistance, there is no reference whatsoever to it as such, either in Pt III of the Act (ss 8–13) nor in any of the regulations. Indeed, to regard the Green Form Scheme as a separate statutory entity leads to considerable difficulty and confusion in attempting to understand the regulations. For this reason it is best to regard the Green Form Scheme as what it is, namely part of the advice and assistance schemes. The comments in this chapter refer, unless otherwise specified, to all forms of advice and assistance, as does the Act and regulations. Separate comment on the Green Form Scheme has therefore been strictly limited to matters which can only refer to that scheme.

(a) 'Advice', 'assistance' and 'representation'

Because of their importance it is worth repeating the statutory definitions of the meaning of advice, assistance and representation.

'Advice' may be oral or written, but it must relate to the application of English law to circumstances which have arisen relating to the person seeking the advice, and as to the steps which that person might take, having regard to the application of English law to those circumstances (s 2(2)).

'Assistance' includes assistance in taking steps with respect to proceedings, whether by taking such steps on behalf of the client or by assisting him in taking them on his own behalf. Assistance must be with regard to the application of English law to circumstances which have arisen in relation to the person seeking the assistance (s 2(3)).

'Representation' means representation for the purposes of proceedings and includes assistance usually given by a solicitor or counsel in:

(1) steps which are preliminary or incidental to proceedings
(2) arriving at or giving effect to a compromise to avoid or bring to an end proceedings.

In criminal proceedings it includes giving advice and assistance as to any appeal. Any step which amounts to representation cannot be given under the advice and assistance schemes, except by one of the various forms of ABWOR created by Pt III of the Act and the Scope Regulations.

The requirement that advice and assistance must relate to a question of English law means that advice about, for example, a Scottish divorce cannot be given under the English Advice and Assistance Scheme, even to a person residing in England and Wales. Such a person could however be advised as to whether applications for custody, access and maintenance could be made in the English courts. Subject to the limitation contained in s 2 of the Act, advice and assistance 'of all descriptions' may be given, unless it is excluded by regulations made under the Act.

The only exclusions which have been made so far are contained in Pt II of the Scope Regs and relate to wills and conveyancing services. These are dealt with in detail later in this chapter.

(b) Advice and assistance from more than one solicitor

The prior authority of the Area Director is required before advice and assistance can be obtained from more than one solicitor on the same matter (Advice and Assistance Regulations 1989, reg 16), unless the initial advice was given by the first solicitor under regs 6, 7 or 8 of the Advice and Assistance Regulations 1989 (advice and assistance at a police station or at a magistrates' court). Without this exception a person who had received advice at a police station from a duty solicitor would not subsequently be able to obtain Green Form advice from his own solicitor with regard to any subsequent summons or charges. If the initial advice was given under reg 6 (Advice and Assistance at Police Stations) the cost of the subsequent advice by a second solicitor must not exceed the costs which would have been incurred, had the advice been given by one solicitor. The Area Director has complete discretion as to the terms and conditions which he can impose on giving his authority.

It is not unknown for clients to seek to change solicitors, but the second solicitor if he has purported to give advice or assistance under any of the Regulations relating to advice and assistance cannot, subject to the exception referred to above, claim payment from the Board without prior authority. Nor, having purported to act under the Advice and Assistance Regulations, will he be able to charge the client privately.

(c) Separate matters

'Separate matters' must be the subject of separate applications for advice and assistance (Advice and Assistance Regulations 1989, reg 17). In order to avoid a plethora of applications in divorce matters, which may involve advice about separation, maintenance, custody and access, reg 17 further provides that matters connected with or arising from divorce proceedings or judicial separation, whether actual or prospective shall not be treated as separate matters for the purpose of advice and assistance. It is for this reason that the question is asked on the back of the Green Form as to whether the solicitor has previously submitted a claim for that client in respect of divorce or judicial separation. Advice about ancillary matters must therefore be given under the same Green Form as the divorce. It is not permissible where a solicitor has obtained the client's decree absolute and submitted his Green Form for payment, to carry out further work under a second Green Form in respect of ancillary matters such as custody, maintenance and property claims.

The Board tends to take a hard line on this point, and if a custody or access dispute arises, even some considerable time after a divorce has been completed, it will not allow that subsequent dispute to be regarded as a separate matter, and certainly not without some detailed explanation as to why it should be. It is important to retain on the file a copy of the Green Form claim for costs, so that if the solicitor is consulted about ancillary matters which arise much later, he will know how much he has been paid on the original claim form and the balance available before the prescribed limit is reached.

(d) Who gives the advice

A solicitor does not have to give the advice himself, and can entrust the work to:
(1) a partner, or
(2) a competent and responsible representative who is employed in his office, or
(3) a competent and responsible representative who is otherwise under the immediate supervision of the solicitor (Advice and Assistance Regulations 1989, reg 20).

This is however subject to further limitations where the work is undertaken by a court duty solicitor or is advice and assistance given at a police station.

2 Eligible persons

The 1988 Act commences with the proposition that advice and assistance shall be available to 'any person', and then gives power for regulations to be made restricting its availability to 'prescribed descriptions of persons' (s 8). In fact, the only prescribed persons are generally children, patients and clients resident outside England and Wales (Advice and Assistance Regulations 1989, regs 14 and 15), although there are separate definitions of eligibility for persons who require advice and assistance under the Advice and Assistance at Police Station (Duty Solicitor) (Remuneration) Regulations 1989 (see 'Duty Solicitor' p 45).

(a) Person applying for advice and assistance

An application for advice and assistance must be made by the client in person (Advice and Assistance Regulations 1989, reg 9), although there is an exception to this for persons who are in custody at a police station and reg 10 cf the Advice and Assistance Regulations permits a client to authorise another person to attend the solicitor on his behalf when the client cannot 'for good reason' attend on the solicitor himself. There is no definition of what will amount to a good reason. The authorised person must give the solicitor all the information necessary to enable the solicitor to assess the client's financial resources and to determine, where the advice required relates to the making of a will, whether the advice or assistance falls within reg 4(2) of the Scope Regulations. There is no similar requirement where the advice required is about a conveyancing transaction.

(b) Children

A child under compulsory school leaving age is not entitled to the benefit of advice and assistance, unless the solicitor has first obtained the authority of the Area Director. The Area Director must withhold his authority unless he is satisfied that the child should receive the advice. An application for advice and assistance on behalf of a child may be accepted directly from:

(1) his parent, guardian or other person in whose care he is; or
(2) a person acting as the child's next friend or guardian ad litem for any proceedings; or
(3) any other person, provided that the Area Director is satisfied that it is reasonable in the circumstances and he has given prior authority for the advice to be given to that person on behalf of the child.

Where the child is arrested, or is being interviewed in connection with a serious service offence or is a volunteer, then a solicitor may accept an application from the child for advice and assistance, if the solicitor is satisfied that the application cannot reasonably be made by one of the persons specified above (Advice and Assistance Regulations 1989, reg 14(1) and (2)).

(c) Patients

An application for advice and assistance can be accepted on behalf of a person who is a patient—in other words a person who, by reason of mental disorder within the meaning of the

Mental Health Act 1983, is incapable of managing and administering his affairs (Advice and Assistance Regulations 1989, reg 14(3)). The application must be made by:

(1) a receiver appointed under Pt VII of the Mental Health Act 1983; or

(2) the patient's nearest relative or guardian within the meaning of Pt II of the Mental Health Act 1983; or

(3) a person acting as the patient's next friend or guardian ad litem for the purpose of any proceedings; or

(4) any other person provided that the Area Director is satisfied that it is reasonable in the circumstances and has given prior authority for the advice to be given to that person on behalf of the patient.

(d) Clients resident outside England and Wales

Clients who reside outside England and Wales may receive advice and assistance, provided that the Area Director is satisfied that it is reasonable in the circumstances and he has given the solicitor prior authority to accept a postal application for such advice (Advice and Assistance Regulations 1989, reg 15). The advice and assistance must still be as to a question of English law, and the application to the solicitor must be made in writing. Telephone calls from distressed clients in the Gulf States or the Isle of Man do not qualify!

(e) Where a legal aid certificate is in force

The Board will not pay for advice and assistance provided under Pt III of the Act, after a legal aid certificate or order has been granted.

Chapter 4

The Green Form Scheme

1 The scope of the scheme

The nature of the advice and assistance which may be given under Pt III of the Act is governed by the definitions of 'advice' and 'assistance' contained in s 2 (see p 24). However, in order to assist practitioners the Board has published Note for Guidance No 2 (1989 edition) which sets out the sort of work which it considers will be covered by the scheme. It should be remembered that the list is not comprehensive and is only a guide, but it does include the following:

(1) advising, correspondence, negotiations;
(2) drafting of documents, excluding most conveyancing matters and wills;
(3) counsel's fees for advice;
(4) disbursements other than court fees and including for example obtaining a copy of a marriage certificate for divorce or judicial separation proceedings;
(5) taking proofs of evidence, interviewing witnesses and visiting sites of accident;
(6) preparation of cases going before administrative tribunals, such as Industrial Tribunals, Social Security Appeal Tribunals etc;
(7) advice as to Social Security and other welfare benefits;
(8) verifying assessments made by the Department of Social Security or by other benefit authorities, such as local authorities;
(9) preparing an application for legal aid or for an appeal to the Area Committee against the refusal of a certificate;
(10) acting as a McKenzie advisor; and
(11) assisting a client to prepare papers enabling him to make

a personal application to the Probate Registry, but in this case the client will have to pay any court fees himself. This list is no longer included in the 1990 edition of the Legal Aid Handbook.

(a) Exclusions from the scheme

For the first time since the introduction of the Green Form Scheme, opportunity has been taken to exclude from the scope of the scheme, advice and assistance in particular areas of law. In fact there is now, under s 8 of the Act, power to close down completely the whole of the advice and assistance schemes, and the fact that it was thought necessary to include such power in the new legislation could bode ill for all types of advice and assistance. The present exclusions to the Green Form Scheme contained in Pt II of the Scope Regulations are as follows:

(1) advice and assistance consisting of conveyancing services, unless:
> (a) they relate to a rental agreement or a conditional sale agreement for the sale of land; or
> (b) they are necessary to give effect to a court order; or
> (c) they are necessary to give effect to the terms of an agreement in proceedings under the Matrimonial Causes Act 1973 or the Matrimonial and Family Proceedings Act 1984.

(2) Advice and assistance in the making of a will, unless given to a client who is:
> (a) aged seventy or over; or
> (b) blind (or partially sighted), or deaf (or hard of hearing), or dumb or suffering from a mental disorder of any description, or substantially and permanently handicapped by illness, injury or congenital deformity; or
> (c) a parent or guardian within the meaning of s 87, Child Care Act 1980 of a person described at (b) above, and a client wishes to provide in the will for that person; or
> (d) the mother or father of a minor living with the client and the client is not living with the minor's other parent, (ie a single parent) and the client wishes to appoint a guardian for that minor under s 4, Guardianship of Minors Act 1971.

The vision of practitioners armed with green forms rushing to obtain will instructions from the mentally deranged, did not appear to cause undue concern to the Lord Chancellor when drafting the Scope Regulations. A new form GF4 relates to advice and assistance in respect of wills.

(b) Legal aid abroad

The Green Form Scheme will cover preparation of legal aid applications for transmission to foreign countries. Furthermore, the Board will pay for this work, even though it does not in any way relate to the application of English law, and does not therefore strictly fall within the definition of advice and assistance under s 2 of the Act. Apart from this, legal aid is not available from the Board for actions or for advice and assistance in foreign countries.

Legal aid must be applied for from the legal aid authorities in the country concerned, but where that country has signed the European Agreement on the transmission of applications for legal aid, it will accept an application on the English legal aid forms, including form L1Rev, as to the applicant's financial circumstances. The completed forms are then submitted in the normal way to the Board, which will send the application to the legal aid authority in the receiving country.

Practitioners should remember that without a properly completed legal aid application and a covering letter, the Area Office will not be able to tell that the application was to be transmitted to a foreign country, and will therefore, deal with it as an incorrect application for legal aid in this country, and this, for obvious reasons, would be automatically refused.

(c) Undefended divorces

Legal aid has not been available since 1977 for undefended divorce or judicial separation proceedings, unless the registrar directs that the petition be heard in open court, or it is impractical for the client to proceed without legal aid by reason of physical or mental incapacity. Subject to these exceptions, it is the Green Form Scheme which must be used for all special procedure divorces. This has the advantage to a client who is financially eligible for the scheme, that the court fees payable on filing the petition and on applying for the decree absolute, at present totalling £50, are not payable, provided the exemptions from fees form is completed and filed with the petition.

A legal aid certificate for divorce or judicial separation proceedings will not be granted, where only an answer has actually been filed even if it becomes likely that the proceedings will be defended.

The Board's Note for Guidance No 1 (1990 edition) lists the work which a solicitor can be expected to carry out in connection with a green form divorce or judicial separation, and for which he can therefore expect to be paid, and gives these examples:

(1) preliminary advice on the grounds for divorce or judicial separation, the effects of a decree on status, the future arrangements for the children, the income and assets of the family and matters relating to housing and the matrimonial home; or

(2) drafting the petition and the statement of arrangements for the children and where necessary, typing or writing the entries on the forms; or

(3) advising on filing the documents at court and the consequential procedure, including service, if no acknowledgement of service has been filed; or

(4) advising a client when the acknowledgement of service is received as to the procedure for applying for directions for trial, and typing or writing the entries on the form of affidavit of evidence; or

(5) advising as to attendances before the judge to explain the arrangements for the children and as to what if any evidence would be required by the judge, other than that of the petitioner; or

(6) advising on obtaining the decree absolute.

Attending court with or on behalf of a client at a children's hearing, even where there is, or is likely to be a dispute as to access or custody, is not within the scope of the Green Form Scheme, because that would amount to representation.

Where the advice and assistance includes advice or assistance to a petitioner in the preparation of a petition for divorce or of judicial separation, the limit on the cost of advice and assistance which can be provided is a sum equivalent to three hours work, as opposed to the general limit for other forms of advice and assistance of two hours work. Because matters connected with or arising from proceedings for divorce or judicial separation cannot be treated as separate from those proceedings for the purpose of advice and assistance, care should be taken as to the work carried out in connection with claims to matrimonial assets.

If negotiations are concluded, for example with regard to the distribution of the proceeds of sale of the matrimonial home or for the matrimonial home to be transferred to the petitioner, the work carried out in connection with the negotiations and agreement cannot be charged for privately, and must be conducted within the financial limit of the costs regulations, ie three hours work, or, at present, £117.75 plus VAT.

Because the client cannot be charged privately for such work, even if it only commences after the grant of the decree absolute, the solicitor must apply for an extension of the green form costs limit. This would only be appropriate where the work was likely to be of short duration, otherwise an application should be made at the earliest opportunity, for a legal aid certificate to cover all ancillary matters. It should be noted that the statutory charge created by s 16 of the Act applies to any property recovered as a result of advice and assistance given under the Green Form Scheme, and will therefore attach to any matrimonial property which has been recovered or preserved.

If application is made to the Area Director for an extension under the Green Form Scheme to cover the cost of negotiating the transfer of the matrimonial home to a petitioner and of the ancillary conveyancing work, a solicitor will not be able to claim payment of his costs under the Green Form Scheme from the Board, either for that work or for the divorce, where his fees will be covered by the statutory charge (which, in the case of advice and assistance, is for the benefit of the solicitor, rather than that of the Board).

(d) Acting as a McKenzie advisor

The Board accepts the principle that the definition of advice and assistance in the Legal Aid Act includes acting as a *McKenzie* advisor (see *McKenzie* v *McKenzie* [1970] 3 WLR 472). The limitations on extensions in *McKenzie* advice cases are referred to earlier in this chapter. The Area Office will wish to see the solicitor's file in any case where he submits, for payment, a green form in respect of *McKenzie* advice. In order to save time and avoid delays in payment, it is sensible to submit the file with the form when it is initially submitted for payment.

(e) Completion of the form

The statutory authority for the green form is to be found in regs 9(6) and 10(4) of the Advice and Assistance Regulations 1989 which provide that the financial information required as to the assessment of the applicant's means shall be furnished on a form approved by the Board. The green form must be signed on the first attendance, and payment of costs will not be allowed for any work carried out before the date of such signature.

One of the most onerous tasks in any Legal Aid Area Office must be that of checking green forms submitted for payment, and it often seems that at least one form in every batch is either incompletely or incorrectly filled in. There is therefore, no alternative to checking and double checking the form prior to submission for payment. Before submission the golden rule is to ask the following questions:

(1) Is the form signed?
(2) Is it dated?
(3) Are the capital and income and deductions sections filled in and completed correctly, both in respect of the client and of the spouse?
(4) Is the contribution correctly calculated and filled in on the back of the form?

On the reverse of the form:

(1) Has (where appropriate) 'no' been entered in the panel asking as to property recovered?
(2) Is there sufficient detail to enable the Area Office to assess the work done?
(3) Is the claim for costs calculated correctly, especially where the work is over a period during which there has been a change in legal advice payment rates?
(4) Has the question about previous advice on divorce or judicial separation been answered?
(5) Are all extensions and authorities granted by the Area Director attached securely to the form?

(f) Extensions

If the cost of giving advice and assistance is likely to exceed the prescribed limit, application can be made to the Area Director on form GF3 for an extension. The Area Director must be given sufficient information to enable him to make a decision, and he has to consider whether the advice and assistance is reasonable and whether the estimate of the cost thereof is reasonable. If he is satisfied on both grounds, he must grant the extension and specify the limit to which costs can be incurred.

If full legal aid is available, it will not be considered reasonable to grant an extension. It is also the Board's policy to regard as unreasonable an application for an extension by a solicitor who is wishing to act as a *McKenzie* advisor, unless the solicitor can satisfy the Area Director that it is necessary (not 'reasonable') for the client to have those services. The Area Director will take into account the difficulty of the case, its importance to the client and the inability of the client to represent himself without legal help.

2 The client's contribution

(a) Assessment of the contribution

The assessment of the client's resources is carried out by the solicitor using the current Key Card issued by the Board. The capital and income of the client must be assessed to determine whether the client is financially eligible to receive advice and assistance. It is only the client's assessed income which determines the amount of the contribution payable, and the relevance of assessing capital is purely to determine eligibility for the scheme. There is no need to assess the client's income where the client or his spouse is in receipt of income support or family income supplement.

The capital and income of a spouse are taken into account in the assessment, unless:

(1) the spouse has a contrary interest to the client; or
(2) the spouse and the client are living separate and apart; or
(3) it would be inequitable or impracticable so to do.

(See Para 7 Sched 2 Legal Advice and Assistance Regulations 1989.)

The following are not to be taken into account in assessing the client's capital:

(1) the value of the subject matter of the claim; or
(2) the main or only dwelling in which he resides; or
(3) his house or furniture and effects; or
(4) the tools of his trade.

The capital allowances referred to on the current Key Card in respect of a spouse and each dependent child or relative, wholly or substantially maintained by the client, are currently £335 for the first, £200 for the second and £100 for each further such person (Para 8 Sched 2 Legal Advice and Assistance Regulations). These have not been increased since 1989.

The following are not to be taken into account in assessing the client's income:

(1) the value of the subject matter of the claim; or
(2) income tax paid or payable by the client or spouse; or
(3) national insurance contributions paid during or in respect of the seven days up to and including the date of the application for advice and assistance; or
(4) bona fide maintenance payments made or to be made in respect of the same seven day period for the maintenance of:
    (a) a spouse who is living apart; or
    (b) a former spouse; or
    (c) a child or relative who is not a member of the client's household; or
(5) the deduction authorised by the current Key Card in respect of:
    (a) a spouse living together with the client; or
    (b) a child or dependent relative being a member of the client's household (Para 9 Sched 2 Legal Advice and Assistance Regulations 1989).

For the purposes of assessing both capital and income 'spouse' includes a cohabitee.

Subject to any authorised deductions, the maximum capital above which the client becomes ineligible for the Green Form Scheme is currently £935, but if, for example, he had a wife and two dependent children, the limit is currently £1570 (£935 plus £335 and £200 and £100). If the maximum disposable income is above £135 per week the client is ineligible for the scheme. Where the disposable income is more than £64 per week but does not exceed £135 per week, the client must pay a contribution in accordance with the table set out in Schedule 3 to the Legal Advice and Assessment Regulations 1989 as amended by the Legal Advice and Assistance (Amendment) Regulations 1990 (see table on p37).

Reference must always be made to the current Key Card issued from time to time by the Board in order to ascertain the correct and up to date figures. If a mistake is made in assessing either income or capital or in calculating the contribution, the solicitor can correct it by making a re-assessment and where necessary amending the contribution.

The solicitor is responsible for collecting the contribution from the client, but it does not have to be collected in one lump sum,

Disposable income not exceeding	Maximum contribution
£64	NIL
£72	£5
£78	£12
£84	£19
£90	£25
£96	£32
£102	£38
£108	£45
£114	£51
£120	£58
£125	£64
£130	£70
£135	£75

and by agreement with the client, it can be collected in instalments (reg 28 of the Advice and Assistance Regulations 1989). If the contribution exceeds the cost of the advice and assistance provided under the scheme, the balance must be returned to the client.

(b) The £5 fixed fee interview

The profession's loss leader is the £5 fixed fee interview available from solicitors willing to offer that facility. The expression 'fixed fee' is in fact misleading, because the official description of the scheme provides for a charge of 'not more than £5 inclusive of VAT.' If the client's contribution under the Green Form Scheme would be nil, then the charge to the client under the fixed fee scheme must also be nil because the charge to the client under the fixed fee scheme cannot exceed the contribution which the client would have to pay under the Green Form Scheme. If the contribution would be nil, then the Green Form Scheme should be used so that some payment can be obtained. The length of interview given under the fixed fee scheme can be up to thirty minutes.

3 Costs

A solicitor cannot require payment of any fee or charge from any assisted person, save for any contribution which the assisted person is assessed by the solicitor as being liable to pay under

the advice and assistance schemes (s 9(5) LAA 1988) and also
save for the amount of the statutory charge to which the solicitor
is entitled under s 11 of the Act in respect of any property
recovered or preserved. Where the green form has been completed, the claim for payment is made on the reverse of the
form, and must show the amount of the contribution payable by
the assisted person, whether or not it has been paid to the
solicitor. The Board pays to the solicitor the assessed costs, less
the amount of any contribution payable. The contribution should
therefore be collected from the client as soon as possible, preferably at the first interview when the form is signed by the client.
Apart from the client's contribution and the amount of any
statutory charge, the solicitor must look solely to the Board for
payment of his costs, and the Board will only allow payment for
work which falls within the strict ambit of the scheme, including
the financial limits as to the amount of work which can be
undertaken. The solicitor's entitlement where ABWOR is not
involved is to payment of the net deficiency after taking into
account the client's contribution and the solicitor's statutory
charge (reg 29(4) Advice and Assistance Regulations 1989).

A claim for costs in respect of advice and assistance given
under regs 7 and 8 Advice and Assistance Regulations 1989 must
be made in accordance with the Legal and Advice and Assistance
(Duty Solicitor) (Remuneration) Regulations 1989.

(a) The amount of work for which payment can be claimed

For advice and assistance given to a petitioner for divorce or
judicial separation, and which includes advice or assistance in
the preparation of the petition, the prescribed limit is a sum
equal to the cost of three hours work. The current rate of
remuneration is £39.25 per hour and the prescribed limit is therefore £117.75 plus VAT. For all other advice and assistance within
the scope of the scheme, the limit is a sum equal to two hours
work, ie £78.50 plus VAT at current rates.

Whilst the prescribed limit does not include VAT it does
include disbursements. If a solicitor pays for a copy marriage
certificate in connection with divorce or judicial separation proceedings and he also carries out three hours work, he will have
to stand the cost of the copy marriage certificate himself. Similarly, if counsel's opinion is taken, counsel's fees together with
VAT thereon have to be borne in mind when calculating the
amount of chargeable time left within the prescribed costs limit.

If the cost of the advice and assistance appears to be likely to exceed the prescribed limit, the solicitor must determine to what extent the prescribed limit is likely to be exceeded and must not then exceed that prescribed limit without the prior authority of the Board (s 10 LAA 1988).

As well as including disbursements and counsel's fees, costs are defined as 'the solicitor's own proper charges' and would not include work unnecessarily carried out, or carried out in the mistaken belief that it was within the scope of the scheme. In fact, s 10 imposes an absolute ban on giving advice in excess of the prescribed limit without the authority of the Board, and a solicitor who chooses to ignore this cannot subsequently attempt to charge the client on a private basis for the work which exceeded the limit. A solicitor can be instructed by a client on a private basis, only if an application for an extension of the prescribed financial limit has been made and has been refused. Even then the solicitor must first advise the client, preferably in writing, that the green form has been exhausted, that an extension has been refused and that any further work must be carried out on a privately paid basis.

The wording of reg 4(1)(b) is such that it is not necessary in divorce or judicial separation proceedings for the solicitor to prepare the petition himself. It is sufficient to enable work to be carried out up to the extended limit and for advice to have been given on the preparation of such a petition. The petitioner can therefore be left to draw the petition personally, although this cannot be recommended as a safe practice, and if anything were to go wrong, it could probably amount to professional negligence.

The prescribed limit is not a fixed fee, whether in divorce proceedings or otherwise. It is the maximum fee which can be claimed where the maximum permitted amount of work has been carried out.

Where advice and assistance has been given in connection with a criminal matter and the same solicitor is assigned to represent the same client under a legal aid order, the costs of the advice and assistance must be included in the claim for costs arising under the order, as if they were part of the costs of that representation (s 26 LAA 1988). This applies even though such costs have been incurred before the grant of the legal aid order.

The cost of advice and assistance given at a police station by an own solicitor cannot be claimed under the Green Form

Scheme. The Advice and Assistance at Police Stations (Remuneration) Regulations 1989 provide that claims for remuneration in respect of such advice and assistance must be in such form and manner as the Board may direct (reg 4). The Board has directed that form DSPS1 must be used to claim payment for all advice and assistance given under reg 6(1) and (2) Advice and Assistance Regulations 1989. Furthermore, advice and assistance on criminal matters which falls within the provisions of reg 6(1), must be given without reference to the client's financial resources, and, under the Green Form Scheme, the client's financial resources have to be assessed. In any event reg 9 Advice and Assistance Regulations 1989 specifically excludes from the Green Form Scheme work carried out under reg 6.

Section 31(3) of the Act prohibits a person who provides advice and assistance under the Act from taking any payment in respect of it, other than such as is authorised by the Act or by Regulations made under it.

Chapter 5

Advice and Assistance at Police Stations and Duty Solicitors

1 Advice and assistance at police stations

References in this part of this chapter are to the Legal Advice and Assistance at Police Stations (Remuneration) Regulations 1989 unless otherwise stated.

Advice and assistance can be given either by a duty solicitor or an own solicitor to any person who:

(1) is arrested and held in custody at a police station or other premises; or

(2) is being interviewed in connection with a serious service offence; or

(3) is a volunteer.

(Advice and Assistance Regulations 1989 reg 6(1).)

An own solicitor is one who gives advice and assistance in accordance with reg 6 above but does so otherwise than as a duty solicitor (reg 2). Such advice and assistance is given without reference to the financial resources of the assisted person, and although it is provided under the Advice and Assistance Regulations 1989, it does not come within the Green Form Scheme, even where the advice and assistance is provided by an own solicitor. The claim for payment must be made on the advice at police stations report, form DSPS1 (reg 29(2) Advice and Assistance Regulations 1989).

A volunteer is described in reg 2 as a person who, for the purpose of assisting with an investigation, and without having been arrested:

(1) attends voluntarily at a police station or at any other place where a constable is present; or

(2) accompanies a constable to a police station or any other such place.

Regulation 6(1)(*a*) of the Advice and Assistance Regulations 1989 makes it clear that if a person is arrested and held in custody, then he must be at a police station or 'other premises' in order to receive advice and assistance. Where he is a volunteer, there is a further restriction in that if he is at other premises a constable must be present. The regulations do not contain any definition of 'other premises', but the use of these words is sufficient to indicate that neither an arrested person nor a volunteer need be at a police station. Advice and assistance can therefore be given under the regulations to persons who have been arrested by other authorities, such as HM Customs & Excise or who are present with such other authorities as a volunteer, provided in the case of a volunteer, that a constable is present at the premises.

Advice and assistance under these regulations is given without reference to the client's financial resources.

(a) The prescribed limit of fees

The normal maximum which can be claimed for advice and assistance given to one person under reg 6 is the prescribed limit of £90 plus VAT (reg 4(1)(*a*) Advice and Assitance Regulations 1989). This sum includes payment for travelling and waiting and applies to advice and assistance given either by a duty solicitor or by an own solicitor. However, where the interests of justice require that the advice and assistance be given as a matter of urgency, there is no prescribed limit as the restrictions imposed by s 10 LAA 1988 (the giving of advice in excess of the prescribed limit), do not apply to advice and assistance under reg 6(1) given in those circumstances, and this is confimed by reg 5(6). It is necessary to specify on the claim form DSPS1 why the advice and assistance was required to be given as a matter of urgency (reg 4(2)(*a*)).

Interviews of suspects by police can be a lengthy business, especially where tape recorded interviews have not been introduced. Often there may be a need for a second interview several hours after the first, and after the duty or own solicitor has returned home. The £90 maximum can easily be eaten up by such interview, but the suspect does have a right to have his solicitor present during an interview, and the time spent by the solicitor in this manner should be allowed even if it exceeds the £90 maximum. Claims for payment in excess of £90 should explain why it was necessary for the advice and assistance to be given in the interest of justice as a matter of urgency.

(b) Remuneration

Payment to a solicitor who is on duty to give advice and assistance at a police station under the statutory twenty-four hour duty solicitor scheme is based firstly on an hourly standby rate for the hours which the solicitor spends on call. Secondly, he is entitled to payment at hourly rates for the time spent actually working as a duty solicitor, ie travelling, waiting, advising and assisting. The claim for a standby fee is reduced by up to a maximum of one half of the amount of fees claimed for work actually done (para 2 of the schedule to the Advice and Assistance at Police Station (Remuneration) Regulations 1989).

There are enhanced rates of payment for work carried out in 'unsocial hours' which are defined as being between 5.30 pm and 9.30 am on weekdays and any time on a Saturday, Sunday or bank holiday. These enhanced rates are only available to a duty solicitor and not to an own solicitor. The duty solicitor also benefits further in that travelling and waiting time are paid at the same rates as time spent in giving advice and assistance whether in office hours or in unsocial hours.

As well as payment for routine telephone calls, there is a separate rate available to both a duty solicitor and an own solicitor for advice and assistance over the telephone, this being one of the exceptions to the rule that the client must attend the solicitor in person to apply for the advice and assistance (reg 9 Advice and Assistance Regulations 1989).

Sloppy draughtsmanship apparently resulted in the need for the Legal Advice and Assistance (Amendment) Regulations 1989, which were brought into force as a matter of extreme urgency to amend the provisions of reg 30 Advice and Assistance Regulations 1989 which as originally drafted provided that a payment for ABWOR in unsocial hours on an application for a warrant of further detention should be at the higher rate paid to a duty solicitor, even if the solicitor involved was an own solicitor. The effect of the amending regulations was to revoke reg 30 on the date on which it was brought into force, and the amendment thereby ensured that only a duty solicitor was entitled to an enhanced rate for unsocial hours ABWOR, and further that the enhanced rate should be calculated on the basis of the remuneration rates set out in the Criminal Costs Regulations 1989 as now amended plus a mark up of one third.

Thus a duty solicitor who in unsocial hours opposes an application for a warrant of further detention under s 43 or s 44 of PACE will be paid £66 per hour. An own solicitor will only be paid £49.50 per hour for the same work, whether he operated in unsocial hours or not.

The provision of ABWOR by a duty solicitor is dealt with in the following chapter. Any representation provided by a twenty-four hour duty solicitor, other than ABWOR, is not within the class of work for which he can claim remuneration under the Legal Advice and Assistance at Police Station (Remuneration) Regulations 1989.

(c) Claims for payment

Claims for payment are made to a determining officer appointed by the Board, who must allow payment for time reasonably spent on work actually and reasonably done by a duty solicitor or by an own solicitor. Claims must be submitted within three months, but they may be extended by the determining officer for good reason. A representative of a duty solicitor is within the definition of 'duty solicitor', and it is not necessary therefore for the duty solicitor personally to have carried out the work in order to claim payment (reg 2) but such a representative must have been approved by the local duty solicitor committee under para 46 of the LAB Duty Solicitor Arrangements 1989. There is no similar provision in these regulations allowing a representative to carry out the work on behalf of an own solicitor but reg 20 of the Advice and Assistance Regulations 1989 will apply in these circumstances, permitting the work to be carried out by a competent and responsible representative employed in his office or under his immediate supervision.

A duty solicitor on a rota is entitled also to claim reimbursement of hotel expenses actually and reasonably incurred. Both a duty solicitor and an own solicitor may claim at the appropriate rates for travelling and waiting time and for disbursements actually and reasonably incurred.

2 Court duty solicitor schemes

References in this part of this chapter are to the Legal Advice and Assistance (Duty Solicitor) (Remuneration) Regulations

1989 unless otherwise stated. All except the smaller magistrates' courts now have court duty solicitor schemes under arrangements made by the Board under Regulation 7 Advice and Assistance Regulations 1989. A court duty solicitor who was providing ABWOR in his role as court duty solicitor under reg 7 is permitted by Regulation 8 Advice and Assistance Regulations 1989 to give advice to the following persons:

(1) a defendant who is in custody; or
(2) a defendant who is before the court as a result of either a failure to pay a fine or other sum ordered to be paid on conviction, or to obey an order of the court where such failure may lead to his being at risk of imprisonment; or
(3) a defendant who is not in custody, but who in the opinion of the solicitor requires advice.

He may also give assistance to a defendant to make an application for representation under the Act in respect of any subsequent appearance which he is to make before the court. Advice by a court duty solicitor is available without reference to the client's financial resources.

The provision of ABWOR by a court duty solicitor is dealt with in the previous chapter on assistance by way of representation.

An application to a court duty solicitor for advice and assistance under Regulations 7 or 8 of the Advice and Assistance Regulations 1989 need not be made by the client in person (reg 9).

(a) Remuneration

The rates of payment for a court duty solicitor are set out in the schedule to the Legal Advice and Assistance (Duty Solicitor) (Remuneration) Regulations 1989. An increase of twenty five per cent is allowed in remuneration for attendance at court and for waiting on a bank holiday, Saturday or Sunday when payment will also be allowed but only at the normal rate for time spent by a duty solicitor in travelling to and from his home and the magistrates' court. The normal hourly rate for attendance and waiting at a magistrates' court under a duty solicitor scheme is the average of the rates from time to time prescribed by the Legal Aid in Criminal and Care Proceedings Costs Regulations 1989 for advocacy and for travelling and waiting. For travelling times the normal travel rates for magistrates' court work is allowed (reg 5).

There is a time limit of three months for the submission of claims, and again this may be extended for good reason.

3 Reviews and appeals

A solicitor dissatisfied with a fees determination, either under the Legal Advice and Assistance (Duty Solicitor) (Remuneration) Regulations or the Legal Advice and Assistance at Police Station (Remuneration) Regulations can apply to the Area Committee for a review of the determination, but he must do so within twenty-one days of receipt of notification of the costs determined. There is a further right of appeal from the Area Committee to a committee appointed by the Board, but only where the Area Committee certifies a point of principle of general importance. The request for such a certificate must be made within twenty-one days of receipt of notice of the review decision, and the appeal must be made within twenty-one days of notification of the certificate by the Area Committee. Both on a review and on an appeal there is power to confirm, increase or decrease the fees previously allowed.

Under neither set of regulations is there any requirement for a notice of assessment or of determination to be issued by the determining officer if he reduces the fees claimed. The only duties imposed on the determining officer are to allow the appropriate fees for the work in respect of which he allows payment, and to authorise payment of the remuneration which he has determined as payable. The first a solicitor may know about any reduction in his claimed fees is when he actually gets paid. As an application for review must be made within twenty-one days of receipt of notification of the costs payable, it is important to keep a weather eye open when the Board's cheque arrives, for any discrepancies between the amounts claimed under these particular regulations and the amounts paid. This is yet another situation which appears to have arisen from bad draughtsmanship. The details attached to the Board's cheque are details of payments made and can hardly be said to fall within the classification of 'notification of the costs payable'.

Chapter 6

Representation (ABWOR)

Assistance by way of representation (ABWOR) is a half-way house between advice and assistance and full Legal Aid. The aim of Pt III of the Act was to provide advice and assistance falling short of representation, and it was therefore felt that the most obvious place to put ABWOR, which, as its name implies, provides representation, was in that part of the Act from which representation was generally excluded. The entrance to this maze is to be found in s 8(2) of the Act which applies Pt III of the Act to ABWOR in so far as regulations provide for the purpose of any proceedings before a court or tribunal, or at a statutory enquiry.

The Regulations which do so provide are Pt III (regs 6–9) of the Scope Regulations 1989, which commence with the strange logic that Pt III of the Act does not apply to ABWOR except as provided by Pt III of the Scope Regulations. Regulations 7 to 9 and the Schedule to the proceedings then list the proceedings for which ABWOR is available. It is here that the confusion really starts, for being part of the Advice and Assistance Scheme the remaining regulations governing the provisions of ABWOR are in the Advice and Assistance Regulations 1989. Advice and assistance is means tested, but some ABWOR is required to be given without reference to the client's financial resources and there are further separate provisions creating financial eligibility rules applicable only to ABWOR. ABWOR must generally be approved by the Board, but some ABWOR has to be given urgently, and there are therefore further regulations catering for the provision of ABWOR without approval of the Board. Under the advice and assistance schemes, work can only be carried out up to the prescribed limit, but the duration of proceedings cannot be predetermined, and further regulations create separate provisions as to the amount of costs which can be incurred under certain types of ABWOR. A green form is essential for some forms of ABWOR but not for others.

There are four ways in which ABWOR may be granted or obtained in respect of various types of proceedings. It can be authorised in limited circumstances by a magistrates' court or county court. Application can be made to the Board for approval of assistance by way of representation, in respect of the proceedings specified both in reg 9 of and in the Schedule to, the Scope Regulations. In all these cases, a green form must have been completed, and the client's financial resources must be such as to make him financially eligible to receive advice and assistance. The third type of ABWOR is available without reference to the client's financial resources, and therefore without the need for a green form to be completed first, or indeed at all, eg in connection with applications for warrants of further detention or extensions of such warrants—reg 5 Advice and Assistance Regulations. Finally, ABWOR can be provided for the proceedings specified in reg 7(2) and (4) Scope Regulations by a solicitor attending court as a court duty solicitor. This is also available without reference to the client's financial resources and without the need to complete a green form (reg 7(3) Advice and Assistance Regulations 1989).

1 Representation authorised by the court

Whilst advice and assistance cannot generally include the taking of any steps in proceedings, a solicitor can be authorised by a magistrates' court or a county court to represent a person under the Green Form Scheme.

A magistrates' court may, under reg 7(1)(b) Scope Regulations 1989, authorise representation for a party to any proceedings in the court, provided that he is not receiving and has not been refused representation in connection with those proceedings. In addition the court must:

(1) be satisfied that the hearing should proceed on the same day; and

(2) be satisfied that the party would not otherwise be represented; and

(3) request a solicitor who is within the precincts of the court, other than for the purpose of obtaining authority under reg 7(1)(b), to represent a person; or

(4) approve a proposal from such a solicitor, that he provides representation to that party.

The wording of reg 7(1)(b) is clearly aimed at ensuring that a person within the financial eligibility regulations of the Green Form Scheme, does not go without representation where the court thinks it is necessary and would like to deal with the case on the same day, rather than adjourn it, in order to enable that party to obtain representation. What Regulation 7(1)(b) does not do, is to allow a solicitor to turn up at court with his client, but without a Legal Aid Certificate or prospects of being paid privately, in the hope that he can persuade the court to authorise representation. Such a solicitor would not fall within (3) or (4) above. The power of the court to grant such authority is wide, in that it includes any proceedings before the court and not just criminal proceedings.

In the county court a solicitor may be authorised to represent a party to any proceedings in the court, provided that he is not receiving, and has not been refused, representation for those proceedings—reg 8 Scope Regulations 1989. The county court has to be satisfied in the same way as the magistrates' court as to the points raised by reg 7(1) and the 'within the precincts' rule also applies.

Authorisation under the Green Form Scheme for representation in a magistrates' or county court should not be used to avoid the need for submitting an application for ABWOR on the appropriate form—Note for Guidance number 4. The authorisation of representation under the 'within the precincts' rule, has the disadvantage that the work is still subject to the prescribed green form costs limit of the equivalent of two hours work, and the Area Director has no power to authorise that limit to be exceeded. The claim for payment is made on the green form. Even though representation has been provided, all work is carried out at the green form rate of remuneration.

2 ABWOR approved by the Board

Regulation 22 of the Advice and Assistance Regulations 1989 specifies the cases in which ABWOR is available, the approval of the Board is not required. The effect of reg 22 is that the approval of the Board is required for ABWOR in respect of the proceedings specified in regs 7(1)(a), (2), or (9) and in the Schedule to the Scope Regulations.

The proceedings in the schedule for which ABWOR is available under reg 7(1)(*a*) are proceedings:

(1) for or in relation to an order under Pt I of the Domestic Proceedings and Magistrates' Court Act 1978; or

(2) under the Guardianship of Minors Act 1971 and 1973; or

(3) under s 43 of the National Assistance Act 1948, s 22 of the Maintenance Orders Act 1950, s 4 of the Maintenance Orders Act 1958, s 18 of the Supplementary Benefits Act 1976 and s 24 of the Social Security Act 1986; or

(4) in relation to an application for leave of the court to remove a child from a person's custody under ss 27 or 28 of the Adoption Act 1976 or proceedings in which the making of an order under Pt II or s 29 or s 55 of the Adoption Act 1976 is opposed by any party to the proceedings; or

(5) under Pt I of the Maintenance Orders (Reciprocal Enforcement) Act 1972 relating to a maintenance order made by a court of a country outside the United Kingdom; or

(6) under Pt II of the Children Act 1975.

If ABWOR is to be provided for the proceedings specified in reg 7(2), then the approval of the Board is required, unless the solicitor who is providing the representation is the court duty solicitor. The proceedings covered by reg 7(2) are set out later in this chapter.

Advice by way of representation is available under reg 9 Scope Regulations 1989 with the approval of the Board to a person in proceedings before a Mental Health Review Tribunal under the Mental Health Act 1983 and to a prisoner for proceedings before a Board of Visitors, and whom the Board of Visitors has permitted to be legally represented in those proceedings.

(a) Obtaining the Board's approval

Two forms are required for an application to the Board for approval of ABWOR. The first is the green form and the second is ABWOR 1. It is only the latter form and not the green form which is submitted to the Board. The ABWOR 1 form requires completing, with details as to the date of the green form, details of any contribution payable by the client and on the reverse side a statement as to the client's case, which must be signed by the client.

The Board's form ABWOR 1 is as confusing as the regulations

which have spawned it. The form provides that whichever of the following is not applicable, has to be deleted from the form:

I am acting for my client under a green form dated _____/or my client is not financially eligible for green form advice, but is eligible for ABWOR.

The form then goes on to state that a green form must be completed, 'irrespective of whether a client is financially eligible for advice and assistance.'

The Board's requirement is therefore that a solicitor must certify if a client is not eligible for the Green Form Scheme and if he is not so eligible, must then complete a form for the scheme for which he is not eligible. It would appear that regs 9 and 13(6) Advice and Assistance Regulations 1989 give legal authority for this contradictory requirement which non-lawyers might regard as being slightly incompatible with the possession of a logical thought process.

The client (except in the case of ABWOR for proceedings before a Mental Health Review Tribunal or a prison Board of Visitors) must have reasonable grounds for taking, defending or being a party to the proceedings, otherwise the application must be refused (reg 22(5) Advice and Assistance Regulations 1989 as amended by the Legal Advice and Assistance (Amendment) Regulations 1990, reg 3(2)) as it may be where it appears to be unreasonable, that approval should be granted in the particular circumstances of a case (reg 22(6)). The Area Director has power to impose conditions as to the conduct of the proceedings, and it is a condition of every approval of ABWOR given by the Board, that the prior permission of the Area Director is required:

(1) to obtain an expert's opinion or report
(2) to tender expert evidence
(3) to perform an unusual act or one which involves unusually large expenditure

(Regulation 22(7) Advice and Assistance Regulations 1989).

The Area Director can be requested to include such permission in the grant of approval (reg 22 of the Advice and Assistance Regulations 1989). Where ABWOR has been granted, a solicitor can apply for approval to instruct counsel, and the Area Director must grant such approval if he considers that the proper conduct of the proceedings requires counsel (reg 23 Advice and Assistance Regulations 1989). A solicitor is under a duty to give notice to any other party to the proceedings and to the court that

ABWOR has been granted in respect of proceedings set out in the schedule to the Scope Regulations 1989 (reg 24 Advice and Assistance Regulations 1989).

The grant of approval of ABWOR by the Board removes the financial limit on costs imposed under the Advice and Assistance Scheme by reg 4 of the Advice and Assistance Regulations 1989. Assistance by way of representation will also cover giving notice of appeal or applying for a case stated within the ordinary time limits for so doing, as well as work preliminary to such notices or application, eg obtaining justices' reasons.

(b) Financial eligibility

Financial eligibility for ABWOR approved by the Board is governed by regs 11, 12 and 13 Advice and Assistance Regulations. The disposable capital limit for ABWOR approved by the Board is £3,000 as against £935 for the Green Form Scheme. The disposable income limit is the same as for the Green Form Scheme. Both disposable capital and disposable income are assessed by the solicitor in the same manner as for the Green Form Scheme, in accordance with the provisions of Sched 2 of the Advice and Assistance Regulations 1989, save that if an applicant for ABWOR is directly or indirectly in receipt of income support, his disposable capital must be taken as not exceeding £3,000 (reg 13(3) Advice and Assistance Regulations 1989).

The solicitor must also assess and collect the contribution payable by the applicant, and details of this must be shown on the application form, ABWOR 1. The contribution is calculated by use of the current Key Card issued by the Board.

(c) ABWOR in proceedings before the Mental Health Review Tribunal

Advice by way of representation is available to the person who is making the application to the tribunal, as well as to a person whose case is to be the subject of the proceedings before the tribunal (reg 9 Scope Regulations 1989). Thus ABWOR is available to a relative who is making the application, as well as to the patient whose case is the subject of the proceedings. Paragraph 5 of the Board's Note for Guidance Number 3 (1989 edition) states that ABWOR will not be available to the patient where the nearest relative has made the application. This would appear to be incorrect and contradict the provisions of reg 9, although the Board is correct when it states that this will not matter, because in most cases the relative will be acting in close consultation with the patient. It is, however, clear from reg 9 that on a relative's application, both the relative and the patient are entitled to apply for approval of ABWOR.

The applicant no longer has to show that he has reasonable grounds for taking, defending or being a party to such proceedings (reg 3(2) Legal Advice and Assistance (Amendment) Regulations 1990), but the application could still be refused on the grounds of unreasonableness under reg 22(6) Advice and Assistance Regulations 1989.

If the patient is the client, then the green form may be signed by the client's spouse, receiver or nearest relative or guardian (reg 14(3) Advice and Assistance Regulations 1989). Permission to obtain a psychiatric report shall be sought when applying for approval of ABWOR. Normally, the Board will not give approval for counsel to be instructed, on the basis that it expects a solicitor undertaking that type of work to be sufficiently experienced to appear before the tribunal without resorting to counsel. There is no duty under the present regulation to give notice to the tribunal of the grant of ABWOR, but the Board advises that it would be helpful so to do.

As there are now provisions for the automatic referral of cases to a tribunal at specific intervals, the Law Society has established a panel of experienced solicitors who are competent to represent patients whose cases have been referred to the tribunal. This in no way places any limitation on the patient's right to choose his own solicitor. The qualifying criteria for panel membership is:

(1) willingness to prepare cases and to conduct tribunal hearings personally, and either:
(2) (a) the representation of at least five clients before the tribunal in the last twelve months; or
    (b) attendance at two tribunal sittings, covering a minimum of three cases where patients are represented, one being a restricted case, one an unrestricted case and the third either restricted or under s 2 Mental Health Act 1983; and
(3) a satisfactory interview for membership of the panel.

The initial preparation under the Green Form Scheme should include obtaining the hospital statement from the regional office of the tribunal, so that this can be forwarded to the Area Director with the application for approval of ABWOR. The Board takes the view that an application for ABWOR by an applicant to a tribunal will be granted, unless it appears unreasonable in the circumstances (para 5 Note for Guidance Number 3, 1989 edition). This is based on the provisions of the 1980 Advice and Assistance Regulations, even though such provision has not been incorporated in the new 1989 Regulations.

(d) ABWOR in proceedings before a Board of Visitors

Before a prisoner can be represented in proceedings before a Board of Visitors, that Board must have granted permission for him to be represented. Advice by way of representation can only be approved where such permission has been granted. A copy of the permission must be forwarded to the Board with form ABWOR 1. It is no longer a requirement for the want of ABWOR for these proceedings that the applicant should have reasonable grounds for defending the proceedings (reg 3(2) Legal Advice and Assistance (Amendment) Regulations 1990).

A prisoner can be advised under the Green Form Scheme about proceedings before a Board of Visitors, and about making the application to them for permission for representation. The factors which the Board of Visitors should take into account are:

(1) the seriousness of the charge and the potential penalty; or
(2) whether any points of law are likely to arise; or
(3) the capacity of the prisoner to put his own case; or
(4) procedural difficulties such as the prisoner's inability to arrange to interview witnesses and cross-examine witnesses called against him, especially expert witnesses; or
(5) the need for reasonable speed in making the adjudication; and
(6) the need for fairness as between prisoners and as between prisoners and prison officers.

R v *Secretary of State ex parte Tarrant and Another* [1984] 1 All ER 799.

(e) Withdrawal of ABWOR

Approval of ABWOR under reg 22 must be withdrawn by the Area Director where he considers, as a result of information which has come to him, that:

(1) there are no longer reasonable grounds for the client taking, defending or being a party to the proceedings or continuing to do so; or
(2) the client has required the proceedings to be conducted

unreasonably, so as to incur unjustifiable expense to the fund; or

(3) it is unreasonable in the circumstances that the client should continue to receive ABWOR (reg 25(1) Advice and Assistance Regulations 1989)

The Area Director must notify the solicitor that approval has been withdrawn, and the solicitor must then forthwith notify his client and, if the proceedings are included in the schedule to the Scope Regulations, and proceedings have been commenced, must send a copy of the notice of withdrawal to the court and to any other party to the proceedings. If approval is withdrawn, it shall not prejudice any further application for representation or ABWOR in respect of the same proceedings (reg 25(2) Advice and Assistance Regulations 1989).

(f) Appeals to the Area Committee

If the Area Director refuses to approve ABWOR under reg 22 or refuses authority for any of the matters referred to in reg 22(7) or withdraws ABWOR, there is a right of appeal to the Area Committee. The appeal must be on the Board's form and must be made within fourteen days of the Area Director's decision, not it should be noted, within fourteen days of receipt of notification of that decision. The Area Committee, whose decision is final, may dismiss the appeal, quash the decision to withdraw ABWOR, or grant an application for approval of ABWOR or for an authority. It may do so subject to such terms and conditions as it thinks fit (reg 27(1) Advice and Assistance Regulations 1989). Notice of the Area Committee's decision must be given in writing and with reasons, both to the solicitor and to the client. If the Area Committee quashes a decision to withdraw ABWOR, the solicitor must notify the court and any other party to the proceedings.

3 ABWOR without Board approval

The approval of the Board is not required for representation provided by a court duty solicitor under reg 7 Advice and Assistance Regulations 1989, but the proceedings in respect of which he can provide such representation are limited to those specified in reg 7(2) and (4) of the Scope Regulations 1989.

Regulation 7(2) provides that the person who is to be represented must not have previously received and not be otherwise receiving representation or ABWOR, in connection with the same criminal proceedings. The representation can only be in respect of:

(1) a bail application; or

(2) a court appearance where the client is in custody and wishes the case to be concluded at that appearance, unless the solicitor considers it should be adjourned in the interests of justice or of the client; or

(3) where the client is before the court as a result of failure to obey a court order, and such failure may lead to his being at risk of imprisonment; or

(4) where the client is not in custody, but in the opinion of the solicitor he requires ABWOR.

ABWOR cannot be given under reg 7(2) for committal proceedings, proceedings where the client pleads not guilty, nor unless the solicitor considers the circumstances to be exceptional, to proceedings in connection with a non-imprisonable offence.

A court duty solicitor may also provide ABWOR under reg 7(4), Scope Regulations 1989 to a defendant who is appearing before a magistrates' court for failing to pay a fine or other sum which he was ordered to pay on a conviction, and the failure may lead to his being at risk of imprisonment. Advice by way of representation provided by a court duty solicitor is available without reference to the client's financial resources.

Advice by way of representation is also available without reference to a person's financial resources, and without Board approval in connection with an application for a warrant of further detention or for an extension of such a warrant under ss 43 or 44 of the Police and Criminal Evidence Act 1984.

4 Costs and counsel's fees

If, where the claim relates to ABWOR, counsel has been instructed either with approval of the Area Director under reg 23, or where the Area Director considers that the proper conduct of the proceedings required counsel, the costs of the solicitor are assessed and the net deficiency paid to him, after taking into account the client's contribution and the affect of any statutory charge in favour of the solicitor. Counsel's fees are then paid to counsel, less any balance left out of the total of the client's contribution and the solicitor's charge, after taking into account the solicitor's assessed costs (reg 29(5) Advice and Assistance

Regulations 1989). Thus if the solicitor's costs are £30 plus VAT, counsel's fees £40 plus VAT and the total of the contribution and of the solicitor's statutory charge amount to £50, the solicitor will receive nothing from the Board because his net deficiency is nil. Counsel will receive £46 less £15.50 being the balance available over and above the solicitor's net deficiency. Whilst the regulations are silent on the point, it appears that counsel must look to his instructing solicitor for his net deficiency.

If in a claim relating to ABWOR counsel has been instructed without approval, and the Area Director is not satisfied that it was proper to instruct counsel, the costs must be assessed by the Area Director, as if the solicitor had conducted the case and counsel had not been instructed. Counsel is entitled to be paid the same fee on the net deficiency basis, as if he had been approved. The balance of any net deficiency, if any, is then paid to the solicitor (reg 29(6) Advice and Assistance Regulations 1989).

If counsel or a solicitor are dissatisfied with an Area Director's decision as to costs, the rights of appeal are the same as those provided for advice and assistance by regs 29(7)–(10) Advice and Assistance Regulations 1989, except that where the claim has been made by a court duty solicitor or for ABWOR in respect of an application for a warrant of further detention or an extension thereof, the appeals procedure is as provided by the relevant regulations for that work.

5 Costs orders

(a) Orders for costs against persons receiving ABWOR

The factors to be taken into account by a court or tribunal before it makes an order for costs against a person in receipt of ABWOR is the amount which it is reasonable for him to pay, having regard to all the circumstances, including:

(1) the financial resources of all the parties; and
(2) their conduct in connection with the dispute (s 12(1) LAA 1988).

The next friend or guardian ad litem of a child or patient is given the benefit of s 12(1), but if the client is a child, his means for the purposes of a costs order include the means of any person whose disposable income or capital has been included in assessing the child's resources.

Except in so far as regulations so provide, no account is to be taken of the assisted person's dwellinghouse, clothes, household furniture and tools of his trade, in assessing what costs he can afford to pay. Nor if an order is made, can it be enforced in the UK against any of those items (s 12(3) LAA 1988).

The amount of an assisted person's liability for costs must be determined in accordance with Sched 5 Advice and Assistance Regulations 1989 (reg 34). To assist the court to make a determination under s 12:

(1) the court can refer any question of fact relevant to the determination to the clerk to the justices for investigation; and

(2) any party other than the assisted person can file an affidavit of means as to his own capital and income and any other relevant facts; and

(3) the client and any party who files an affidavit of means may be ordered to attend an oral examination as to means and any other relevant fact. At the examination, evidence can be given and witnesses called.

If any order for costs is made, the court has a discretion as to how they shall be paid, and it may be by instalments or otherwise. If the costs are not to be paid immediately, the court may order that payment be suspended either sine die or to such date as the court may determine (sched 5 para 6 Advice and Assistance Regulations 1989). A person in whose favour a costs order is made, can apply to the court within six years from the date of the order for it to be varied, if there has been a change in the assisted person's circumstances, or on the grounds that material additional information is available, which could not with reasonable diligence have been available at the time of the order (Sched 5 para 7 Advice and Assistance Regulations 1989).

(b) Order for costs against the Board

A court or tribunal may, in any proceedings which are finally decided in favour of an unassisted party, make an order that the Board shall pay the costs of that successful unassisted party, if the unsuccessful party has been in receipt of ABWOR (s 13 LAA 1988). Before such an order can be made, the court must consider what order for costs should be made against the assisted person, and must determine his liability in respect thereof. Section 13(4) further provides that the order can only be made if:

(1) an order for costs would be made apart from the Legal Aid Act 1988;

(2) in a court of first instance, the proceedings were instituted by the assisted party and the court is satisfied that the unassisted party would suffer severe financial hardship if the costs order was not made; and

(3) the court is satisfied that it is just and equitable that costs should be paid out of public funds.

If an assisted party to the proceedings was only in receipt of ABWOR for part of those proceedings, a costs order against the Board can only relate to the unassisted person's party and party costs incurred during that part of the proceedings. There is no appeal against a costs order made under s 13, nor against the refusal to make such an order. The Area Director who dealt with the ABWOR application under reg 22 Advice and Assistance Regulations 1989 must first be given an opportunity to make representations before the costs order can be made against the Board (reg 35 Advice and Assistance Regulations 1989).

A costs order against the Board does not take effect where an appeal lies against the decision in favour of the unassisted party, until the time has expired for appealing or applying for leave to appeal and no appeal or application for leave has been made (s 13(8) Legal Aid Act 1988). Proceedings are only to be treated as 'finally decided' where those time limits have expired or no appeal lies against the decision (s 13(7)).

As an order for costs against the Board can only be made when the proceedings are 'finally concluded', the effect of s 13(7) is that where an appeal may lie, the costs order cannot be made until the time limits referred to in s 13(7) have expired.

If an appeal is brought out of time, the appellate court has power to order the unassisted party to repay in whole or in part, any costs which he has received from the Board under s 13.

Chapter 7

The Statutory Charge

The statutory charge applies to any property which has been recovered or preserved in connection with any matter for which a person has received advice and assistance under Pt III of the Legal Aid Act 1988 and to any costs which are payable to him in respect of the matter for which advice and assistance was given (s 11 LAA 1988). The major distinction between the statutory charge in these circumstances and the statutory charge where a legal aid certificate has been granted, is that it is a charge, not for the benefit of the Board, but for the benefit of the solicitor who has given the advice and assistance (s 11(2)). The charge arises in respect of the costs and fees, payment of which would be payable by the Board to the solicitor (s 11(3)).

The charge for the benefit of the solicitor attaches to any costs payable 'by virtue of a judgment, order of a court or otherwise, and to any property of whatever its nature and wherever it is situate, including the assisted person's rights under a compromise or settlement reached to avoid or conclude proceedings (s 11(4)). The exceptions to the charge are set out in Sched 4 Advice and Assistance Regulations 1989. They are not the same as the exceptions contained in reg 94 of the Civil Legal Aid (General) Regulations 1989 and there is one important addition in that one half of any redundancy payment recovered or preserved for the client is exempt from the solicitors statutory charge. There is no similar provision for payment made in respect of a claim for unfair dismissal. The exceptions contained in Sched 4 are as follows:

The provisions of s 11(2)(*b*) of the Act shall not apply to—
(*a*) any periodical payment of maintenance, which for this purpose means money or money's worth paid towards the support of a spouse, former spouse, child or any other person for whose sup-

port the payer has previously been responsible or has made payments;

(b) any property recovered or preserved for the client as a result of advice and assistance given to him by the solicitor which comprises the client's main or only dwelling, or any household furniture or tools of trade;

(c) (without prejudice to (b) above) the first £2,500 of any money or of the value of any property recovered or preserved by virtue of—

   (i) an order made or deemed to be made, under the provisions of s 23(1)(c) or (f), 23(2), 24, 27(6)(c) or (f), or 35 of the Matrimonial Causes Act 1973(a);

   (ii) an order made, or deemed to be made, under the provisions of ss 2 or 6 of the Inheritance (Provision for Family and Dependants) Act 1975(b);

   (iii) an order made, or deemed to be made, under s 17 of the Married Women's Property Act 1882(c); or

   (iv) an order made, or deemed to be made, under the provisions of s 4(2)(b) of the Affiliation Proceedings Act 1957(a); or

   (v) an order for the payment of a lump sum made, or deemed to be made, under the provisions of s 60 of the Magistrates' Courts Act 1980(b); or

   (vi) an order made, or deemed to be made, under the provisions of s 2(1)(b) or (d), 6(1) or (5), 11(2)(b) or (3)(b) or 20(2) of the Domestic Proceedings and Magistrates' Courts Act 1978(c); or

   (vii) an order made, or deemed to be made, under s 9(2)(b), 10(1)(b)(ii), 11(b)(ii) of the Guardianship of Minors Act 1971(d) or under s 11B, 11C or 1D of that Act (e); or

   (viii) an order made, or deemed to be made, under s 34(1)(c) or s 35 of the Children Act 1975(f); or

   (ix) an agreement which has the same effect as an order made, or deemed to be made, under any of the provisions specified in this sub-paragraph;

(d) one-half of any redundancy payment within the meaning of Pt VI of the Employment Protection (Consolidation) Act 1978(g) recovered or preserved for the client;

(e) any payment of money in accordance with an order made under s 136 of the Employment Protection (Consolidation) Act 1978 by the Employment Appeal Tribunal;

(f) any sum, payment or benefit which, by virtue of any provision of or made under an Act of Parliament, cannot be assigned or charged.

(a) Authority not to enforce the charge

Where the solicitor is of the opinion that it would cause grave hardship or distress to the client to enforce the charge on any particular money or property, or if because of the nature of the property it could be enforced only with unreasonable difficulty, he may apply for authority not to enforce the charge, either wholly or in part (reg 33 Advice & Assistance Regulations 1989). The application is made to the Area Committee and if it is granted in respect of the whole of the property, the Board will then pay the solicitor his costs in the usual manner for the advice and assistance given. If it is granted in respect of part of the property, the Board will pay any deficiency to the solicitor.

There are no indications as to what would amount to hardship, but one arguable example would be the recovery of clothing or furniture desperately needed by the assisted person, and worth perhaps only a few pounds at second hand value, but nonetheless costing much more to replace.

Part II

Criminal Legal Aid

Chapter 8

The Grant of Legal Aid

The grant of legal aid in the magistrates' court in particular, became such a lottery that an attempt was made many years ago by the introduction of the Widgery criteria to provide a basis for some semblance of uniformity. As voluntary guidelines these were hardly a roaring success, and ss 21 and 22 of the Legal Aid Act 1988 now contain 'statutory criteria', although these only apply to certain types of cases. Experience so far indicates that statutory guidelines have had little, if any, of the desired effect.

The aim of the legislation is to endeavour to ensure that the grant of criminal legal aid depends on two factors only, namely whether it is in the interests of justice and secondly, whether the applicant is financially eligible.

1 The vagaries of the present system

It is regrettable for a country which purports to take pride in its system of criminal justice, that the chance of geography and the whims of a local bench, all too often override these basic concepts, although no doubt it would be claimed in support of the system that the difference arises only because of a difference in interpretation. The published figures for 1988 show that Claro in North Yorkshire (which is not particularly noted as a hotbed of do-gooders and social reformers) refused only 0.4 per cent of legal aid applications, whereas Newcastle and Ogmore in South Wales refused 28 per cent and Bury in Greater Manchester refused 25 per cent. Differences of this extent cannot be properly explained, nor can they be tolerated and urgent action is required to bring about speedy reform.

Clearly, there can be no substitute for the practitioner knowing the 'whims' of his local bench, and using his best endeavours to overcome these by carefully drawn up application.

It is little wonder that the Lord Chancellor's office felt that it was essential to spell out in statute that a person committed for trial charged with murder must, subject to his financial eligibility, be granted legal aid.

There can never be total uniformity where the exercise of judgment is called for, but it is a nonsense that neighbouring courts can have wildly differing unofficial policies as to the grant of legal aid for serious charges such as assault occasioning bodily harm and theft. Many courts would of course deny that there ever is, or had been, any 'policy' with regard to the grant of legal aid, because a court cannot lawfully restrict its discretion to grant legal aid by having such a policy; *R* v *Highgate Justices ex parte Lewis* (1977) 142 JP 178. Despite this, policy memoranda as to the refusal of legal aid for certain classes of offences are now beginning to appear. Each case must be dealt with on its merits. Many courts will automatically refuse legal aid for offences of drunk and disorderliness and for offences under the Public Order Acts, convictions for which can have disastrous consequences for a person's reputation and employment prospects.

Cases of this nature can involve allegations against the police. Incidents during the miners strike and at Wapping when prosecution after prosecution collapsed, may then have made national headlines, but they are repeated unnoticed at a local level almost on a daily basis. Without skilful and proper cross examination of prosecution witnesses, an accused person's chances of a fair trial and perhaps of a complete acquittal are reduced alarmingly.

There may even be a more cogent argument for criminal legal aid being more widely available, now that the Crown Prosecution Service conducts all prosecutions. It cannot do any harm to add to a legal aid application as a supporting factor the 'Pollard' ground, namely that the prosecution is legally represented at public expense, and the accused will be disadvantaged if he is deprived of similar professional representation. Even if it does not persuade sufficiently, it lays the ground for a possible appeal, if an unrepresented client is wrongly convicted. Legal aid may then be more readily available for the appeal.

So called minor charges can produce lengthy trials, as the number of witnesses, both for the prosecution and defence bears no relationship to the seriousness of the charge. Reference, where appropriate, on the legal aid application to the fact that a trial may well last for a full day or even longer, will often bring forth a legal aid certificate from a clerk who does not want to have to sit through such a trial with a defendant conducting his own case.

Special features of a case should always be set out on the application form. A bench which is likely to refuse an application in respect of an offence of assault occasioning actual bodily harm where the plea is to be guilty, may well be persuaded to grant it, if they are made aware that the assault involves an allegation of head butting or of kicking a person who is on the ground. If the complainant's injuries are known to be at all serious, reference should be made to that as a factor in the application. A practitioner has only himself to blame if an application is refused because he has failed to put forward any special features affecting his client's case, eg failing where the charge is theft to point out that the amount is large or that there are other aggravating circumstances such as that the accused is alleged to have abused a position of trust, perhaps by stealing during the course of his employment.

2 The statutory criteria

The criteria set out in ss 21 and 22 Legal Aid Act 1988 are not exhaustive and legal aid can be granted where they do not apply. Section 21 lists the circumstances in which legal aid must be granted, subject to financial eligibility, and s 22 sets out the factors to be taken into account in determining whether legal aid should be granted for trials or for appeals to the Crown Court.

For the purposes of Part V of the Act 'criminal proceedings' include:

(1) proceedings for dealing with an offender:
    (*a*) for an offence, or
    (*b*) in respect of a sentence, or
    (*c*) as a fugitive offender;
(2) proceedings instituted under s 115 MCA 1980 (binding over) in respect of an actual or apprehended breach of the peace, or other misbehaviour; and
(3) proceedings for dealing with a person for a failure to comply with a condition of a reconnaissance to keep the peace or to be of good behaviour

(Section 19 (5) LAA 1988).

(a) Where legal aid must be granted

Section 21 of the Act provides that legal aid must be granted subject to financial eligibility in the following cases:

(1) by examining justices, when a person is committed for trial charged with murder;

(2) for an appeal in the House of Lords, where the prosecution appeals or applies for leave to appeal;

(3) for proceedings in a magistrates' court relating to bail, when a person has been charged, and:

(a) has been remanded in custody without being legally represented; and

(b) may again be remanded or committed in custody; and

(c) he is still not represented but wishes to be;

(4) for proceedings in a magistrates' court or Crown Court when a person is to be:

(a) sentenced or dealt with for an offence; and

(b) kept in custody for enquiries or for a report to be made.

The provisions at (3) above also apply to persons under the age of eighteen who have been remanded to the care of a local authority or to a remand centre.

A custodial sentence cannot be imposed for the first time on a defendant who is not legally represented, unless legal aid has been refused because the defendant is not financially eligible, or he has failed to apply for legal aid after having been given the right and the opportunity so to do (Powers of Criminal Courts Act 1973, s 21). Section 21 applies to a person who has been the subject of a previous suspended sentence provided it has not been implemented. For the purposes of the section, a person is legally represented only if he has been represented by counsel or a solicitor after conviction.

A person under twenty-one, whether or not he has previously been the subject of a custodial sentence, must similarly be given the right and opportunity to apply for legal aid before a custodial sentence may be passed on him, and such an application may only be refused on the grounds of financial ineligibility (Criminal Justice Act 1982, s 3).

(b) Where legal aid may be granted

The factors to be taken into account for determining whether legal aid should be granted in the interests of justice include the following:

(1) The likelihood of a sentence involving:
  (*a*) deprivation of liberty; or
  (*b*) loss of livelihood; or
  (*c*) serious damage to reputation;
(2) a substantial question of law being involved;
(3) the accused being unable to understand the proceedings or to state his own case because of inadequate knowledge of English, mental illness or physical disability;
(4) the nature of the offence involves:
  (*a*) tracing and interviewing witnesses; or
  (*b*) expert cross-examination of a prosecution witness;
(5) it is in the interests of someone other than the accused that the accused should be represented.
(LAA 1988, s 22.)

This final factor would be of particular relevance in cases where the complainant should not be cross examined directly by an accused, and would apply to cases of indecency or where the complainant was a juvenile, or perhaps an elderly person who could expect to be frightened of direct cross examination by the accused.

The factors set out in s 22 may be varied by the Lord Chancellor. Where there is doubt as to whether legal aid should be granted, the doubt must be resolved in favour of the applicant (LAA 1988 s 21(7)).

Because the statutory factors are not exhaustive, applications can still be made where there is some other reasonable factor justifying the grant of legal aid. The Act has specifically included blemishes of the peace within the definition of criminal proceedings, and this has not been done without reason. Where there is a suspicion that a refusal is based on a bench's unofficial policy, nothing is lost in renewing the application to the court or the clerk, or, where permitted in applying for review to the Area Committee.

Self defence, the admissibility of evidence, compliance with the code of conduct under the Police and Criminal Evidence Act are all matters where a substantial question of law is involved, and whereby one of the statutory factors would be satisfied.

The criteria set out in s 22 are only to be applied in the limited number of cases where there is to be a trial either in the magistrates or in the Crown Court, or an appeal in the Crown Court. They do not apply to the great majority of cases where pleas of guilty are to be entered, but as neither the Act nor any regulations made under it give any further guidance as to the factors to be applied in guilty pleas, it can be reasonably assumed that in practice the courts will continue to seek guidance from the statutory criteria for these cases.

There is a general overriding power for a court, judge or registrar to make a legal aid order whether or not it has been applied for. Similarly, nothing in the Act or the Criminal General Regulations affects the right of a person to apply to the court at the trial or in other proceedings, even if his application for legal aid has been previously refused, or his legal aid order has previously been revoked for failure to pay the contribution (Criminal General Regulations 1989, reg 10). The only requirements for the grant of legal aid under reg 10 are that it is in the interests of justice so to do and the applicant is financially eligible.

Article 6(3)(c) of the European Convention on Human Rights provides that every person charged with a criminal offence has the right if he has not sufficient means to pay for legal assistance, to be given it free when the interests of justice so require. Breach of this article could lead to an application by an accused person to the European Court of Human Rights (*Kamascinski* v *Austria* Case Number 9/1988/153/207). A separate legal aid scheme is available under the Convention for proceedings before the European Court.

(c) Criteria for guilty pleas

Most practical difficulty in obtaining the legal aid order is likely to continue to occur in cases to which the statutory criteria laid down in s 22 do not apply because there is to be a guilty plea. Those statutory criteria which are relevant could still be referred to by the magistrates for guidance in exercising their discretion, as could the Widgery criteria which are virtually identical. It should be emphasised that article 6(3) of the European Convention on Human Rights provides that legal aid must be granted in criminal proceedings where the interests of justice require it, and this is irrespective of whether there is to be a trial or a plea of guilty. It would not have done any harm to have drafted s 22 without the limiting words 'by way of a trial'.

The relevant factors which should be taken into account in exercising discretion in these circumstances, should be the criteria set out in s 22(2)(a) namely loss of liberty, loss of livelihood or serious damage to reputation. The application form should be completed with as much detail as necessary as to why any of those factors are relevant. If necessary details of any previous convictions should be disclosed or other factors which put the client's liberty at stake. A conviction for a minor theft may place a nurse, teacher or shop assistant and many others, who are in a position of trust, in danger of instant dismissal. The court cannot be expected to know what it is not told.

Despite the fact that a court cannot fetter its discretion by having a policy, official or unofficial as to the grant or refusal of criminal legal aid, nor by the use of internal memoranda, some courts have devised policy statements restricting the availability of criminal legal aid, and excluding altogether certain types of offences from the scope of the Act and of the regulations. A startling and open example of this is the guideline document issued in January, 1990 by the Clerk to the Batley and Dewsbury magistrates' court 'after consultation with other clerks in West Yorkshire'.

After a reminder that each application must be considered on its merits and after setting out the statutory criteria, the guidelines set out a further nine 'criteria key points' as follows:

(1) Loss of liberty—real and practical risk of imprisonment. The likelihood of simply a conviction for an imprisonable offence is *not* a factor to be taken into consideration.

(2) Loss of livelihood—Real risk of loss of employment. Must therefore assess not only the likely sentence, but the possible direct consequence of conviction of penalty on the accused.

(3) Damage to reputation—'Reputation' means good character, trustworthiness and standing in the community. But where a guilty plea or there are recent similar previous convictions there would be no avoidable damage.

(4) Substantial question of law—'Substantial' means more than merely technical and it must be central to the applicant's defence of the charge. Some questions of law have clear guidelines and require simply application of facts to the guidelines, ie Not Substantial.

(5) Language difficulties—Knowledge of English must be insufficient to enable understanding of the charge or to follow the proceedings. Note, an interpreter's fees are less than a solicitors!

(6) Mental or physical—Would not necessarily indicate simple

illiteracy. The disability should be relevant to the accused's ability to prepare a defence to the charge or conduct himself in court.

(7) Interviewing witnesses—Be cautious: such work can be carried out by a solicitor as legal advice and assistance under the Green Form Scheme.

(8) Expert cross examination—This head includes not only the cross examination of expert witnesses but also where skilled cross examination is necessary. It may be necessary to consider this in conjunction with No 9 below.

(9) Desirable, for someone other than the accused—Where cross examination by the accused might put one of the chief prosecution witnesses under unreasonable strain. Examples of this would be:

(a) victims of all sexual offences; or

(b) an elderly victim in a theft or robbery; or

(c) a close relative giving evidence; and

(d) all cases where a child is giving evidence.

The guidelines then list classes of offences accompanied by a statement as to where legal aid should be refused, including a first offence for:

(1) section 20 wounding and grievous bodily harm (unless it is an unprovoked attack of a serious nature or upon a person exposed to violence because of their position, or unless a weapon is used);

(2) first and second offences for possession of class B drugs;

(3) threats to damage property;

(4) theft, deception, handling and going equipped for theft unless the offender is persistent, a perpetrator of a sophisticated crime, or in a position of trust or unless a substantial amount is involved.

Neither Parliament nor the Lord Chancellor has excluded these offences from the legal aid scheme. What is really alarming about circulars of this nature is that the criteria key points are to be used in applying the statutory criteria contained in s 22, ie for trials in the magistrates' court or Crown Court. The list of offences referred to in the circular for which legal aid will be refused is not confined to guilty pleas. Batley and Dewsbury and it appears soon much of West Yorkshire, will have the privilege of seeing unrepresented defendants being forced to conduct their own defences on serious charges such as wounding, stealing and handling stolen property. Furthermore, they will be expected to have sufficient knowledge to make technical legal points themselves and also apply the facts to those technical legal points. No doubt the learned clerk and his assistants will do their utmost to help such unrepresented defendants to become DIY advocates, but can any of this be said to be in the interests of justice, or is it not more in the interests of cost cutting and economy, at the expense of justice? The most glaring omission from the guidelines is the absence of any reference whatsoever to s 21(7) of the Act, which provides that where there is a doubt as to whether legal aid should be granted 'it shall be resolved' in the applicant's favour.

It is to be hoped that other courts do not follow this example of modern thinking towards criminal legal aid. If they do the number of appeals is likely to increase substantially, as is the number of applications to the High Court for judicial review of refusals to grant legal aid.

(d) Legal aid for a criminal prosecution

Legal aid is not available to bring a prosecution for a criminal offence in either the magistrates' court or the Crown Court. However, by virtue of s 17 of the Prosecution of Offences Act 1985:

(1) in any proceedings in respect of an indictable offence; and

(2) in any proceedings before the Divisional Court or the House of Lords in respect of a summary offence,

the court may order that the expenses of a private prosecutor be paid out of central funds. The order may be for the whole of the costs or such part as is just and reasonable. There is no requirement that the order must be made only at the conclusion of the proceedings. The section is not designed to encourage wild cat prosecutions, but it does mean that from an expense point of view, a decision by the Crown Prosecution Service not to bring proceedings need not be the end of the matter for an aggrieved complainant. Provided the private prosecution is properly prepared and presented, an application for costs out of central funds for expenses properly incurred may be met with a sympathetic reception.

Legal Aid is available to the prosecution to resist an appeal in the Crown Court against conviction or sentence, but only where the prosecutor is a private person not acting in an official capacity (LAA 1988, s 21(1)).

3 Grounds for refusal

There are only two grounds on which an application for a criminal legal aid order can be refused. The first is that it does not appear to be desirable in the interests of justice to make such an order, and the second is that the applicant's financial resources render him ineligible.

Where in refusing to grant an application for legal aid magistrates have made an error of law, acted ultra vires or come to a decision which no reasonable court could have made, application can be made in the High Court for judicial review. In considering an application for judicial review, the High Court will not substitute its own views for those of the magistrates, but it will not permit magistrates to fetter the discretion which the Act has given them by adopting a policy as to the refusal of legal aid for certain types of cases.

Now that there are statutory provisions for renewing applications and in certain circumstances applying for a review to the Area Committee, the High Court will be unlikely to grant leave to apply for judicial review until all the statutory procedures available under Criminal General Regulations 1989 have been exhausted.

Chapter 9

Making the Application

Legal aid is available for criminal proceedings in the magistrates and juvenile courts, the Crown Court and in the criminal division of the Courts of Appeal and the Courts Martial Appeal Court (the Appeal Courts). It is also available for criminal proceedings in the House of Lords, but only in respect of appeals from the Appeal Courts.

The determination of a legal aid application, unless it is made to a court, is to be done in private unless regulations otherwise provide, and must be made in the absence of the applicant, the appropriate contributor or person concerned (Criminal General Regulations 1989 reg 7).

1 Scope of the order

Once granted, a criminal legal aid order includes proceedings which are preliminary or incidental to the main proceedings, such as bail applications and other preliminary arguments which are dealt with separately from the main proceedings. A legal aid order in the magistrates' court also covers bail applications to a judge in chambers in the Crown Court (Legal Aid Act 1988 s 19(2)).

'Criminal proceedings' includes applications for a binding over in respect of an actual or apprehended breach of the peace, although few are the courts which could normally be persuaded to grant legal aid in respect of a 'blemish the peace', for the English criminal courts are not readily disposed to regard an allegation that a person is a 'peeping Tom', as being likely to cause serious damage to his reputation, or at least not when it comes to granting him legal aid. The position is similar for those who appear before a court for failing to comply with a recognizance to keep the peace or be of good behaviour (LAA 1988, s 19(5)).

A person who has been arrested cannot be said at that stage to be the subject of any criminal proceedings, but he may still apply for legal aid to the magistrates' court, and the legal aid order is to be granted for proceedings in respect of the offence for which he has been arrested (LAA 1988, s 20). This provision applies, it would seem, even though the person has not been charged with any offence, but Form 1 being the form of application for criminal legal aid does not cater for it.

Once a legal aid order has been made in the magistrates' court it covers representation in any other magistrates' or juvenile court to which the case is remitted, LAA 1988, s 19(3). It also covers advice on appeal and the serving of a notice of appeal and proceedings in the Court of Justice of the European Community, provided they are a stage in the original proceedings for which legal aid was granted.

Legal aid in criminal proceedings is granted by the 'competent authority' which is normally the court in which the proceedings are to take place, save that for criminal proceedings in the House of Lords the only competent authority is the Appeal Courts.

2 Making the application to the magistrates' court

(a) Making the application

Legal aid applications for criminal proceedings in the magistrates' court are made either on Form 1 to the clerk to the justices or orally to the court. Prior to 1 April, 1989 the clerk had no power to refuse an application, but since then both the clerk and the court have power to grant or to refuse an application. An oral application made to the court can be referred to the clerk for determination (Criminal General Regulations 1989, reg 11).

A legal aid order cannot be made until a statement of means on Form 5 has been filed and considered, save where the applicant is physically or mentally incapable of providing one.

The magistrates' court is competent to grant legal aid for Crown Court proceedings where:

(1) it has committed a person for sentence or trial; or

(2) it has been given notice of transfer in serious fraud cases under s 4 Criminal Justice Act 1987; or

(3) a person appeals against conviction or sentence (LAA 1988, s 20(4)); or

(4) it is enquiring into an offence as examining justices, but only before it decides whether or not to commit that person for trial (LAA 1988, s 20(5)).

(b) Refusal of legal aid

The applicant must be served with notice of refusal in Form 2, specifying on which ground his application is refused, and advising him of his right to renew his application, or where applicable to apply to the Area Committee for a review (Criminal General Regulations 1989, reg 12).

There is no requirement that the applicant must be given any further detail as to why it is deemed not to be in the interests of justice to grant his application. The applicant's financial resources must still be assessed, even though his application is refused, and he must still be notified of any contribution which he would have had to pay, had his application been granted (Criminal General Regulations 1989, reg 13).

(c) Renewing the application

Where an application has been refused it may be renewed, either orally to the court or to the justices' clerk (Criminal General Regulations 1989, reg 14(1)). The regulation does not specify that a renewed application to the clerk must be in writing, but it does specify that only the court can receive an oral application. The clerk can grant the renewed application, or refer it to the court or to a single magistrate who is not on the retired list. The clerk cannot refuse a renewed application himself. The court may grant or refuse the renewed application and may also refer it to the clerk, who may then grant it or refer it back to the court or to a single magistrate. Again the clerk cannot refuse it. The court or single magistrate to whom a renewed application is referred may grant or refuse it. If it is refused, notice under reg 12 must be given to the applicant.

(d) Review by the area committee

Where an application has been refused, a choice may be available as to whether the application should be renewed under reg 14 or whether an application for review should be made to the Area Committee under reg 15 of the Criminal General Regulations 1989. There is no right to apply for a review where the right to renew an application has been exercised, even if the renewed application was unsuccessful.

An application for review may be made to the Area Committee where:

(1) the applicant is either charged with an offence which is indictable or triable either way, or is brought before the court to be dealt with in respect of a sentence or order made in connection with such an offence; and

(2) legal aid was refused on the grounds that it was not in the interests of justice; and

(3) legal aid was applied for more than twenty-one days before the trial or committal date, provided that date had been fixed at the time of the application. The twenty-one day period is not to be computed by reference to the date of the applicant's first appearance before the court, but by reference to the date actually fixed for the trial or committal (*R* v *Bury Magistrates ex parte N (a minor)* [1986] 3 All ER 789). This decision supported the view contained in an agreement of a joint committee of the Law Society and the Justices' Clerks Society of 11 July, 1984 and which had been ignored by a number of courts which took a contrary view, namely that the relevant date was the date of the first appearance before the court.

The Area Committee may refuse the application or grant legal aid, it must also make a contribution order in accordance with the assessment order already made and notified to the applicant under reg 12, when his original application was refused. If the contribution is to be paid out of capital before the legal aid order can take effect, the Area Committee must send the order to the clerk to the justices and not to the applicant. Application is made to the Area Committee by giving notice in Form 3, accompanied by a copy of the original statement of means and of the notice of refusal. Form 3 must be served within fourteen days of the notice of refusal, although for good reason the Area Committee may extend the time limit or waive it altogether. A copy of Form 3 must also be served on the clerk to the justices.

The Area Committee has power to require further information and documents from the applicant, but he has no statutory right to appear in person before the Committee.

There can be no general rule as to whether it is best to appeal by way of renewal or by way of review. The choice must depend on local knowledge of the local court and its clerk, and of any unofficial policy which they may have with regard to the grant of legal aid for certain types of cases. If refusal appears to be based on policy, then there may be more chance of success if a review is applied for to the Area Committee, rather than going back to the court or its clerk and asking, in effect, for it to reconsider and overturn its own unofficial policies.

3 Applying for legal aid for criminal proceedings in the Crown Court

The Crown Court has power to grant legal aid for all criminal proceedings before it. It is not therefore fatal if an advocate has forgotten to ask for Crown Court legal aid at the conclusion of the proceedings in the magistrates' court, but an application directly to the Crown Court involves completing a new application form and a further statement of means. It is therefore more cost effective to remember to make the application to the magistrates' court, on the basis of the forms already submitted to it.

The Crown Court can also deal with legal aid applications for leave to appeal to the Court of Appeal and for appeals under s 9(11) CJA 1987 in respect of appeals against decisions made at preparatory hearings in the Crown Court.

The application to the Crown Court is made to:

(1) the chief clerk on Form 1; or
(2) orally to the Crown Court, or to a magistrates' court at the conclusion of proceedings in a magistrates' court; or
(3) to the magistrates or to the justices clerk on Form 1 where notice of transfer in respect of serious fraud cases has been given; or
(4) to the justices clerk on Form 1 in the case of an appeal from the magistrates to the Crown Court; or
(5) to the justices clerk in such form as may be required where the magistrates have committed a person for trial under s 6(2) MCA 1980; or
(6) orally to the court ordering a re-trial under s 7 Criminal Appeal Act 1968.

A legal aid order cannot be made until a statement of means on Form 5 has been considered, unless the applicant is not required to file one because of physical or mental incapacity.

(a) Refusal of legal aid

Whether the application is refused by the Crown Court, the chief clerk or the justices clerk, a notice of refusal must be sent, together with a determination of means and of any contribution payable. Regulations 19 and 20 Crim Gen Regs 1989.

(b) Renewal of the application

Application for renewal following a refusal, must be made either orally to the Crown Court or in writing to the chief clerk and must be accompanied by the notice of refusal. The chief clerk cannot refuse a renewed application, but he can grant it or refer it to a Crown Court judge, who may grant or refuse it.

The Crown Court may refuse a renewed application, grant it or refer it to the chief clerk, who again cannot refuse it. He must grant it or refer it back to a judge. The statement of means where required must be considered before legal aid can be granted on a renewed application. There is no right to apply for review to the Area Committee once a legal aid application has been refused in the Crown Court.

4 Criminal legal aid in the Appeal Courts

Applications for legal aid in the Criminal Division of the Court of Appeal and in the Courts Martial Appeal Court can be made orally to the Court of Appeal, to a judge thereof or to a registrar thereof. Alternatively, a written application can be made on the form provided by the court.

An oral application to the Appeal Courts may be referred by the court to a judge thereof or to the registrar. An oral application to a judge may be referred to the registrar. If a judge refuses to make a legal aid order, the application can be renewed to the Court of Appeal, but there is no right to renew an application which has been refused by the full court. The registrar has no power to refuse an application, if he does not grant the application, he must refer it, or as the case may be, refer it back to the court.

There is no right to apply for review to the Area Committee following refusal of an application.

A statement of means must have been filed and considered before a legal aid order can be granted, and in addition, notice of appeal or of application for leave to appeal must also have been given. In proceedings in the Court of Appeal, the stage at which legal aid is to commence may be specified in the order.

Only a judge of the Court of Appeal can revoke a legal aid order, unless revocation is applied for by the assisted person when the registrar can deal with the application. For the purposes of the Criminal General Regulations 1989 'Court of Appeal' includes the Courts Martial Appeal Court.

5 Proceedings in the House of Lords

The House of Lords is the only court with criminal jurisdiction which has no power to grant legal aid. Applications are made to the Court of Appeal in accordance with reg 22 of the Criminal General Regulations 1989, once notice of appeal or notice of application for leave to appeal has been given.

6 The Legal Aid Order

When granted a legal aid order must be in Form 11 for proceedings in the magistrates' court or Crown Court and Form 13 for the Appeal Courts. If granted by the Area Committee it must be in Form 12. A magistrates' court sitting as examining justices may make or amend an order so that it applies to the committal proceedings, and if the assisted person is committed for trial at the Crown Court (a through order). (Criminal General Regulations 1989, reg 41). The making of a through order does not affect the way in which costs are claimed.

A copy of the legal aid order must be sent to the assisted person, subject to regs 17(3) and 29(3) as to payment of the contribution. Where the order is granted in respect of proceedings in the magistrates' court, a further copy marked 'Board Copy' must also be sent to the solicitor. This applies whether the order is made by the court or by the Area Committee. This second copy is eventually sent to the Board with the claim for costs at the conclusion of the case.

If counsel is instructed, whether or not he is assigned, a copy of the legal aid order must be included with the instructions and counsel must also be notified of any amendment to the order.

7 Withdrawal revocation and amendment of orders

(a) Withdrawal

A legal aid order may be withdrawn if the assisted person does not accept the terms on which the order is offered, or at the request of the assisted person, or if the legal representative assigned under the order withdraws and the assisted person's conduct is such that it is not desirable to amend the order by substituting another legal representative (LAA 1988, s 24(2) and regs 36 and 50 of the Criminal General Regulations 1989).

An order withdrawing a legal aid order must be on Form 14 and a copy must be sent to the assisted person, the solicitor assigned or if none, to counsel, and if withdrawal is by the Area Committee, to the proper officer of the court.

(b) Revocation

A legal order may be revoked by the court in which the proceedings are being heard if the assisted person fails to pay any relevant contribution which is due (LAA 1988, s 24(2)). For these purposes 'relevant contribution' means any sum which the assisted person is required to pay under a contribution order and which falls due after the making of the order but before the conclusion of the proceedings (LAA 1988, s 24(4)). The power to revoke a legal order cannot be exercised before the assisted person has been given an opportunity of making representations, and unless the court is satisfied firstly, that he was able to pay the relevant contribution when it was due and secondly, that he is able to pay the whole or part of it but has failed or refused so to do (LAA 1988, s 24(3)).

Regulation 36 of the Criminal General Regulations 1989 requires further procedural formalities to be carried out before an order can be revoked. A notice in Form 9 must be served on the legally assisted person requiring him to comply with the contribution order and to pay any sums due under it within seven days of receiving the notice. If he does not comply with that notice, a further notice in Form 10 must be served on him, inviting him to make representations as to why he cannot comply with the contribution order. Copies of both notices must be served on the assisted person's solicitor or if counsel only is assigned, on his counsel. Regulation 36(3) of the Criminal General Regulations 1989 repeats the provisions of s 24(2) of the Act. Revocation does not affect the right of the assigned legal representative to be paid for work done before the date of the revocation.

An order of revocation in Form 14 must be served as on a withdrawal of a legal aid order.

(c) Amendment

Power to amend a legal aid order is contained in regs 50 and 51 of the Criminal General Regulations 1989. Regulation 50 relates to amendments required where the assisted person wishes to change a legal representative (ie solicitor or counsel) assigned under the order, or if such legal representative withdraws from the case. Regulation 51 caters for an amendment to include representation by counsel in the magistrates' court and the specified cases set out in reg 44(3). Regulation 51 also sets out the procedure for applying for such amendments, and where the application is refused, for renewing it to the court or to the Area Committee.

A general power to amend a legal aid order is conferred by Legal Aid Act 1988, s 21(9) on any appropriate authority. If further charges are brought against an assisted person after the granting of a legal aid order, application must be made for the order to be amended to include them, as otherwise work carried out in relation to those new charges would be outside the scope of the certificate.

Chapter 10

Financial Eligibility

1 Assessment of means

Criminal legal aid is means tested and cannot be granted to any person unless his financial resources are such as to make him eligible. LAA 1988, s 21(5). The person whose means are tested is the applicant, the applicant's 'spouse' and where the applicant is under sixteen years of age, 'the appropriate contributor' which is his parent or guardian. A statement of means on Form 5 must be submitted together with sufficient payslips to enable the average net weekly income to be assessed.

If the applicant is in receipt of income support or family credit, no determination of his means is to be made, and the remainder of Form 5 as to capital and income does not have to be completed. A statement of means is not required from a person who is incapable of furnishing one by reason of his physical or mental condition, nor where a previous application, accompanied by a statement of means has been made, and there has been no change in the applicant's financial resources (Criminal General Regulations 1989, reg 23(4)).

The applicant can be required to provide evidence of any information given in the statement of means, or of any change in those means, as well as any additional information required to make the assessment. If the evidence or information is not supplied, the disposable capital and income are deemed to exceed the limit below which no contribution is payable. In those circumstances, the court will fix the amount of the contribution.

(a) 'Spouse or cohabitee'

The capital and income of a spouse or cohabitee are to be treated as those of the person submitting the statement of means, unless they are living apart or the spouse has a contrary interest in the proceedings, or it is not equitable in all the circumstances to take them into account.

'Cohabitee' means a man and woman living together in the same household as husband and wife. It will not therefore include a lodger of either sex, or a person who only comes to stay for part of the time such as weekends.

(b) Disposable income

For persons in employment their income is their wage or salary. For those who are self employed it is the actual profit at the time, or an estimate of income based on the last period for which accounts have been prepared. In arriving at the assessment of disposable income, certain deductions can be made from actual gross income and certain payments and expenses can also be deducted. Disposable income does not include any of the following:

(1) attendance allowance; or
(2) mobility allowance; or
(3) constant attendance allowance paid as an increase to a disablement pension; or
(4) housing benefit; or
(5) payments under s 32 Social Security Act 1986.

In assessing disposable income a deduction has to be made in respect of:

(1) income tax payable;
(2) national insurance contributions payable;
(3) reasonable travelling expenses to and from work;
(4) contributions paid to an occupational pension scheme or to a personal pension scheme; and
(5) reasonable expenses in making reasonable provision for a dependent child living with the person whose means are being assessed because of that person's absence from home by reason of employment. This would include expenses of a nanny or child minder whose services were needed whilst a parent or spouse was at work.

Deductions must be made in assessing disposable income of:

(1) The net rent payable for the main or only dwelling: 'Net rent' includes the annual rent, poll tax, a reasonable allowance for repairs, insurance premiums and mortgage repayments both as to capital and interest.

(2) Reasonable board and lodging where the person concerned is not a householder.

(3) Maintenance of a spouse where the couple are living together.

(4) Maintenance of any dependent child or relative who are members of the household, although any income of such dependants can be taken into account to reduce the deduction. If the dependent's financial resources are sufficient they would not be treated as being dependent.

(5) Bona fide maintenance payments for any of the following who are not members of the household (the deduction to be made is either the amount of the payment or a deduction at such rate as is reasonable):
   (a) a spouse who is living apart;
   (b) a former spouse;
   (c) a child;
   (d) a relative.

(6) Payments under orders of the High Court, Crown Court, county court or magistrates' court, and which arise from proceedings other than those in respect of which legal aid is granted.

2 Disposable capital

Any resource of a capital nature must be taken into account in determining disposable capital. If the resource is not money, its value is the amount which it would fetch if sold in the market, whether the market is an open one or restricted.

The following must be disregarded in assessing capital:

(1) savings made out of mobility allowance and intended to be used for mobility;

(2) arrears of attendance allowance, mobility allowance, income support or family credit, for a period not exceeding twelve months from the date of receipt of the arrears;

(3) payments made under s 32 of the Social Security Act 1986.

(4) household furniture and effects of the main or only residence of the person concerned, articles of personal clothing and tools and equipment of his trade (these can however be taken into account in exceptional circumstances, and presumably this justifies the question about furs and jewellery on Form 5);

(5) the value of the main or only residence in which the person concerned resides;

(6) any capital which, having regard to its nature or in the circumstances of the case, the determining officer decides should be disregarded.

(a) Deprivation of resources

A person who deprives himself of resources or converts his resources into resources which, under the regulations are to be disregarded, will have those resources taken into account for the purposes of assessing his financial eligibility for criminal legal aid. The Criminal Costs (Amendment) Regulations 1990 do not contain any provision limiting the reason for the deprivation as do the 1990 regulations relating to Civil Legal Aid and Advice and Assistance.

3 Contributions

The assessment of means is not only made for the purpose of ascertaining whether the person concerned is financially eligible for legal aid. If he is financially eligible, then the assessment determines what, if anything, his contribution is to be. The contribution may be ordered to be paid in a lump sum, or by weekly or at the discretion of the court, fortnightly or monthly instalments. If it is to be paid out of income, it must be paid by instalments, payable within the contribution period which is a maximum of six months from the date of the legal aid order. If it is to be paid out of capital, it must be paid immediately, or if the capital is not readily available, within such time as the court considers reasonable.

If the contribution paid exceeds the costs eventually paid by the Board under the order, the excess must be refunded to the assisted person. Clients can be alarmed at the size of the contribution which they are ordered to pay under criminal legal aid orders, and it should be explained to them at the outset that any contribution which they have to pay will be assessed purely on their means, and will bear no relationship to the eventual cost of their case. This will help to save alarmed or even irate telephone calls and visits from clients who have a contribution to pay of perhaps £500 when they are pleading guilty to a comparatively minor case, which will not involve many hours work.

The amount of the contribution must be reduced by the

amount of any contribution paid by the client for advice and assistance under the Green Form Scheme in connection with the same matter. The Green Form Scheme contribution should always therefore be shown on the statement of means Form 5.

There is power for a court to order that a legal aid order shall not take effect until the contribution has been paid. The solicitor is always supplied with a copy of the contribution order as well as of the legal aid order. He has only himself to blame if he does not check them carefully, and then discovers that he has done work for which the Board cannot make payment.

Payment of a contribution can only be ordered once in the same case. If the case goes to a higher court, whether for trial or by way of appeal, the higher court cannot, provided a contribution order was made in the lower, make any further determination of means or order the payment of any further contribution (Criminal General Regulations, reg 28 1989).

(a) Change in financial circumstances

Any change in the financial circumstances of the person concerned must be notified to the court, which must then redetermine whether a contribution is payable, even if it was not originally. The amount of the contribution payable must be redetermined if disposable income has increased by more than £750 per annum, or decreased by more than £300 per annum, or if disposable capital has increased by more than £300 Criminal General Regulations 1989, reg 33. If a contribution is reduced or revoked, any sum over paid must be refunded.

(b) The amount of the contribution

The contribution payable out of disposal income by weekly instalments is set out in the table in sched 4 to the Criminal General Regulations 1989 and is increased by £1 for each £4 or part thereof, by which weekly disposable income exceeds £85. The contribution payable out of disposal capital is equal to the amount by which that capital exceeds £3,000.

(c) Remission, refund and repayment of contributions

At the conclusion of proceedings, the court may, if it thinks fit, remit any unpaid contribution. If the assisted person is acquitted or is successful on an appeal which he brings or opposes, the court may remit any unpaid contribution or order repayment of any contribution made. Such an order should be made unless there are circumstances which make it inappropriate (Practice Note [1989] 2 All ER 608 Para 10).

No further contributions are to be paid if the person concerned starts to receive income support or family credit, or if the assisted person is sentenced to an immediate term of imprisonment or detention (Criminal General Regulations 1989, reg 37).

Chapter 11

The Assignment of Solicitor and Counsel

Representation must generally provide for both solicitor and counsel, save that a criminal legal aid order cannot provide for representation by counsel on a bail application in the magistrates' court, nor can it provide for representation by counsel in any other proceedings in a magistrates' court unless the court thinks it desirable because the offence is unusually grave or difficult, as well as being indictable, and in addition, in the case of offences under s 1 of the Children and Young Persons Act 1969 the conditions set out in subsection 2(*f*) of that section are also satisfied.

In urgent cases where there is no time to instruct a solicitor, the Crown Court may grant representation limited to counsel only. This power is limited to appeals and committals for trial or for sentence. Legal aid for Crown Court appeals and committals may also be limited to representation by a solicitor only, and this applies whether legal aid is granted in a magistrates' or Crown Court. Criminal General Regulations 1989, regs 45(5) and (9). What some judges may say, were this power ever exercised, is perhaps best left to the imagination.

The assisted person must generally have assigned to him the solicitor of his own choice, unless there is another legally aided defendant in the same case and the cases are to be heard together, in which case the same solicitor may be assigned to two or more defendants, unless the interests of justice require separate representation. Criminal General Regulations 1989, regs 45 and 45(9).The usual argument which is put forward to justify separate representation is that there is a conflict of interest between the accused. Such a conflict would arise where one accused was blaming the other, whether by way of defence or mitigation, or where one accused had far more previous convictions than the other, thereby enabling a comparison of respective criminal experience to be brought to the court's attention.

Just as the client has freedom of choice in selecting a solicitor, so the solicitor has freedom in selecting counsel within the terms of the order Regulation 45(2) of the Criminal General Regulations 1989 subject to the power to assign one counsel to two defendants under the provisions of reg 49. Selection of counsel by a solicitor in cases where counsel is not assigned by the Court is entirely a matter for the solicitor, even as to choosing separate counsel in cases where the solicitor represents more than one defendant *R v O'Brien* [1985] 1 All ER 971. For proceedings in the Court of Appeal and the House of Lords, counsel may be assigned by the court, the judge or the proper officer and must be so assigned where a legal aid order is made or amended so as to provide for representation by counsel only. In the case of an appeal in those courts regard must be had so far as is reasonably practicable to the wishes of the assisted person to have the counsel or solicitor who represented him in the lower court. For other proceedings in those courts, counsel can be assigned without any regard being paid to those matters (Criminal General Regulations 1989, reg 47).

1 Orders for two counsel

A legal aid order for two counsel can only be made for specified cases namely trials in the Crown Court or for proceedings in the Court of Appeal and the House of Lords where the charge is murder or one of exceptional difficulty, gravity or complexity and the services of two counsel are required in the interests of justice. The only power which the magistrates court has to specify the type of counsel to be instructed or to make a two counsel order is on a charge of murder where the order must provide for Queen's Counsel with junior counsel (Criminal General Regulations 1989, reg 48(4)).

A High Court judge or a circuit judge in proceedings in the Crown Court, a judge of the Court of Appeal or the registrar in proceedings in the Court of Appeal may specify in a two counsel order that counsel shall be:

(1) a Queen's Counsel with a junior counsel; or
(2) a Queen's Counsel with a noting junior counsel; or
(3) two junior counsel; or
(4) a junior counsel with a noting junior counsel.

Before making any such order, consideration must be given as to whether Queen's Counsel alone will suffice and in considering which type of order to make, regard must be had to the choice by the legally aided person of any one particular counsel (Criminal General Regulations 1989, reg 48(3)).

A national legal aid authority is required by Article 6(3) of European Convention on Human Rights to intervene, if a failure by legal aid counsel to provide effective representation, was either manifest or sufficiently brought to its attention in some other way; *Kamczinihi* v *Austria* (1990) *The Independent* 3 January.

2 Amendments to representation

If a legal aid order in a specified case under reg 48(2) Criminal General Regulations 1989 provides for one counsel only, application can be made for it to be amended to include two counsel. If the order provides for two counsel it may be amended to any of the other alternatives set out at (1) to (4) above reg 48(6) Criminal General Regulations 1989.

Application for a two counsel order for proceedings in the Crown Court are made:

(1) to the judge if at a pre-trial review or during the trial; or
(2) otherwise to the resident or designated judge of that Crown Court, or in his absence, to a judge nominated by the presiding judge of the circuit. If the case is to be heard before a named High Court judge or circuit judge, he should refer it to the named judge for consideration (Practice Direction [1989] 1 WLR 359).

A court which has power to make a legal aid order may amend it by substituting any legal representative whom the court could assign were it then making the order (Criminal General Regulations 1989, reg 51). If because of an assisted person's conduct it is not desirable to amend an order by substituting another legal representative where the one originally assigned has withdrawn from the case, the court may withdraw the legal aid order (reg 52). An order amending a legal aid order under reg 50 must be in Form 15 and a copy must be sent to the assisted person and to the solicitor originally assigned, as well as to the substituted solicitor. If the amendment is by the Area Committee, Form 15 must also be sent to the proper officer of the court to which the application for an amendment was originally made. If counsel only is assigned under the original order, he must be sent a copy of Form 15 (reg 53).

An application for amendment either under reg 50 or by allowing representation by counsel in a magistrates' court where such representation is permitted under reg 44(3) must be made to the proper officer of the court and must also state the grounds for the application. If the application is refused, it may always be renewed, both to the court and in certain circumstances to the Area Committee.

Such applications cannot be renewed to the Area Committee if:

(1) the application has previously been refused by the court or the Area Committee; or

(2) in Crown Court proceedings, more than fourteen days has elapsed since the committal or the giving of notice of appeal; or

(3) in the magistrates' court there is less than fourteen days before the trial or committal, and the date of such trial or committal has been fixed when the application was made; or

(4) it is in respect of proceedings in the Appeal Courts or the House of Lords.

A renewal of an application to the Area Committee must be accompanied by a copy of a legal aid order, notice of refusal of the application, any papers submitted in support of the original application, and any other relevant document or information. The Area Committee may grant or refuse the application and amend or revoke the legal aid order accordingly.

Chapter 12

Costs

1 The assesssing authorities

The appropriate authority for assessing costs and paying costs after 1 April, 1989 is:

(1) the officer prescribed by order of the House of Lords for proceedings in the House of Lords (Criminal Costs Regulations 1989, reg 18); or

(2) the Registrar for proceedings in the Court of Appeal; or

(3) the appointed officer for proceedings in the Crown Court; or

(4) the Board for proceedings in the magistrates' court, including advice or assistance for an appeal to the Crown Court.

Criminal Costs Regulations 1989, reg 3.

Once costs have been determined, solicitor or counsel must be notified by the appropriate authority of the costs payable and payment must be authorised accordingly (reg 10(1)). Counsel's fees must be paid directly to counsel.

(a) Time limits

Claims for costs must be submitted within three months of the conclusion of the proceedings (Criminal Costs Regulations 1989, reg 5). This period may be extended where there is good reason, and also where provided that there are exceptional circumstances, a claim for payment has been submitted late and there is no good reason for the delay. It is difficult to think of circumstances being exceptional which would not also amount to a good reason for delay.

The appropriate authority may reduce a claim for costs because of delay, even where there are exceptional circumstances, provided that the reduction is reasonable in the circumstances

(Criminal Costs Regulations 1989, reg 17). The solicitor must first be given a reasonable opportunity to show, either orally or in writing, why the costs should not be so reduced.

(b) Completing the claim form

The claim for costs must be completed on the appropriate claim form and must be submitted with the legal aid order and receipts for any disbursements. If a claim is submitted to the Board it must be accompanied by the copy legal aid order marked 'Board Copy'. There are different claim forms for each of the appropriate authorities. The claim must include the following information:

(1) a summary of the work done by a fee earner;
(2) the date when the work was carried out and the time spent on each item;
(3) whether the work was done for more than one legally aided client;
(4) the amount of any disbursements and the circumstances in which they were incurred;
(5) work done in relation to more than one indictment or a re-trial;
(6) any circumstances justifying a claim for payment at a rate in excess of the prescribed rate;
(7) any special circumstances which should be drawn to the attention of the appropriate authority; and
(8) in the Crown Court and Court of Appeal the class of fee earner undertaking the work.

(c) Payment on account and increased hourly rates

Where cases require particularly heavy preparation or there is to be a lengthy or complex criminal trial, payment on account of costs will be made during the course of the case. Towards the end of 1989 a judge agreed in *R* v *Saunders* (the Guinness case) for monthly payment of costs to be paid on account to the solicitors involved.

The judge also stressed that in cases where higher rates are likely to be paid under the Criminal Costs Regulations 1989 and although the Regulations only provide for an assessment of costs to be made after the conclusion of the case, the Board should give an indication as to the probable higher rate which it would approve in a particular case. Such an indication is not an offer and does not prevent or in any way limit, proper assessment after the conclusion of the case.

2 The work for which payment will be made

Payment will only be made for work reasonably carried out by a fee earner, ie a solicitor, legal executive or a clerk who regularly does work for which it is appropriate to make a direct charge to clients (Criminal Costs Regulations, reg 2). Because there are different rates of payment the types of work for which payment will be allowed are split into the following classes:
   (1) preparation;
   (2) advocacy;
   (3) attendance at court with counsel—but only where counsel has been assigned;
   (4) travel and waiting;
   (5) routine letters and telephone calls; and
   (6) advice on appeal or case stated.

Preparation includes all the work which it is reasonable to carry out in getting the case ready for court, such as interviewing witnesses, taking instructions from the client, perusing prosecution statements, instructing counsel (where counsel is assigned), preparing documents, non-routine letters and telephone calls and preparing for advocacy.

Long letters and telephone calls which are not routine should always be timed, as otherwise they can only be paid at the standard rate and this can lead to a substantial reduction in the amount claimed. Three long telephone calls of ten minutes each are worth a total of £19.62 at current rates outside London. If claimed as routine because no record has been kept of their length, they are worth £9.15. Repeated once per week over a year, such neglect results in a loss of income in excess of £500, purely through failure to observe the most elementary of time recording practices.

Preparation for advocacy is often difficult to time and record accurately, but the discipline of time recording is essential. Many a cross examination has been plotted in the bath or a mitigation prepared whilst driving to the office. Thinking time of this nature must be recorded at the first available opportunity. Half an hour per week not recorded brings a further loss of £500 per annum.

If any of the work done is unreasonable it will not qualify for payment. The test of reasonableness applies not only to the nature of the work, but to the time spent on it. It is not normally reasonable to spend two hours taking instructions from a shop-lifter who is pleading guilty, even if the competence of the fee earner concerned is such that he actually spends two hours doing it.

(a) Committal proceedings

In order to reduce the call on the Legal Aid fund, solicitors are expected to exercise the option available under s 6(2) MCA 1980 as amended by s 61 Criminal Justice Act 1982, not to attend committal proceedings involving written statements only.

Payment will not be made either to a solicitor or counsel for attending committal proceedings unless:

(1) a submission is to be made of no case to answer or there is no need to take oral evidence from a witness; or

(2) there is to be an application for bail or for variation of bail conditions; or

(3) there is to be an application to lift reporting restrictions; or

(4) there is to be an application in relation to the venue of the trial; or

(5) the written statements have been served less than fourteen days before the date fixed for the committal proceedings; or

(6) the solicitor has to attend to make an oral legal aid application to the court, or to make representations about the grant of legal aid for the Crown Court; or

(7) there is any other matter reasonably requiring the attendance of solicitor or counsel at the hearing.

The claim for costs form includes a section setting out the circumstances in which payment can be claimed, and the solicitor has to indicate by ticking the appropriate boxes which of them, if any, apply. The widespread failure of the police to submit files to the Crown Prosecution Service in reasonable time before the date fixed for a committal hearing, means that the ability of the Prosecution to serve statements more than fourteen days before the committal is extremely limited. All too often committal proceedings have to be adjourned completely unnecessarily because the police have not bothered to get the file ready in time. The cost to public funds of wasted court time and of keeping defendants further remanded in custody for no reason other than this, makes the savings to be obtained from insisting on accused persons going to court without their solicitor, appear miniscule. If only as in so many instances the authorities would put their own house in order, ample money could be made available for a properly funded legal aid system.

(b) Pre-certificate work

If representation or advice is given before a legal aid order is made for proceedings in the magistrates' court, it is deemed to have been given under the order if:

(1) the interests of justice required it to be given urgently; or
(2) legal aid was applied for without undue delay; or
(3) it was given by the solicitor who was subsequently assigned under the order (Criminal General Regulations 1989, reg 44(7)).

This regulation applies to any advice or representation in connection with those proceedings and is not limited to advice and assistance within either the scope of, or the financial eligibility regulations relating to, advice and assistance.

If advice or assistance under Pt III of the Legal Aid Act 1988 has been given on any matter which becomes the subject of criminal proceedings for which a legal aid order is made, the cost of the advice and assistance must be paid as if it were carried out under the order, provided that the solicitor assigned under the order also gave the advice and assistance (LAA 1988, s 26). As this is mandatory, any green form work or advice and assistance at the police station must be included in the claim for payment under any subsequent legal aid order, and should not be claimed separately. This cannot apply where there is a delay between the advice and assistance given and the bringing of subsequent proceedings in respect of which a legal aid order can be applied for. In any event the Act and the regulations on this point are confusing because it is also mandatory to claim on the appropriate forms for advice and assistance given.

(c) Disbursements, counsel's fees and prior authorities

A claim for disbursements reasonably incurred must be allowed, Criminal Costs Regulations 1989, reg 7. If excessive travelling is involved, either to the court or to the client's premises, a claim for travelling expenses will be limited to what is considered reasonable. If there are valid reasons as to why 'excessive' travel was necessary, they should be set out on the claim for costs or in an accompanying letter. In cases in the Court of

Appeal, it is not regarded as being reasonable to obtain a transcript, either in whole or in part, from the official shorthand writer, save through the registrar. A claim for the cost of a transcript obtained directly from the shorthand writer will be disallowed unless the proper officer can be persuaded that it was reasonable (Criminal Costs Regulations 1989, reg 7(1)(*b*)).

If a legal aid order is made for an appeal in the Crown Court the justices clerk must on request, supply the legally aided person or his solicitor with a copy of the notes of evidence or depositions (Criminal General Regulations 1989, reg 42).

Counsel's fees in the magistrates' court may be claimed as a disbursement, even where counsel was not assigned, but the amount will be limited to the amount which would have been paid to the solicitor, had he undertaken the case without counsel. Counsel's and Solicitor's costs together must not exceed that sum (Criminal Costs Regulations 1989, regs 7(2) and (3)).

Prior authority can be obtained from the Area Committee for the following steps in the magistrates' or Crown Courts:

(1) obtaining a written expert's report or opinion;
(2) employing a person other than an expert to provide a written report or opinion;
(3) obtaining transcripts of shorthand notes or of tape recordings;
(4) where counsel is assigned, instructing Queen's Counsel;
(5) incurring expenditure which is unusual in its nature or amount.

(Criminal General Regulations 1989, reg 54.)

It is always prudent to apply for the necessary authority, because if it is granted, the expenditure cannot be challenged and must be allowed without determination when the claim for payment is made, unless the solicitor knew or ought to have known that the purpose for which the authority was given had become irrelevant or unnecessary before the cost was incurred. Applications for prior authority can be made by letter, setting out the relevant circumstances, including the amount of the expenditure in respect of which the prior authority is sought. The Board's copy of the legal aid order must also be submitted, so that if granted, the authority and the maximum expenditure can be endorsed on it.

If authority is refused under reg 54, the solicitor can be paid privately by the legally aided client for anything which is the subject of the refusal (Criminal General Regulations 1989, reg

55). This is one statutory exception to the golden rule that solicitor and counsel acting for a legally aided client cannot receive or be a party to the making of any work done in those proceedings, unless the payment is made out of the legal aid fund (Criminal General Regulations 1989, reg 55(*a*)).

(d) Witness expenses and interpreters

Witness expenses and the fees of any interpreter required for an accused cannot be claimed out of the legal aid fund, but are allowed instead out of central funds unless the court otherwise directs (Practice Note [1989] 2 All ER 605). This direction also applies to the costs of a medical practitioner for an oral report. In the Crown Court a medical report as to the mental condition of a person charged with murder may be ordered by the court to be paid for out of central funds.

(e) Judges disallowing costs

There is no power for any judge to order that any legal aid costs should be disallowed for any reason in respect of any item of work. In the Crown Court or the Court of Appeal the proper procedure is for the judge to make observations for the attention of the appropriate authority, as to any specified items which the judge feels should be considered when costs are determined.

These observations should be made if the case has been conducted unreasonably so as to cause unjustifiable expense or, without reasonable competence or expedition, resulting in costs being wasted. Where standard fees are payable in the Crown Court and the judge is dissatisfied with the conduct of the case, he can direct that the fees should be determined and not paid as standard fees.

Solicitor and counsel whose work is being called into question must be given proper notice, as well as an opportunity to make representations to the appropriate officer and to show cause—normally in chambers and not in open court—why the observations or direction by the judge should not be made. The judge's decision may then be announced in open court if it is in the interests of justice to do so. Practice Direction [1989] 2 All ER 607.

(f) Advice on appeal

Advice as to an appeal or case stated is specifically included by reg 6(1)(*a*) Criminal Costs Regulations 1989 as work within the scope of a legal aid order and for which payment may be allowed. This includes preparing and serving notice of appeal or of an application for leave to appeal. A legal aid order for an appeal to the Court of Appeal or the Court Martial Appeal Court may be limited to advice as to whether there are reasonable grounds for the appeal and to assistance in preparing a notice of appeal or of an application for leave to appeal.

Counsel or solicitor are under a duty to give written advice to a defendant within twenty-one days of conviction or sentence in the Crown Court. If the advice is positive and notice of appeal or application for leave to appeal is lodged, the costs in respect of the advice and notice will be determined by the Registrar of criminal appeals.

The Crown Court can only determine those costs if either the notice was not given on counsel or solicitor's advice or if, following the receipt of positive advice no notice of appeal was given. No costs are to be allowed for advice on appeal where counsel's immediate and final view is that there are no reasonable grounds for appeal (Practice Direction [1989] 2 All ER 605).

3 The fees payable

Regulation 4(1) of the Criminal Costs Regulations 1989 provides that costs for work done under a legal aid order must be determined by the appropriate authority in accordance with the Criminal Costs Regulations. The remainder of reg 4 shows a certain confusion in the mind of the parliamentary draughtsman, because reg 4(2) continues by providing that a reasonable amount must be allowed 'subject to and in accordance with these Regulations' for all work reasonably done. Despite this the schedule to those Regulations sets out hourly rates of pay and the amount of standard fees.

The question therefore arises as to how the appropriate authority can, in assessing costs, take into account matters which reg 4(2)(b) requires it to take into account, namely the nature, importance, complexity and difficulty of a case, when it is permitted by reg 6(3) to authorise only payment of the fees specified in the schedule. The answer lies partly in para 3 of Pt I Schedule 1 to the Costs Regulations, which permit the appropriate authority to allow fees greater than those in para 1 of that schedule, where those fees would not reflect the exceptional competence and dispatch with which the work was done, or the exceptional circumstances of the case.

However, this really is only a partial answer, because nothing in para 3 permits the appropriate authority to take into account the matters such as complexity or difficulty referred in reg 4(2).

In *R v Saunders* (1989) *The Independent* 12 May Mr Justice Henry is reported as having said, rather kindly, that solicitors are entitled to 'reasonable remuneration'. Presumably he was looking at reg 4(2) without considering the effects of the other regulations referred to above. The only thing that is certain about these conflicting regulations is that they intended to give a right to reasonable remuneration where the basic rates were insufficient, but because of bad draughtsmanship, patently failed so to do.

Two important points did however come out of the Saunders case:

(1) the Board will make payments on account, but these cannot be claimed as of right. The Board's directions state that the practice of making payments on account should not be encouraged and should only be made very occasionally.

(2) there is a right to request in advance from the Board, an indication of the likely hourly rates which it will pay, however, such an inclination is not an offer.

Where solicitors fees are to be determined under reg 6 of the Criminal Costs Regulations 1989, the fees which are to be allowed are those set out in Sched 1 Pt 1 of the Criminal Costs Regulations 1989 as amended by the Criminal Costs (Amendment) Regulations 1990. The Schedule sets out the rates of payments for magistrates' court and Crown Court proceedings classified as to the types of work, eg preparation, waiting, travelling and advocacy. In addition the Schedule and reg 6(4) of the Criminal Costs Regulations 1989 also provide for a further classification in Crown Court proceedings, namely the qualification and experience of the fee earner who has carried out the work, for example senior solicitor, solicitor, legal executive or articled clerk. A fee earner with experience equivalent to that of a legal executive or an articled clerk also qualifies. 'A fee earner' is defined as a solicitor, legal executive or any clerk who regularly does work for which it is appropriate to make a direct charge to a client (Criminal Costs Regulations 1989, reg 2).

The effect of reg 2 is that it is no use sending a typist or office junior to sit behind counsel at Crown Court and then expect to be paid for it. It is in fact far more economical and profitable to draw a brief which in appropriate cases will allow counsel to appear on his own, so that an enhanced rate can be claimed for the preparation of such a brief.

(a) Standard fees for solicitors in the Crown Court

Part II of Schedule 1 of the Criminal Costs Regulations 1989 also specifies standard fees which are payable to solicitors for work in Crown Court proceedings. These are payable irrespective of the grade of fee earner involved in the work. Standard fees are payable in respect of:

(1) committals for trial where the indictment consists of counts for class 3 or 4 offences, and:

    (a) the trial lasted for two days or less (this includes cases prepared for trial but in which no jury was sworn); and

    (b) when listed the case was reasonably expected to last two days or less; or

    (c) the case was listed and disposed of as a guilty plea;

(2) appeals against conviction and sentence;

(3) committals for sentence including proceedings arising from breach of a Crown Court order and proceedings in respect of sentence was deferred.

If the trial judge was dissatisfied with the solicitor's conduct of the case or, if there are other exceptional reasons, he may direct that instead of receiving the standard fee the solicitor's costs should be determined in the normal manner as if the case was not one in which a standard fee was payable. There is no power to reduce a standard fee for any reason and the purposes of a judge's direction would be to give the chief clerk power to pay only for work reasonably undertaken. If because of incompetence or inefficiency, the cost of the work reasonably undertaken was less than the standard fee, no payment would then be made for incompetence or inefficient work and the solicitor would quite properly be penalised for his inefficiency or incompetence.

A solicitor may elect to claim standard fees, even though the case is not within the classification of cases where standard fees are payable, for example a trial lasting more than two days.

(b) Work covered by standard fees

Standard fees are payable in respect of:
(1) preparation including routine letters written and telephone calls;
(2) advocacy on bail applications;
(3) attending and waiting at court where counsel is assigned;
(4) travelling, unless:
   (a) it is to undertake work for which no standard fee is payable, or
   (b) it is in respect of a bail application.
(5) waiting in connection with preparation, in which case for standard fee purposes, the waiting is deemed to be travelling.

The standard fees are set out in the table in Pt II Sched 1 Criminal Costs Regulations 1989 (as amended).

The standard fees which are claimed must be paid unless in the case of the principle standard fee for preparation it is considered excessive, in which case the lower standard fee must be allowed (Criminal Costs Regulations 1989, para 2(1), Pt II, Sched 1).

(c) The lower and upper fee limits

The question as to which level of standard fee is the appropriate one is governed by the cost of the work involved in that part of the case. If the cost of the work does not exceed the lower fee limit, then the lower standard fee is payable. If those fees exceed the lower limit but do not exceed the upper limit, then the higher standard fee is paid. If the fees exceed the higher fee limit, then no standard fee is payable and the costs are determined under reg 6.

(d) Attendance at court

The standard hourly rate for attendance at court where counsel is assigned is charged for the period beginning thirty minutes before the case is listed and ending fifteen minutes after the hearing ended, provided that the client was present. If the client was not present, it ends when the hearing ends. No claim can be made save in exceptional circumstances for the luncheon adjournment (Criminal Costs Regulations 1989, para 5, Sched 1 para 5).

If the fee earner attends court for more than one case, the hourly rate can only be charged in respect of time actually spent on the second and subsequent cases (para 6). This is in addition to the claim for time spent on the first case.

(e) Travelling to bail applications

The standard travel rate does not apply to travel to bail applications. For some reason best known to our legislators, such travel is paid at the rate appropriate to the fee earner under the table set out in para *(c)* of Sched 1 Pt 1 of the cost regulations provided that the fee earner travelling is also the advocate, ie counsel is not being used to make the bail application.

(f) Increasing the standard fees payable

The standard fees are increased by twenty per cent:

(1) for preparation and advocacy on a bail application where the solicitor represents more than one defendant. The increase is 20 per cent for each additional defendant. There is no such increase for travel to a bail application nor for attendance with counsel.

(2) Where there is more than one or a combination of more than one indictment, appeal against conviction or sentence, or committal for sentence, there is an increase of 20 per cent for each allowable additional item (Criminal Costs Regulations 1989 Pt II, Sched 1, para 9).

Standard fees are increased by £26.25 (£28.00 if London weighting applies) if the solicitor prepares the case with a view to counsel appearing at the substantive hearing, without the solicitor or his representative being present (Criminal Costs Regulations 1989 Pt II, Sched 1, para 10 as amended).

The standard preparation fee is increased where a fee earner listens to a tape recording of a police interview conducted under PACE, by £9.40 for each ten minutes of the tapes listened to and for the remaining period of any such tape. Where the standard fees are increased, the respective fee limits are increased by the same amount.

Where a percentage increase is payable in a standard fee, that percentage increase is ascertained before the addition of any increase by a fixed amount. The percentage increases apply only to the standard preparation fee and cannot be cumulative. For example, if the principle standard fee applies without London weighting, and:

(1) there are two defendants each with two indictments; and

(2) the case was prepared for counsel to appear alone; and

(3) Tape recordings were listened to, for 20 minutes.
   The fees are calculated as follows:

principle standard preparation fee	£220.00
add 20 per cent for second defendant	£44.00
add 20 per cent for each additional indictment	£88.00
increase for brief to counsel to enable to appear alone	£26.25
addition for tape recordings	£18.80

4 Counsel's fees

Claims for counsel's fees must be submitted to the appropriate authority within three months and must provide the following information:

(1) the classes of work for which a fee is claimed;
(2) the date on which each item of work was done;
(3) the time taken;
(4) whether the work was done for more than one assisted person;
(5) the sums claimed;
(6) particulars of any work done in relation to more than one indictment or a re-trial;
(7) particulars to support any claim that:
   (a) it would be inappropriate to allow a standard fee or
   (b) fees under Pt II Sched 2 Criminal Costs Regulations 1989 would be inappropriate.
(8) specify any special circumstances which should be drawn to the attention of the appropriate authority (Criminal Costs Regulations 1989, reg 8).

If the work has been done by junior counsel in the Crown Court, only the standard fee as set out in Pt I, Sched 2 of the Criminal Costs Regulations 1989 are to be allowed, unless they are inappropriate, having regard to all the circumstances (reg 9(2)). A standard fee is not to be allowed unless counsel requests it for:

(1) committals for trial where the indictment includes counts for a Class 1 or 2 offence; or
(2) proceedings which:
   (a) lasted more than three days; or
   (b) at the time of listing were reasonably expected to last more than three days; or
   (c) are disposed of by a guilty plea, but if contested would

reasonably have been expected to last more than three days (Criminal Costs Regulations 1989 reg 9(3)).

Unless a Crown Court standard fee is allowed to counsel under reg 9(2)· the appropriate authority must allow counsel for work in the magistrates' court or Crown Court, such fee as is reasonable under the provisions of Pt II Sched 2 of the Criminal Costs Regulations 1989. For work done after 30 June, 1990 there shall instead be allowed such fees as are reasonable, having regard to the fees specified in Pt II Sched 2 (Criminal Costs Regulations 1989, reg 5(a)).

If those fees do not provide reasonable remuneration because of the exceptional circumstances of the case, such fees as do provide reasonable remuneration are to be allowed (reg 9(5)(*b*)).

The classes of fee which are to be allowed to counsel where a standard fee is not payable are:

(1) a basic fee for preparation;

(2) a refresher fee for any day or part of a day during which a hearing continues;

(3) subsidiary fees for:

(*a*) attendances at conferences, consultations and views not covered by (1) or (2).

(*b*) written advice on evidence, plea, appeal, case stated or other written work.

(*c*) attendance at pre-trial reviews, applications and appearances (including bail applications and adjournments for sentences) not covered by (1) or (2) supra.

'Preparation', includes preparation for a pre-trial review and the first day's hearing. Both preparation and refresher fees include where they take place on the same day, short conferences, consultations, applications and appearances, (including bail applications) views and any other preparation (Criminal Costs Regulations 1989 reg 9(4)).

Counsel's fees for the Court of Appeal are allowed at a reasonable rate of remuneration for work reasonably undertaken.

5 Counsel's fees in the Crown Court

Provisions relating to the payment of counsel are set out in Sched 2 of the Criminal Costs Regulations 1989 and in the tables set out in Parts I and II.

(a) Standard fees

There are four types of standard fee available to counsel, these are:

(1) a standard basic fee which covers preparation, the first day's hearing and the amount of which depends on the type of case, eg trial or guilty plea;

(2) a standard refresher fee to cover any day after the first day and on which the hearing continues (Both the basic and the refresher fees, including bail applications, preparation and views carried out on the day in respect of which the standard fee applies);

(3) a standard written work fee for written advice as to evidence, plea, appeal, case stated and other written work;

(4) a standard appearance fee for applications and appearances including bail applications and adjournments for sentence and any short conferences taking place on that day, not covered by a basic or refresher fee. A standard appearance fee is not paid for a pre-trial review.

Refresher fees are of three kinds, a half day refresher, a full day refresher and a refresher of more than a full day. For the half day refresher fee, the beginning and the end of the hearing must be before the lunch adjournment or after that adjournment but before 5.30 pm. A full day refresher is paid for a hearing beginning before lunch and ending before 5.30 pm or beginning after the lunch adjournment and ending after 5.30 pm. A refresher fee for more than a full day must be allowed for a hearing beginning before lunch and ending after 5.30 pm.

(b) Cases not proceeded with

Half of the standard basic fee for a jury trial is payable where the case is listed for trial but does not proceed on the same day. If a case listed for plea is:

(1) adjourned for trial, the standard appearance fee is allowed, or if greater and counsel has no other effective case on that day, half the standard basic fee is allowed; or

(2) adjourned part heard after a guilty plea, the standard basic fee is allowed for the first hearing and the standard appearance fee is allowed on the disposal hearing.

If a case listed for hearing is not opened because a defendant or witness does not attend or a social enquiry report is not available or there is other good reason, counsel is allowed the

standard appearance fee, Criminal Costs Regulations 1989, Pt I
Sched 2 paras 3–7 as amended by the Criminal Costs Amendment
Regulations 1990.

(c) Increases in standard fees

Increases in the standard fees are similar and in some cases
identical to those which are allowed to solicitors. An addition of
20 per cent is allowed to the standard basic fee for each
additional defendant substantively dealt with at the hearing and
also to the fee payable where a case is adjourned or not proceeded with. The standard basic fee is increased by 20 per cent
if counsel appears for a defendant on the same day for more
than one indictment, appeal against conviction or sentence, or
committal for sentence. There is also an increase of 20 per cent
for any combination of these.

The standard basic fee which is increased, is the greater of
those applicable. In a case where one defendant had two indictments and one committal for sentence, the relevant standard
basic fee for a guilty plea is increased by 20 per cent for the
second indictment and 20 per cent for the committal for sentence.
An increase of £17 is allowed to counsel who appears alone
without his instructing solicitor. The increases for listening to
tape recordings of Police and Criminal Evidence Act (PACE)
interviews are identical to those allowed to solicitors.

The fixed increases cannot be subject to any of the percentage
increases and must be added on after the percentage increases
have been calculated.

(d) Waiting time

There is no provision for counsel to be allowed waiting time
or travelling time under the standard fees systems, as allowances
for waiting are built into the system of calculating fees for parts
of days and also in the half fees provisions. This can result in
some financial hardship, especially if counsel has to wait nearly
all day to start a short mitigation. The regulations do recognise
this and make provision for reasonable remuneration to be paid
instead of the fixed fee.

(e) Time limits

A claim for counsel's fees for standard fees must be submitted
within three months of the conclusion of the proceedings,
although there is the same power under reg 17 of the Criminal

Costs Regulations 1989 for this time limit to be extended, as there is with solicitor's costs, as well as the power to reduce the costs because of delay in submitting the claim.

(f) Assessment of counsel's fees

If the standard fees set out in Sched 2, Pt I of the Criminal Costs Regulations 1989 are inappropriate, counsel will be allowed a basic fee, a refresher and a subsidiary fee in accordance with the table set out in the regulations. If because of exceptional circumstances those fees do not provide reasonable remuneration for some or all of the work, then a sum may be allowed which does provide reasonable remuneration.

Pt II Sched 2 also determines counsel's fees in the magistrates' court, subject to the same reasonable remuneration rule.

The fact that the tables in the Regulations contain maximum fees for Counsel, distinguishes them unfairly from solicitors who are paid by the hour. Five hours advocacy on the second day of a trial will earn counsel at most £155 by way of a refresher where he has been assigned under the order unless there are exceptional circumstances justifying an increase. A solicitor advocate in the magistrates' court would earn £248.50 for the same five hours. If counsel is not assigned, he can be paid at the same rate as a solicitor.

6 Redeterminations, reviews and appeals

Where, as the result of a redetermination, review or appeal the costs are increased, the appropriate authority must authorise payment of the increase. Where they are decreased, the amount of any overpayment must be returned by solicitor or counsel. If counsel or solicitors costs of an appeal to a taxing master or the High Court are allowed, payment of those must also be authorised by the appropriate authority (Criminal Costs Regulations 1989, reg 10(2)).

(a) Reviews of determinations by the board

The Board's determination of costs claimed either by counsel or solicitor in respect of proceedings in the magistrates' court may be reviewed by the Area Committee. An application for review must be made within twenty-one days of notification of the assessment. The Area Committee has power not only to confirm or increase the assessment, but also to reduce it still further (Criminal Costs Regulations 1989, reg 12).

The Board has issued a Practice Note dated 31 May, 1989, setting out guidelines to be applied by the Area Committee to ensure that a costs review is seen to be independent. The Area Committee should only have before it, a copy of the report on case, a breakdown of the assessment made and a copy of any representations made by a solicitor or counsel. Any comment by the area office should be kept to a minimum and restricted to issues of fact.

The Area Committee should give reasons for its decision and where necessary refer to the relevant regulations.

(b) Appeal to a board committee

There is no further right of appeal, unless the Area Committee on being requested so to do, certifies that a point of principle of general importance exists. The request must be made within twenty-one days of receipt of the Area Committee's decision. If the Area Committee does so certify, the dissatisfied solicitor or counsel may within twenty-one days of receipt of the certificate, appeal in writing to a committee appointed by the Board. That committee has power to amend the decision of the Area Committee, which includes power to decrease the costs as well as to increase them, or to confirm the Area Committee's decision (Criminal Costs Regulations 1989, reg 13).

The Board takes the view that points of principle are not generally based on issues of fact, but would include interpretation of the regulations and the principles governing their application.

(c) Redetermination of assessment by other appropriate authorities

A solicitor who is dissatisfied with a costs determination, other than as to the standard fees, made by an appropriate authority other than the Board, may apply for his costs to be redetermined (Criminal Costs Regulations 1989, reg 14). The application must be made to that authority within twenty-one days of receipt of the notice of assessment by giving written notice specifying the matters in respect of which the application is made and the grounds of objection. It must be accompanied by all the documents and other information and particulars which the solicitor supplied under reg 5 with his original claim.

If the applicant wishes to appear or to be represented, he must state so in the notice of application and he will then be given notice of the time when those representations may be made.

The appropriate authority has power to decrease or increase the costs assessed, as well as to confirm the original determination. The applicant may require the authority to give written reasons for its decisions (Criminal Costs Regulations, reg 14(7)), and must do so if he wishes to appeal further to a taxing master.

(d) Solicitor's standard fees in the Crown Court

A solicitor who has claimed the principle standard fee but only been allowed the lower standard fee by the Crown Court, may either request in writing a review of that decision or submit a detailed claim form, together with a written request for the fees for preparation to be determined under reg 6 of the Criminal Costs Regulations 1989, as if the case was not a standard fee case. If a review is requested, the appropriate authority must either allow the principal fee or request the solicitor to provide a detailed claim form (Criminal Costs Regulations 1989, Pt II, Sched 1, para 2).

The lower standard fee is deemed to be confirmed if an application for review is not requested, nor the detailed claim form submitted within six weeks of the decision to allow the lower standard fee. It is also deemed to be confirmed if the solicitor fails, within six weeks therefrom, to comply with a request that he submit a detailed claim form.

In any case in which a detailed claim is submitted, the fees for preparation must first be determined, and if they are less than the lower fee limit, the lower standard fee for preparation must be allowed and paid. If they are not less than the lower fee limit and not more than the upper limit, the principle standard fee must be allowed and paid. If the fees as determined exceed the upper fee limit, the fees to be paid must be determined under reg 6 as if no standard fee was payable (Criminal Costs Regulations 1989, Pt II, Sched 1, para 3).

In addition to the fees eventually allowed for preparation, the standard fees must still be paid for the remaining classes of work undertaken during the case.

A solicitor may apply under para 6 Sched 1 Pt II of the Criminal Costs Regulations 1989 for redetermination of his costs, where he is dissatisfied with the original determination under para 3. The redetermination may result in the allowance of the lower standard fee, the principle standard fee or if the fees as redetermined exceed the upper fee limit, an allowance of fees in accordance with the table in Pt I Sched 1. The provisions of reg 14(2)–(8) apply to applications for redetermination under para 6.

In addition to the right to apply for a redetermination, a solicitor may make a written request for a review if he is dissatisfied because either the standard fee is not apt for that type of work or any of the provisions of para 4(4)–(12) of Pt II Sched 1 have been incorrectly applied (Criminal Costs Regulations 1989 Sched 1, Pt II, para 7). Such request must set out the reasons and must be made within six weeks of receipt of the decision. If on a review the decision is confirmed, written reasons must be given to the solicitor.

(e) Counsel's fees

Despite the fact that Pt II of Sched 1 of the Criminal Costs Regulations 1989 contains detailed provisions as to how solicitors can apply for redeterminations, reviews and appeals in respect of their standard fees in the Crown Court, there are no provisions whatsoever in Sched 2 for counsel to have such rights in respect of their standard fees. Counsel's rights to reviews, redeterminations and appeals, whether relating to standard fees or otherwise, are set out in regs 12 to 16 of the Criminal Costs Regulations 1989 which also relate to solicitor's rights with regard to all non standard fee cases.

Where counsel's fees have been determined by the Board, counsel has the same right as a solicitor under regs 12 and 13 to apply for a review to the Area Committee, with a further right of appeal on a certified point of principle of general importance to a committee appointed by the Board.

If the assessment of costs has been carried out by an appropriate authority, other than the Board, counsel may apply under reg 14(1)(a) Costs Regs 1989 to that authority for a redetermination of his costs or for a review under reg 14(1)(b) where he is dissatisfied with a decision to allow standard fees the procedure is the same as with the solicitor's costs. Counsel may also apply for a redetermination or review under reg 14 where he is dissatisfied with a decision to allow standard fees, as well as where he is dissatisfied with the standard fees themselves.

The remaining provisions of reg 14 apply to application by counsel for redetermination and review as they do to application by solicitor in respect of their costs.

7 Appeals to a taxing master

A solicitor who is dissatisfied with a redetermination under para 6 Sched 1 Pt I or a review under para 7 (both relating to fixed fees) may appeal to a taxing master of the High Court (Criminal Costs Regulations 1989 Part II, Sched 1, para 8). On an appeal against a redetermination under para 6 the master has the same powers as the appropriate authority had when making the redetermination. If the appeal is against a review under para 7, the master must allow whichever standard fee he considers apt for the type of work done, or re-apply the provisions relating to standard fees, including those paragraphs dealing with percentages or fixed increases in the standard fees.

If the appeal is allowed in whole or in part, the taxing master may also allow all or part of the reasonable costs of the solicitor in connection with the appeal. Appeals to a taxing master under para 8 can only be made in respect of proceedings for which standard fees are payable, otherwise the appeal must be made under reg 15 by way of an appeal from a decision under reg 14.

If a solicitor or counsel is dissatisfied with a redetermination under reg 14 or counsel is dissatisfied with a review under the same regulation of a decision to allow standard fees an appeal lies to a taxing master (Criminal Costs Regulations 1989, reg 15). Written notice of appeal must be given within twenty-one days of receipt of the appropriate authority's reasons. As reg 14 does not apply to costs determined by the Board, there can be no appeal to a taxing master in respect of fees originally determined by the Board. Similarly, reg 14 does not apply to standard fees of solicitors in the Crown Court to a solicitor wishing to appeal in respect of those.

The following documents must accompany the notice of appeal:

(1) a copy of the written representations made under reg 14(2); and

(2) the reasons given by the appropriate authority under reg 14(7); and

(3) all documents, particulars and information supplied to the appropriate authority under reg 14.

The provisions of reg 15(5) must be complied with as to the form and contents of the notice of appeal which must:

(1) be in such form as the chief taxing master may direct; and

(2) specify separately each item appealed against and showing:

(*a*) the amount claimed for that item;

(*b*) the amount determined for it; and

(*c*) the objections to the determination; and

(3) state whether the appellant wishes to appear in person or be represented, or whether he will accept a decision given in his absence.

The Lord Chancellor can require the chief taxing master to send to him a copy of the notice of appeal and of any other documents submitted in connection with the appeal. Oral or written representations may be made by or on behalf of the Lord Chancellor, but he must first give, both to the appellant and to the chief taxing master, notice of his intention so to do. A copy of any written representations made by the Lord Chancellor must be sent to the appellant. If the representations are to be oral, the Lord Chancellor must give the chief taxing master and the appellant, the grounds on which the representations are made. The appellant must be allowed a reasonable opportunity to make a reply and informed of any hearing date.

No objections can be raised on an appeal to a taxing master which were not raised under reg 14, although the taxing master does have power to consult the trial judge. No further evidence can be raised on the hearing of the appeal, unless the taxing master so directs, although he does have power to require the appellant to provide any further information required (Criminal Costs Regulations 1989, reg 15(11)).

The taxing master's powers are the same as those of the appropriate authority, and he may increase or decrease the amount of the redetermination, confirm a decision to allow standard fees under reg 9(2) (junior counsel's fees only) or allow fees under reg 9(4) and (5). The appellant may be allowed his reasonable costs of the appeal, unless the sum determined under reg 14 is confirmed or decreased or the decision to allow standard fees is confirmed.

Counsel is entitled to a professional fee and out of pocket expenses, for preparing for and attending a successful appeal to a taxing master, whether on his own behalf or on behalf of another member of the bar. *R* v *Boswell*; *R* v *Halliwell* [1987] 2 All ER 513.

(a) Appeals to the High Court

Where a solicitor or counsel is dissatisfied with the decision of a taxing master on an appeal under reg 15, a further appeal lies to the High Court, but only if the taxing master certifies a point of principle of general importance. The application for the taxing master's certificate must be made within twenty-one days of his decision, and the appeal must be made with the Lord Chancellor as respondent, within twenty-one days of receipt of the certificate (Criminal Costs Regulations 1989, reg 16(1)–(4)).

If the Lord Chancellor is dissatisfied with the decision of the taxing master, he may appeal to the High Court, if the solicitor or counsel does not do so. An appeal by the Lord Chancellor must be made within twenty-one days of receipt of the taxing master's decision. An appeal to the High Court is by way of originating summons in the Queen's Bench Division and is heard by a single Judge who has the same powers as the appropriate authority and the taxing master.

8 Time limits

The Criminal Costs Regulations 1989 contain a number of provisions imposing time limits. Various time limits apply for the original submission of a bill of costs and for subsequent applications for reviews, redeterminations and for appeals. Regulation 17(1) provides that any time limit referred to in the Criminal Costs Regulations 1989 may be extended by the appropriate authority where there is good reason. If the application is for an extension of time in respect of a time limit imposed by regs 15 or 16 (Appeals to a Taxing Master and to the High Court) only the taxing master or the High Court can grant the extension.

There is no definition as to what would amount to good reason, nor can reg 17(1) be used if the time limit has already expired. In those circumstances, reg 17(2) can be employed, but only where without good reason the solicitor or counsel has failed to comply with the time limit. It must be shown that there are exceptional circumstances for the failure to comply with the time limit. Regulation 17(2) can also be used where the time limit would not be met unless an extension was granted.

If counsel or solicitor is forced to resort to reg 17(2) that is sufficient to justify a reduction in his costs, but not until he has been given opportunity, orally or in writing, to show cause why they should not be reduced. There is a right of appeal to the chief taxing master against any decision made under reg 17 against refusal of an extension or a decision to reduce costs for failing to comply with the time limit.

Chapter 13

Legal Aid in Care Proceedings and Other Special Cases

1 Care proceedings

(a) In the juvenile court

An application for a Legal Aid Order for care proceedings in the juvenile court can be made to the justices' clerk on Form 16 or orally to the court. The powers of the court can be exercised by a single justice who is entitled to sit as a member of the juvenile court. A single justice may also receive oral applications in proceedings under s 12E of the Child Care Act 1980, but the applicant's statement of means, which in this one instance may be oral, must always be considered before Legal Aid can be granted (Criminal General Regulations 1989, regs 60 and 61).

All the provisions of Regs 11–14 of the Criminal General Regulations 1989 apply to applications for Legal Aid in care proceedings, save for regs 15–17 inclusive which are specifically excluded. There is therefore no right to apply to the Area Committee for review of a refusal to grant Legal Aid, but as reg 14 does apply, there is still a right to renew an application either orally to the court or to the Justices Clerk.

(b) Appeals to the Crown Court

A Legal Aid application for an appeal to the Crown Court from the juvenile court can be made orally to the juvenile court at the conclusion of the proceedings, orally to the Crown Court or on Form 16 either to the justices' clerk or the appropriate officer of the Crown Court. The powers of the juvenile court to grant legal aid for an appeal to Crown Court may be exercised by a single justice entitled to sit as a member of a juvenile court or by the justices' clerk (Criminal General Regulations 1989, reg 62).

Regulations 18 to 21 relating to legal aid for criminal proceedings in the Crown Court apply to appeals in care proceedings from the juvenile court. A renewed application can therefore be made under reg 21 if there is an initial refusal.

(c) Appeals to the High Court

Legal Aid for appeals from the juvenile court to the High Court is applied for to the Board. There is an overlap between Pts 4 and 6 of the Legal Aid Act which provide a choice between civil legal aid or criminal legal aid for these appeals. The Board takes the view that it is normally in the interests of the client for him to apply for criminal legal aid under Pt 6 because criminal legal aid contributions out of income are lower than those for civil legal aid. Also the criminal legal aid means test has no higher capital or income limit to disqualify the applicant.

The Criminal General Regulations 1989 do not specify an application form for applications to the Board, and the Board suggests that Form 16 be used with the necessary modifications. There is a right of appeal to the Area Committee against the refusal of civil legal aid under Pt 4, and the Board suggests that an application for civil legal aid should be made under Pt 4 if an application for criminal legal aid under Pt 6 has been refused. Civil legal aid is applied for on Form CLA1; Note for Guidance, Number 50 (1989 edition).

(d) Availability of legal aid in care proceedings

Legal aid is available to any person other than a local authority who is a party to the proceedings. The criteria for the grant of legal aid is that it must be granted where it is desirable in the interests of justice. Where there is a doubt, it must be resolved in favour of the applicant. Legal aid must be granted where a child who is not legally represented but wishes to be, is brought before the juvenile court under Child Care Act 1980 s 21A (Section 28 Legal Aid Act 1988). In all cases availability of legal aid is subject to assessment and determination of the applicant's financial resources, and the regulations apply as they do for an application for legal aid in criminal proceedings, save that a guardian ad litem cannot be an appropriate contributor for the purposes of legal aid in care proceedings. Nor can a person who has beem made a party to care proceedings because he has a contrary interest, be required to pay a contribution to the child's legal aid in addition to the cost of his own representation.

A parent of a child the subject of care proceedings cannot therefore be treated as an appropriate contributor in assessing the child's means, if that parent is a party to the proceedings and whether or not he has the benefit of legal aid for himself in those proceedings.

(e) 'Care proceedings'

Care proceedings are defined by s 27 of the Legal Aid Act 1989 as being:
  (1) care proceedings under s 1 of the 1969 Children and Young Persons Act;
  (2) variation and discharge of supervision or care orders under ss 15 or 21 of the Children and Young Persons Act 1969;
  (3) appeals in such proceedings;
  (4) applications under s 3 of the Children and Young Persons Act 1963 by a parent or guardian for an order directing a local authority to take care proceedings under s 1 of the Children and Young Persons Act 1969;
  (5) proceedings under ss 3, 5 or 67(2) of the Child Care Act 1980 in connection with resolutions by local authorities with respect to the assumption of parental rights and duties;
  (6) proceedings relating to access orders under Part 1A of the Child Care Act 1980.

(f) Payment allowed

For the first time since the introduction of the legal aid system, the tendency to specialisation has been encouraged by providing a higher rate of remuneration for work done in care cases, than in other cases in the magistrates' courts. The rates for preparation and advocacy in care cases are substantially higher than the standard rates in the magistrates' court. There is also a separate rate for attendance with counsel, where counsel is assigned, reg 44(3)(b) of the Criminal General Regulations permitting counsel to be assigned under a magistrates' legal aid order for care proceedings under s 1 Children and Young Persons Act 1969 where the condition in subsection (2)(f) is satisfied in consequence of an indictable offence and the court is satisfied that there are circumstances which make the case unusually grave or difficult.

The fees allowed for care proceedings in the Crown Court are assessed on the reasonable remuneration basis and not in accordance with the provisions relating to criminal proceedings in the Crown Court (Criminal Costs Regulations 1989, reg 6(5)).

2 Contempt proceedings

Where any person is liable to be committed or fined in proceedings for contempt, the court may order that he be granted representation if it appears to the court to be desirable to do so in the interests of justice (LAA 1988, s 29). Contempt proceedings are defined as being:

(1) proceedings in a magistrates' court under s 12 of the Contempt of Court Act 1981;

(2) proceedings in a county court under ss 14, 19 or 118 of the County Courts Act 1984; and

(3) proceedings in a superior court, ie Court of Appeal, High Court, Crown Court, Courts Martial Appeal Court, Restrictive Practices Court, Employment Appeal Tribunal and any other court exercising powers equivalent to those of the High Court and including the House of Lords when acting as an Appellate Court for appeals from courts in England and Wales.

The grant of representation may be made only by the court, and the person facing the contempt proceedings does not have the right to solicitor or counsel of his choice (LAA 1988, s 31(4)). The court has power to assign any counsel or solicitor who is within the precincts of the court at the time (s 31(5)). There are no regulations as to assessment of the client's financial resources in assessing eligibility for representation under s 29, nor as to claims for payment of costs.

Part III

Civil Legal Aid

Chapter 14

Administration of Civil Legal Aid

1 The structure of the scheme

The Board is under a statutory duty to appoint Area Committees and Area Directors for the purposes of administering the Act and to exercise the functions either delegated to them by the Board, or conferred by the Civil Legal Aid (General) Regulations 1989. The Area Director is given power to perform any function on behalf of the Area Committee, save that he cannot determine an appeal against a refusal of a certificate (reg 6 of the General Regulations 1989). He has power to grant an extension of any time limit imposed by the General Regulations, even if the application for an extension is not made until the time limit has expired (reg 7 of the General Regulations 1989).

Unless the Area Director refuses an application for civil legal aid, it is his duty to refer to the assessment officer that part of the application relating to the applicant's means. The Area Director cannot generally approve an application until the assessment officer has assessed both the disposable capital, disposable income and maximum contribution of the applicant. A re-assessment of the applicant's financial resources cannot be required by the Area Director, where the application for legal aid relates to proceedings:

(1) in the House of Lords or an appeal from a magistrates' court, provided that the applicant was an assisted person in the court below; or

(2) by way of a new trial ordered by a court in which the applicant was an assisted person.

The Area Director can also notify any party to the proceedings in respect of which an application has been made that he has received an application for legal aid, and ask that party if he is willing to delay taking any further steps until the application has been determined (reg 26 of the General Regulations 1989). The Area Director must then inform any person he has so notified, when he has determined the application.

Where a court is given any power, jurisdiction or discretion to do any act under the General Regulations, provided that it is not exercisable only during a hearing or trial, it may be exercised:

(1) by a registrar in the county court or Family Division of the High Court;

(2) by a judge, master or district registrar in the Chancery or Queen's Bench Divisions;

(3) by a single judge or the registrar of civil appeals in the Court of Appeal;

(4) by the Clerk of Parliaments in the House of Lords (reg 5 of the General Regulations 1989).

(a) Service of documents

Service of any document required to be served by virtue of the Civil Legal Aid (General) Regulations 1989, must be in the manner prescribed, as follows:

(1) where the person to be served is acting in person and has an address for service:

    (*a*) by delivering it to him personally;

    (*b*) by delivering it to his address for service;

    (*c*) by posting it to his address for service; or

(2) where the person to be served is acting in person and does not have an address for service:

    (*a*) by delivering it to his residence or the place of any business of which he is proprietor;

    (*b*) by posting it to his last known residence or last known place of any business of which he is proprietor; or

(3) where the person to be served is acting by a solicitor:

    (*a*) by delivering it to the solicitor's address for service;

    (*b*) by posting it to the solicitor's address for service; or

    (*c*) if the address for service includes a document exchange number, by leaving it at that document exchange or at a document exchange which transmits documents daily to that document exchange, in which case the document shall be deemed to have been served on the second day after the day on which it was left (reg 8 of the General Regulations 1989).

Service is good if it is carried out in any of these ways, irrespective of whether a particular regulation requires it to be 'served', 'sent', or 'sent by post' (reg 8(1)).

(b) Matrimonial proceedings

For the purposes of the Civil Legal Aid (General) Regulations 1989, 'matrimonial proceedings' are defined as being:
  (1) any proceedings for which rules may be made under s 50 of the Matrimonial Causes Act 1973;
  (2) any county court proceedings under s 17 of the Married Women's Property Act 1882 or s 1 of or Sched 1 to the Matrimonial Homes Act 1983;
  (3) any proceedings under the Domestic Violence and Matrimonial Proceedings Act 1976.
(reg 3 of the General Regulations).

(c) Authorised summary proceedings

For the purposes of the Civil Legal Aid (General) Regulations 1989 'authorised summary proceedings' means proceedings in a magistrates' court for which legal aid is available by virtue of para 2 Pt I Sched 2 of the Legal Aid Act 1988 (see page 131 below).

(d) Specified proceedings

The proceedings for which civil legal aid is available before courts or tribunals in England and Wales are specified in Pt I of Sched 2 to the Act which is reproduced below:

PART I
DESCRIPTION OF PROCEEDINGS
 1 Proceedings in, or before any person to whom a case is referred in whole or in part by, any of the following courts, namely:
  (*a*) the House of Lords in the exercise of its jurisdiction in relation to appeals from courts in England and Wales;
  (*b*) the Court of Appeal;
  (*c*) the High Court;
  (*d*) any county court.
 2 The following proceedings in a magistrates' court namely:
  (*a*) proceedings under the Guardianship of Minors Acts 1971 and 1973;
  (*b*) proceedings under section 43 of the National Assistance Act 1948, section 22 of the Maintenance Orders Act 1950, section 4 of the Maintenance Orders Act 1958, or section 18 of the Supplementary Benefits Act 1976;
  (*c*) proceedings in relation to an application for leave of the court to remove a child from a person's custody under section 27 or 28

of the Adoption Act 1976 or proceedings in which the making of an order under Part II or section 29 or 55 of the Adoption Act 1976 is opposed by any party to the proceedings;

(d) proceedings under Part I of the Maintenance Orders (Reciprocal Enforcement) Act 1972 relating to a maintenance order made by a court of a country outside the United Kingdom;

(e) proceedings under Part II of the Children Act 1975;

(f) proceedings for or in relation to an order under Part I of the Domestic Proceedings and Magistrates' Courts Act 1978.

3 Proceedings in the Employment Appeal Tribunal.

4 Proceedings in the Lands Tribunal.

5 Proceedings before a Commons Commissioner appointed under section 17(1) of the Commons Registration Act 1965.

6 Proceedings in the Restrictive Practices Court under Part III of the Fair Trading Act 1973, and any proceedings in that court in consequence of an order made, or undertaking given to the court, under the Part of that Act.

Part II of the Schedule as amended by the Civil Legal Aid (Matrimonial Proceedings) Regulations 1989 sets out a list of excepted cases for which legal aid is not available. These are:

PART II
EXCEPTED PROCEEDINGS

1 Proceedings wholly or partly in respect of defamation, but so that the making of a counterclaim for defamation in proceedings for which representation may be granted shall not of itself affect any right of the defendant to the counterclaim, to representation for the purposes of the proceedings and so that representation may be granted to enable him to defend the counterclaim.

2 Relator actions.

3 Proceedings for the recovery of a penalty where the proceedings may be taken by any person and the whole or part of the penalty is payable to the person taking the proceedings.

4 Election petitions under the Representation of the People Act 1983.

5 In a county court, proceedings for or consequent on the issue of a judgment summons and, in the case of a defendant, proceedings where the only question to be brought before the court is as to the time and mode of payment by him of a debt (including liquidated damages) and costs.

6 Proceedings incidental to any proceedings excepted by this Part of this Schedule.

An amendment made by the Civil Legal Aid (Matrimonial Proceedings) Regulations 1989 adds a new paragraph to Pt II of Sched 2 to the Act, and specifies that except in limited circumstances, legal aid is not available for divorce or judicial separation proceedings, save for ancillary matters such as injunctions, ancillary relief, custody and access applications. The detailed provisions of the new para 5A are as follows:

Proceedings for a decree of divorce or judicial separation, unless the cause is defended, or the petition is directed to be heard in open court, or it is not practicable by reason of physical or mental incapacity for the applicant to proceed without representation; except that representation shall be available for the purpose of making or opposing an application:

(a) for an injunction;
(b) for ancillary relief, excluding representation for the purpose only of inserting a prayer for ancillary relief in the petition;
(c) for an order relating to the custody of (or access to) a child, or the education, care or supervision of a child, excluding representation for the purpose only of making such an application where there is no reason to believe that the application will be opposed;
(d) for an order declaring that the court is satisfied as to arrangements for the welfare of the children of the family, excluding representation for the purpose only of making such an application where there is no reason to believe that the application will be opposed; or
(e) for the purpose of making or opposing any other application, or satisfying the court on any other matter which raises a substantial question for determination by the court.

It is perhaps symptomatic of the parliamentary draftsman's mind that details of cases in which legal aid are available should be included in that part of the Schedule to the Act which deals with proceedings for which it is not available.

(e) 'Any person'

Legal aid for proceedings within the scope of the Acts and General Regulations is available to 'any person' whether resident in England and Wales or abroad, subject only to the applicant's means, his liability to pay a contribution under s 15 and the Board's right to reimbursement under s 16 of the Act from costs and property recovered or preserved for the assisted person.

'Any person' does not include a body of persons, corporate or unincorporate, unless it is concerned in a representative, fiduciary or official capacity (LAA 1988, s 2(1)). Legal aid cannot therefore be granted to a firm as such, nor to a partnership because it has no separate legal entity, but it can be granted to any individual partner. In those circumstances the Area Director would look at the interests of the other partners and consider whether they should contribute to the costs of the proceedings under reg 32(1) and (3) of the General Regulations 1989.

2 Applications for certificates

(a) Form and content of application

An application for legal aid must be made on the appropriate form (CLA2 matrimonial; CLA1 non matrimonial; SJ1 summary jurisdiction and CLA3 emergency certificates) or in such other written form as the Area Director shall accept. Only in exceptional circumstances will an application be accepted in advance of a written application, and only on condition that the proper and completed form is submitted as soon as possible. Applications can be submitted to any Area Director, although normally it should be submitted to the legal aid office for the area in which the solicitor practices and if it is not, the Area Director will exercise his power under reg 17 to transfer it to that area, unless there is good reason for not doing so. In the case of a person resident outside the United Kingdom, an application must be submitted to the Area Director nominated by the Board (regs 10 and 11 of the General Regulations 1989).

The application must state the name of the solicitor selected by the applicant and must contain sufficient information to enable the Area Director to determine the nature of the proceedings and whether it is reasonable for representation to be granted (s 12(1)(b)).

As from 3 September 1990 new forms CLA 4A and LI7A have replaced the old statement of means form. This follows a trial system introduced by the Board in the Manchester area and is designed to reduce delay caused by waiting for the DSS to issue and have returned to it the assessment form previously in use. All the information needed for the assessment will now have to be collected by the applicant and his solicitor and submitted on the new forms. A person applying for a certificate for authorised summary proceedings for which it is not possible to obtain an emergency certificate can lodge with the Area Director an undertaking to pay any contribution which he will be assessed as being liable to pay, and this will enable the issue of the certificate to be expedited (reg 12(2)). An applicant can be required to provide additional information or documents in support of the application, even where a summary jurisdiction certificate has been issued on an undertaking given under reg 12(3).

(b) Persons resident outside the United Kingdom

An applicant who resides outside the United Kingdom and cannot be present in England or Wales whilst his application is considered, must submit an application:

(1) written in English or French; and

(2) except where he is a member of HM forces, sworn either:

    (a) before a Justice of the Peace, magistrate or any other person authorised to administer oaths where the applicant resides in a Commonwealth country or the Republic of Ireland; or

    (b) if he resides elsewhere, before a British Consul or person authorised to exercise his functions or any other person authorised to administer oaths in that place; and

(3) accompanied by a written statement from a responsible person with knowledge of the facts, certifying that part of the application which relates to the applicant's disposal income and capital

(reg 13 of the General Regulations 1989).

There is a separate means form, L1RevA for civilian applicants residing outside the United Kingdom and for members of HM forces. The requirements of reg 13 relating to applications for civil legal aid by persons resident outside the United Kingdom may be waived by the Area Director if serious difficulty, inconvenience or delay would otherwise be caused, and provided that the application otherwise satisfies the requirements imposed on an applicant residing within the United Kingdom.

(c) Child abduction and registration of foreign orders and judgments

There are special provisions under regs 14 and 15 of the General Regulations 1989 relating to the grant of legal aid for cases where children have been abducted abroad, and with regard to applications to register certain foreign orders or judgments. The effect of the special provisions is that legal aid is available whether or not the applicant's financial resources are such as to make him eligible, and cannot be refused under s 15 of the Act on the grounds that he has not satisfied the Board that he has reasonable grounds for taking, defending or being a party to the proceedings, nor because it is unreasonable to grant representation, or more appropriate to grant ABWOR. Furthermore, the applicant cannot be required to pay a contribution to the legal aid fund. The proceedings in respect of which these special provisions apply are:

(1) applications under the Hague Convention or the European Convention pursuant to s 3(2) or s 14(2) of the Child Abduction and Custody Act 1985, where a solicitor in England and Wales has been instructed in connection with that application; or

(2) appeals to a magistrates' court either against the registration or against the refusal to register a maintenance order made in a Hague Convention country, pursuant to the Maintenance Orders (Reciprocal Enforcement) Act 1972; or

(3) where applications for registration of a foreign judgment under s 4 of the Civil Jurisdiction and Judgments Act 1982.

(d) Minors and patients

Applications for legal aid for a minor or for a patient, ie a person who by reason of mental disorder within the meaning of the Mental Health Act 1983 is incapable of managing and administering his property and affairs (reg 3(1) of the General Regulations 1989), must be made by a person of full age and capacity. If the proceedings require the appointment of a next friend or guardian ad litem, the application must be by the person so appointed, or if the proceedings have not commenced, who intends to act in either of those capacities (reg 16(1) of the General Regulations 1989). Unless the application is made by the official solicitor, the next friend or guardian must give a written undertaking before a certificate can be issued, to pay to the Board any sum which an applicant would be required to pay on the issue of a certificate, during its currency, or upon its discharge or revocation (reg 16(2) of the General Regulations 1989).

The certificate is issued in the name of the minor or patient, and the person named in the certificate as his next friend or guardian is treated for all purposes, except the receipt of notices, as his agent (reg 16(4) of the General Regulations 1989). The Area Director has power to waive any or all of the provisions of reg 16.

(e) Civil legal aid in the magistrates' court

Where an application is made on form SJ1 for legal aid in the magistrates' court for proceedings specified in para 2 of Pt I Sched 2 to the Act, the Board requires at least three weeks between the lodging of the application and the date of the hearing. If a hearing date has already been fixed, then it should be stated on the form.

The Board says in its Note for Guidance Number 11 (1989 edition), that only in exceptionally urgent cases, should a summons be issued before the application for a certificate has been determined. This request however, can be very problematic. It would cause great difficulty for example in the case of a wife and mother going through the trauma of a separation. If a summons is issued first and the hearing date put on the form, then the application can be determined with greater speed, and the client is not jeopardised by two delays, the first waiting for the Board and then the second of waiting for the eventual hearing.

Unless otherwise specified the Civil Legal Aid (General) (Regulations) 1989 apply to certificates for authorised summary proceedings (summary jurisdiction certificates) as they do to legal aid generally. There are however a number of regulations, the provisions of which apply only to authorised summary proceedings. These are as follows:

(1) The certificate does not need to specify the parties to the proceedings (reg 47).

(2) There is no need to serve notice of issue of the certificate, nor of the amendment, revocation or discharge thereof, but the certificate itself, an amended certificate and the revocation or discharge thereof must be filed with the clerk to the justices at or before the first hearing after the issue, amendment, revocation or discharge of the certificate (regs 50(5), 54(4) and 82(4)).

(3) Counsel cannot be instructed without authority, either in the certificate itself or from the Area Director and the authority must be included with any instructions to counsel (reg 59(1)(a) and (c)). Counsel's fees cannot be paid by the Board where counsel has been instructed, without authority.

(4) Solicitors and counsels fees must be assessed by the Area Director and the assessment is made as if the Criminal

Costs Regulations 1989 (reg 6 and Sched 1 Pt 1 para 1(*a*))
applied to the work (reg 104(1)).

(5) There is no provision for taxation of costs relating to a
summary jurisdiction certificate. Regulations 105 to 110
concerning costs and taxation do not apply except for paras
4 to 8 of reg 105 which deal with applications for reviews
and appeals. Thus although costs are assessed under the
Criminal Costs Regulations, the right to apply for reviews
and to appeal are the same as where civil costs have been
assessed.

(6) Payment of costs ordered in favour of an assisted person
must be made to the clerk to the justices and only he can
give a good discharge for those costs. The clerk must then
account for the costs, either to the Board or as the Board
may direct (reg 89(*a*)).

A certificate for authorised summary proceedings will normally
only be issued where the applicant is financially ineligible for
ABWOR.

3 Determination of applications

(a) Eligibility on the merits

Before approving an application for a certificate, the Area
Director must consider all the questions of fact or law arising in
connection with the application, as well as the circumstances in
which it was made (reg 28 of the General Regulations 1989).
This is in addition to the criteria imposed by s 15(2) of the
Act that the applicant must have reasonable grounds for taking,
defending or being a party to the proceedings, and to the discretion given to the Board by s 15(3) to refuse an application where
it appears unreasonable that representation should be granted or
that ABWOR should be granted as an alternative.

A further discretion is given to the Area Director to refuse
an application where:

(1) only a trivial advantage would be gained by the applicant
from the proceedings; or

(2) because of the nature of the proceedings a solicitor would
not normally be employed (reg 29 of the General Regulations 1989); or

(3) the applicant has available to him rights or facilities which
make it unnecessary for him to obtain legal aid; or

(4) the applicant has a reasonable expectation of obtaining financial or other help from a body of which he is a member (reg 30 of the General Regulations 1989).

(b) The criteria of reasonableness

The Board has tried to assist Area Directors and the profession as to where, even though the legal merits justify the grant of legal aid, the particular circumstances of a case may make it unreasonable to do so (see Note for Guidance Number 9, 1989 edition). The following are the principles which the Board will take into account:

(1) The applicant's moral character and conduct do not justify refusal unless a court would regard either as relevant to its decision.

(2) The propriety of expending public money on a particular case is irrelevant if a client with sufficient or not superabundant means would, with competent advice, fund the litigation privately. This is of particular importance for appeals to the Criminal Division of the Court of Appeal on a point of law. Even where a crime has been admitted and the sentence is a proper one, that is not sufficient to justify refusal where on a point of law the conviction or sentence may be quashed.

(3) There are cases where the benefit to be achieved does not justify the cost of the proceedings, especially where the financial plight of the applicant is the reason for the proceedings, eg proceedings for maintenance and those relating to welfare benefits. The test as to whether a client of adequate means would fund litigation in those circumstances is not an appropriate one, and regard must be had to the benefits sought by the particular applicant.

(4) In possession cases, it is relevant to consider whether the applicant has reasonable grounds for asking the court, even though there are rent arrears, not to make an order for possession or to suspend it on reasonable terms. Regard should be had to the seriousness to the applicant of potential homelessness and of the hardship which might occur if an unreasonable order for payment of arrears were to be made against him.

(5) If the applicant's status, reputation or dignity is affected the non-financial benefits which would accrue from the proceedings may be sufficiently important to justify a

certificate, even though the amount of damages may be small compared to the costs. Proceedings under the Race Relations Act 1976 or the Sex Discrimination Act 1975 are intended to eliminate discrimination, as well as obtain financial recompense, and in those cases the distress caused to the applicant may justify a certificate. Solicitors should bear in mind that the Commission for Racial Equality has power to arrange legal representation and to pay legal fees.

(6) The Equal Opportunities Commission has power in certain cases to provide advice and assistance as well as legal representation, but its resources and powers are limited. It is not generally a valid ground for refusing a legal aid application to refer it to the Commission, nor should the application be delayed by referring it to the Commission.

A decision of the Area Committee refusing or discharging a civil aid certificate was quashed where, following a test case on causation in the whooping cough vaccine cases, counsel had advised that the outcome of the test case should not be treated as a reliable guide to the outcome of further litigation, nor as a ground for refusing legal aid. The Area Committee was required to re-determine the appeal because there had been a want of proper consideration, such as to constitute an error of law *R v Legal Aid Area No 8 Appeal Committee, ex parte Parkinson and Others* (1990) *The Independent* 13 March.

(c) The criteria of 'trivial advantage'

The factors in reg 29 of the General Regulations 1989 are intended to prevent abuse of the scheme and the waste of public money, but should not be used without good reason to deprive any applicant of legal aid. The Board does not regard reg 29 as either adding to or subtracting from the statutory criteria. Where the benefit to the applicant for proceedings is so small that the cost is not justified, but there would be benefit to other individuals, groups, or the community at large, the Board will apply the following principles:

(1) the mere fact that the proceedings will benefit others is not in itself a reason for refusal; or

(2) if the applicant has been persuaded to make an application which he would not otherwise have made on his own behalf, in order to achieve a benefit to others who can

afford to take proceedings themselves, legal aid should not be granted because it is an abuse of the scheme; or

(3) if a common calamity has affected a group or they have a common interest in a particular action which they could afford to fund privately, the Area Director must be satisfied that it is impossible for the applicant to obtain the benefit desired, were he to be refused legal aid. If the Area Director has difficulty in being so satisfied, the application should be granted if there is any probability that a refusal would cause the applicant to be denied justice and suffer as a result.

(d) Cases where a solicitor would not normally be employed

The Board accepts that this provision of reg 29 can cause difficulty, especially with regard to proceedings in the magistrates' court for variation of a maintenance order. In some cases the assessment of a proper level of maintenance is little more than an arithmetical calculation, and this is true where the parties are open and honest about their financial resources and expenditure. There are, however, many cases and a cynic may say a majority, where at least one party is less than honest about his or her finances. Attempts may be made to conceal from the court cohabitation with a partner who is working (but never with a partner who has numerous children which need maintaining), foreign holidays, the costs of a new house or car, or the existence of a second job. All these are matters which require investigation and more importantly cross examination at the hearing.

The Board states that it is prepared to consider each application on its merits, but the solicitor should not hesitate to submit applications for legal aid (or presumably for ABWOR where appropriate) if there is reason to believe that without representation the order may not be fair to the client.

(e) Legal aid for groups

The Area Director must consider whether the rights of an applicant would be substantially prejudiced by a refusal, where an application for legal aid is made for proceedings in which:

(1) numerous persons have the same interest; or

(2) one or more persons may sue or be sued; or

(3) one or more persons may be authorised by a court to defend any such proceedings on behalf of or for the benefit of all persons so interested.

(Reg 32(2) of the General Regulations 1989.)

If the Area Director considers it reasonable for persons concerned jointly with, or having the same interest as the applicant, to contribute to the costs of the proceedings, the amount which would be payable by them must be added to the contribution payable by the applicant (reg 32(3) of the General Regulations 1989). The applicant must be given notice of this addition, and it is then for him to take reasonable steps to recover it from those other persons, and if unsuccessful in so doing, to permit the Area Director so to do. If the Area Director is satisfied that the applicant has unsuccessfully taken all reasonable steps to obtain payment and has given the necessary permission to the Area Director, he may then redetermine the amount of the additional contribution (reg 32(4) of the General Regulations 1989).

Legal aid cannot be granted if the applicant will obtain no personal benefit for himself. If the personal benefit to the applicant is limited, that can be taken into account by the Area Director in considering whether it is reasonable for a contribution to be made by the other interested parties. If the applicant's personal benefit is substantial, then it would not be reasonable to require an additional contribution under reg 32(3) (Note for Guidance No 12).

(f) Determining the contribution

In determining an application, the Area Director must also decide the sums payable by the applicant on account of the contribution which he has been assessed as being liable to pay. In fixing these sums, regard must be had to the probable cost of the proceedings (reg 31(1) of the General Regulations 1989). If that cost is likely to exceed the maximum assessed contribution, the sum payable on account shall be the maximum contribution.

If an application is made by a person in a representative, fiduciary or official capacity, the financial resources of any person who might benefit from the action will be taken into account, as will any property or fund out of which the applicant is entitled to be indemnified. The application can be granted, subject to payment out of that property or fund, of such sum as the Area Director determines. An application by a representative or fiduciary applicant can be refused if it will not cause undue hardship (reg 33 of the General Regulations 1989).

4 Refusal of applications

(a) Notice of refusal of legal aid

The applicant must be given notice of the grounds on which his application has been refused, where:

(1) his disposable income renders him ineligible or, if it does not, his disposable capital renders him liable to be refused and the probable cost of the proceedings would not exceed the contribution payable; or

(2) legal aid is not available for those proceedings; or

(3) reasonable grounds for taking, defending or being a party to proceedings have not been shown; or

(4) it appears unreasonable in the circumstances to grant legal aid.

In the last two cases the applicant must also be given a brief statement as to why that ground applied to his case (reg 34 of the General Regulations 1989). This enables an applicant who wishes to appeal to know what he is fighting against.

(b) Repeated applications and refusals

There is no statutory limit to the number of times a person can submit an application in respect of the same matter. In theory, although an appeal against a refusal is final, there is nothing to prevent a further application being submitted and this would be quite proper, where for example, additional evidence or information had come to light, or there had been a change in the applicant's financial resources, where these were relevant. However, in order to prevent abuse of the scheme the Area Director has power to report the Area Committee where a person has been refused a certificate on three separate occasions (reg 40 of the General Regulations 1989). The refusals need not have been in respect of the same matter.

The Area Committee can enquire whether any other area office has received an application from the same person, and if so, can call for a report about them. If it appears that the facilities of the Act are being abused, the Area Committee can make a report to the Board together with recommendations.

On receipt of such a report the Board must give the named person an opportunity to make written representations, either by himself or by some other person acting on his behalf. If the Board is then satisfied after making any other enquiries that there has been abuse, it may make a prohibitory direction, which gives the Area Director power for five years to refuse to consider any future application by that person with regard to a particular matter, or even in exceptional circumstances, to any future application whatsoever. The Lord Chancellor must be informed of any prohibitory direction (reg 41 of the General Regulations 1989).

(c) Appeals against refusals

An appeal lies to the Area Committee against a refusal of a certificate and against the terms on which it is offered, but there is no right of appeal from the assessment of the Assessment Officer, nor against the Area Director's decision as to how sums payable on account of the contribution or the method by which the contribution shall be paid. There is a right of appeal to the Area Committee against decisions made by the Area Director relating to additional contributions under reg 32(3) and sums payable under reg 33 where the application has been made by a person acting in a representative, fiduciary or official capacity.

The Board's Note for Guidance No 19 (1989 edition) sets out the Board's view that there is no right of appeal where refusal is on the grounds that the disposable income exceeds the amount which makes legal aid available. The actual provisions of reg 35(2)(b) however, are somewhat different, in that that sub-section only provides that there can be no appeal from the assessment of the Assessment Officer. A right of appeal is given against a decision of the Area Director refusing an application, and is not specifically excluded where the refusal is based on assessment of income. It may therefore be arguable that whilst there is no appeal against the Assessment Officer's assessment, there could possibly be a right of appeal against the Area Director's refusal of a certificate based on that assessment.

Note for Guidance No 19 also states that there is no right of appeal against any decision of the Area Director about the amount of the contribution. Again this is not supported by reg 35(2) which provides that there is no appeal against any decision by the Area Director as to the sums payable on account of the contribution or the method by which they shall be paid. In fact it is the assessment officer who assesses the contribution and not the Area Director. These however obviously are arguments which will not find favour with the Board. The normal method of challenging the assessment officer is by an application to the High Court.

Written notice of appeal against the refusal of a certificate must be given within fourteen days of the date of the notice of refusal or of the terms upon which a certificate would be issued (reg 36 of the General Regulations 1989). The appeal is by way of a full reconsideration of the application. In order to keep paper work to a minimum, the Board's staff, will, on occasions, omit to give members of the Area Committee copies of all documents necessary to enable such full reconsideration to be given. If the Committee feels inclined to refuse an appeal, it should always ask the Area Director if it has been given all the information and documents presented to him.

The appellant can furnish further oral or written statements in support of his appeal, and has a right at the determination of his appeal to conduct it himself or with the assistance of any other person he appoints, as well as the right to be represented by counsel or solicitor (reg 38).

The Area Committee's decision is final. Notice of the decision and of the reasons for it must be given to the appellant and his solicitor. The decision which the Area Committee must reach is one which appears to it to be just, and the Area Committee may:

(1) dismiss the appeal; or
(2) direct that a certificate be offered on such terms and conditions as it thinks fit; or
(3) direct the Area Director to settle terms and conditions on which the certificate may be offered; or
(4) refer the matter or any part of it back to the Area Director for his determination or report.

(reg 39 of the General Regulations 1989.)

Advice and assistance under the Green Form Scheme is available to an appellant in respect of any appeal to the Area Committee, but the Green Form Scheme will not cover representation at the hearing of the appeal.

Chapter 15

Issue and Effect of Certificates

1 Contributions

(a) Where a contribution is payable

Where an application is approved and a contribution is payable, the applicant must be required to pay any part of the contribution which is payable out of capital, either forthwith or if the capital is not readily available, within such time as is reasonable in all the circumstances (LAA 1988, s 16). Any sums payable out of income must be paid by instalments. The Area Director must notify the applicant of the amount of the contribution, and of the terms upon which the certificate will be issued. He must also draw the applicant's attention to the Board's entitlement to the statutory charge under s 16(6) of the Act in respect of any deficiency to the fund, as well as to the power contained in s 17 of the Act for an order for costs to be made against an assisted person. All these matters are included on the blue offer of legal aid form sent to the applicant and his solicitor.

An applicant who has received an offer of legal aid has twenty-eight days to lodge, with the Area Director, the signed acceptance of the offer and an undertaking to pay any contribution payable by instalments. If any part of the contribution is to be paid before the certificate is issued, it must be paid within the twenty-eight days (reg 45(1) of the General Regulations 1989). Once those requirements have been complied with, the certificate is issued and sent to the applicant's solicitor. If the applicant appears to be a member of a body which can reasonably be expected to give him financial assistance for the proceedings, but he does not appear to have any right to be indemnified by that body against the costs of the proceedings, the Area Director must make it a term of the offer, issued to the applicant, that he signs an undertaking to pay to the Board any sum which he does receive from the organisation on account of his costs, as well as his ordinary contribution and any additional contribution payable under reg 31.

(b) Where no contribution is payable

Where a contribution is not payable by the applicant, the Area Director must, having approved an application, issue the certificate and send it, together with a copy, to the applicant's solicitor. A copy must also be sent to the applicant, together with a notice drawing his attention to the effects of s 16(6) and 17(1) of the Act (reg 42 of the General Regulations 1989).

2 Scope of a certificate

A certificate can be issued for either the whole or part of proceedings, and except in matrimonial or authorised summary proceedings, it must specify the parties to the proceedings. It is important to ensure that on the application for legal aid the name of the applicant's opponent is set out exactly and correctly, and also that the name is correct on the certificate once it is issued, otherwise it would be necessary to apply for the certificate to be amended, with all the delays to the client which such an application involves.

A certificate can be extended to cover appeals, other than in the House of Lords or from a magistrates' court (reg 46(1) and (2)). The certificate cannot relate to more than one action, cause or matter except in the case of:

(1) authorised summary proceedings; or
(2) matrimonial proceedings; or
(3) proceedings under the Guardianship of Minors Act 1971 or the Guardianship Act 1973 and proceedings under the Domestic Violence and Matrimonial Proceedings Act 1976; or
(4) an application for a grant of representation which is necessary to enable the action which is the subject matter of the certificate to be brought; or
(5) an application under s 33 of the Supreme Court Act 1981 or s 52 of the County Courts Act 1984 and subsequent court proceedings; or
(6) proceedings which under the Act may be taken to enforce or give effect to any order or agreement made in the

proceedings to which the certificate relates and, for these purposes, proceedings to enforce or give effect to an agreement or order, shall include proceedings in bankruptcy or to wind up a company.

(Reg 46(3) of the General Regulations 1989.)

The certificate covers all work which is reasonably necessary within the scope of the certificate to obtain a successful outcome to the proceedings. Limitations on the scope of the certificate arise in a number of ways. Firstly, even if the certificate is a full one issued without specific limitations, it is still issued for a specific purpose and that purpose must be adhered to. If it is issued to defend proceedings, it will not include making a counterclaim against the plaintiff. Secondly, there may be a specific limitation incorporated in the certificate. This would arise where the Area Committee felt that whilst the issue of a certificate may be justified, the outcome of any proceedings is far from certain at that stage, and in those circumstances, a limitation would be placed on the steps which could be taken under the certificate. It may only authorise the obtaining of specialists' reports or counsel's opinion, or all stages up to and excluding the issue of proceedings. Even if it does go so far as to authorise the issue of proceedings, it may be limited up to and including a particular stage in the proceedings. In that way the Area Committee and the Area Director can keep a watch on the progress of cases, about which at the start they could not be certain. The applicant's solicitors must ensure that as the initial limitations on the certificate are reached, an application is made for an amendment to authorise further stages in the proceedings or the removal of any specific limitations. Often counsel's opinion approving the proposed amendment will be required.

(a) Authority to incur costs

The third limitation is as to steps which cannot be taken without the authority of the Area Director, unless that authority is given by way of a general authority under reg 60. The Board has power under reg 60 to give general authority in any particular class of case for a solicitor to incur costs up to a maximum specified fee by:

(1) obtaining a report or opinion from one or more experts, or tendering expert evidence; or

(2) employing a person to provide a report or opinion, other than as an expert; or

(3) requesting transcripts of shorthand notes or tape recordings of any proceedings.

If a solicitor considers it necessary for the proper conduct of
the proceedings to take any of the steps set out below, he can
apply to the Area Director for authority to take them. If that
authority is given, it must specify the number of any reports or
opinions to which it refers, the number of persons who are
authorised to give expert evidence and the maximum fee to be
paid to each (reg 61). The steps referred to in reg 61 are:

(1) in a case of a class not included in any general authority
under reg 60:
  (a) obtaining an expert's report or opinion or tendering
  expert evidence;
  (b) paying a fee to a person other than an expert witness
  to prepare a report and give evidence;
(2) in a case of a class which is included in a general authority
under reg 60;
  (a) paying a higher fee than that specified by the Board;
  (b) obtaining more reports or opinions or tendering more
  evidence, expert or otherwise, than has been specified;
(3) performing any act which is unusual in its nature or
involves unusually large expenditure;
(4) bespeaking transcripts of shorthand notes or tape recordings of any proceedings are not included in a general
authority under reg 60.

Queen's Counsel or more than one counsel may not be
instructed without authority (reg 59 of the General Regulations
1989), although leave of the Area Director is not required where
counsel entrusts a case to another counsel under s 32 of the Act.
If Queen's Counsel or more than one counsel have been
instructed without authority either in the certificate or under reg
59(1), no payment on taxation in respect of those costs and
counsel's fees is to be allowed unless they are also allowed on
an inter partes taxation (reg 63(3)).

Even though the work can be done and the expenditure
incurred without authority, the advantage of obtaining an authority is that no question can be raised on taxation, as to the
propriety of a step or act for which prior authority has been
given, nor as to the amount of any payment to be allowed for
it, unless the assisted person or his solicitor knew or ought
reasonably to have known, that the purpose for which the

authority was required had become irrelevant or unnecessary before the costs were incurred.

There is no power for the Area Director to give retrospective consent and an authority must be obtained before the step for which it is required is taken (*Wallace* v *Freeman Heating Co Ltd* [1955] All ER 418). If the authority is refused, the Area Director must give written reasons for the refusal (reg 62 of the General Regulations 1989). If authority is not applied for or is refused, payment in respect of the costs incurred may still be allowed on taxation (reg 63(4)), but neither solicitor nor counsel can be paid privately in respect of work done during the currency of a certificate, whether or not the work is within the scope of the certificate (reg 64). Regulation 64 is not however as drastic as it may seem, and the Board's Note for Guidance Numbers 30 (1990 edition) and 46 (1989 edition) set out in detail its views as to the interpretation of that regulation in the light of *Littaur* v *Steggles-Palmer* [1986] 1 WLR 780. There is no right of appeal against the refusal of an authority under regs 59 to 61.

In addition to the authority of the Area Director, the prior approval of the client must also be sought for any step involving unusual expense. The client may well, even though he is legally aided, have to pay for it in the end, either through his contribution or the statutory charge. The full implications of the cost and its effect must first be explained to the client.

The wary solicitor must be on his guard against incurring expenditure which is not authorised by the Board or the client. If there is any doubt, the approval of both should be obtained.

(b) Amending the scope of the certificate

Some matters are outside the scope of the certificate altogether, unless they were originally specifically authorised by the certificate. Regulation 52 sets out a list where amendment of the certificate is obligatory from the solicitor's point of view, if he is to be able to obtain payment for that work. The Area Director can amend the certificate where there is a mistake in it, and where:

(1) it has become desirable for the certificate to extend to:
    (*a*) proceedings,
    (*b*) other steps,
    (*c*) subject to reg 46(3), other proceedings,
    (*d*) enforcement proceedings which may be taken under

the Act to give effect to any order or agreement made in the legally aided proceedings,

(e) bringing an interlocutory appeal,

(f) proceedings in the Court of Justice of the European Community on a reference to that court for a preliminary ruling, or

(g) representation by an EEC lawyer;

(2) it has become desirable to add or subtract parties to the proceedings; or

(3) it has become desirable for a certificate to extend to any steps having the same effect as cross action, a reply thereto or a cross appeal; or

(4) a change of solicitor should be authorised.

Applications can also be made to amend the certificate so that certain of the proceedings for which it was issued are excluded from the scope of the certificate. The Area Director must amend the certificate where the amount payable on account of the assisted person's contribution is redetermined. The Area Director cannot refuse to amend a certificate by deleting a limitation on it, until notice has been served on the assisted person that his application may be refused and his certificate discharged, and he has been given an opportunity to show cause why the application should not be granted (reg 55).

The relevant parts of the general regulations which relate to applications for certificates and the procedure on refusal, also apply to applications for amendments of certificates (reg 53). Where a certificate is amended, two copies are sent to the assisted person's solicitor and one copy to the assisted person. If the application for amendment is refused, notice in writing together with the reasons for refusal must be given to the assisted person's solicitor. An appeal against a refusal must be made on the appropriate form to the Area Committee, within fourteen days of the date of the decision (reg 57).

The Area Committee deals with the appeal by way of reconsidering the application for amendment. There is no right for the assisted person to appear at the hearing, nor to be represented, if the Area Committee considers it unnecessary (reg 58(3)), in which case the representation must be made in writing. The Board's Note for Guidance Number 19 (1989 edition) is technically incorrect when it states that the applicant may only make written representations: it is a matter for the Area Committee to decide in the light of reg 58(3). The Area Committee may dismiss the appeal or direct that the certificate be amended in such manner as it thinks fit. The Area Committee's decision is final, and notice of its decision together with reasons must be given to the assisted person and his solicitor (reg 58(1) and (2)).

3 Certificates and authorities in special cases

(a) Probate

Where an action can be brought only by a personal representative, reg 46 provides that a certificate may include an application for a grant of representation which enables the action to be brought. If the assets of the estate are sufficient to cover the cost of obtaining a grant, authority for it should not be included in the certificate (Note for Guidance No 14, 1989 edition). In probate action the Area Director must have regard to the size of the estate in deciding whether or not to grant a certificate. Because probate actions are lengthy and therefore expensive, the action could produce only a trivial benefit to the applicant, after taking into account the effect of the statutory charge, if the costs of the assisted person are not ordered to be paid out of the estate. Area Directors are advised to place limitations on certificates, so that progress can be reviewed no later than at the close of pleadings (Note for Guidance No 15).

(b) Arbitration

Legal Aid is not generally available for arbitration proceedings, but if a legal aid certificate has been issued for county court proceedings, a subsequent reference to arbitration by that court will, in the unlikely absence of a specific exclusion, be covered by that certificate. Legal aid will not be granted in proceedings involving claims not exceeding £500 where there is a compulsory reference to arbitration, save to apply for rescission of that reference (Note for Guidance No 16).

The existence of an arbitration clause in an insurance policy is not necessarily a bar to legal aid being granted for proceedings, where the insurers are bound by an agreement made in 1956 under which members of the British Insurance Association and Lloyd's Underwriters agreed not to insist on enforcing such arbitration clauses where the insured preferred to take court proceedings (Note for Guidance No 17, 1989 edition).

4 Legal aid for appeals

For an appeal from a magistrates' court or to the House of Lords, a new legal aid certificate is required to make or defend the appeal. In other cases an existing certificate may be amended by the Area Director to include making or defending an appeal or making an interlocutory appeal. Defending an interlocutory appeal is within the scope of the original certificate (Note for Guidance No 20).

Where an appeal is to be made to the Divisional Court of the Family Division, prompt notice should be given to the other side, of the intentions to appeal and to apply for a legal aid certificate. The notice of appeal should contain an application to extend the time for appeal. The Divisional Court can then be expected to give leave at the hearing without any prior application (Note for Guidance No 21). In order to avoid delay, applications for legal aid or for the amendment of existing certificates for an appeal to the Court of Appeal should be made as soon as possible after the original hearing. The Area Director will respond 'very quickly', but initially the certificate will be limited to obtaining relevant transcripts and counsel's opinion. A warning to the shorthand writer that an appeal is being considered is advisable, and prompt notice of the intention to appeal, accompanied by a request for an extension of time should be given to the other party. A request for such an extension should be granted, and failure to consent may lead to that party having to pay the costs of an application to the court for an extension (Note for Guidance No 22).

Legal aid will not normally be granted for an appeal to the High Court from a decision of the Pensions Appeal Tribunal, as that tribunal must, under Rule 28 of the Pensions Appeal (England and Wales) Rules 1980, meet the costs of the appellant. The appellant will not therefore benefit from the grant of legal aid. The Area Director will ask any solicitor submitting such application to clarify any possible benefit to the client without which the application will be refused on the grounds of unreasonableness.

Every notice of appeal to the Employment Appeal Tribunal which is not delivered within the forty-two days time limit must be accompanied by an application for an extension of time, which must also set out the reasons for the delay. The fact that a legal aid certificate has been applied for, is not a good reason for delay. Both the Registrar and the other party should therefore be informed within the time limit of the client's intentions, and the other party's consent sought, to an extension.

5 The conduct of legally aided litigation

(a) Notice of issue of certificate

The assisted person's solicitor must file a copy of the certificate and of any amendment thereto with the court, either when the certificate or amendment is received or when proceedings are commenced. Notice of issue of the certificate must be given to all parties to the proceedings or on persons who subsequently become parties to the proceedings. If the copy notice of issue is filed when proceedings are commenced, a copy of it must be annexed to the originating process for service (reg 50).

Notice of issue of an amendment, revocation or discharge of a certificate must be filed and served in similar manner, save where the amendment relates only to the contribution payable by the assisted person (reg 54). A copy of the certificate and any amendment to it must be included with any instructions delivered to counsel, as must a copy of any authority granted by the Area Director. The instructions must be endorsed with the legal aid reference number and must not be marked with a fee (reg 59).

(b) Entrusting cases to others

Neither solicitor nor counsel can entrust the conduct of any part of an assisted person's case to another solicitor or counsel unless they are selected in accordance with s 32(1) of the Act. A solicitor may, however, entrust that work to a partner, to a competent and responsible representative employed in his office or otherwise under his immediate supervision (reg 65).

(c) Duties to report

The assisted person must notify his solicitor of any change in his circumstances or in the circumstances of the case, which he has reason to believe may affect the terms or continuation of the certificate (reg 66).

The assisted person's solicitor or counsel must notify the Area Director and also have a right to give up a case, if they have reason to believe that the assisted person has:

(1) required his case to be conducted unreasonably, so as to incur unjustifiable expense, or has required unreasonably that the case be continued; or

(2) intentionally failed to comply with any regulations as to the provision of information to be furnished by him; or

(3) knowingly made a false statement or representation in furnishing such information.

They must also report to the Area Director if they become uncertain as to whether it would be reasonable to continue to act (reg 67).

If counsel or solicitor give up a case or refuse to act or accept instructions, they must give reasons to the Area Director. If any of the circumstances specified in reg 67 exist, the solicitor must specify which one it is.

The Area Director can require counsel and solicitor to provide him with information as to the progress and disposal of the proceedings. Further duties on the assisted person's solicitor are to:

(1) report the refusal to accept a reasonable offer of settlement or of a sum paid into court;

(2) notify the Area Director of the issue of a legal aid certificate to another party in the proceedings;

(3) if required so to do by the Board, certify to the Area Director the grounds on which it is reasonable for legal aid to continue. (If the solicitor fails to comply with this request within twenty-one days, the Area Director must give the solicitor and the assisted person notice that the certificate may be discharged, and invite the assisted person to show cause why it should not be (reg 70). The request for information contained in the new Annual Report on Case form is made under reg 70.);

(4) report to the Area Director:

(a) the death of the assisted person; or

(b) the making of a bankruptcy order against him (reg 71); or

(c) the completion of the work authorised by the certificate; or

(d) any reason why he is unable to complete the work (reg 72);

(5) inform the Area Director of any property recovered or preserved for the assisted person (reg 90);

(6) pay to the Board forthwith all monies received by him

under an order or agreement made in favour of the assisted person—reg 90 (subject to any arrangement to the contrary made with the Board on an undertaking being given by the solicitor); and

(7) comply with reg 96 where the statutory charge is to be postponed.

Privilege does not preclude the disclosure of any information required to be disclosed by the Act or by the General Regulations 1989 (reg 73).

(d) The new case control system

The Board has introduced a new system of controlling cases, which is operative from 1 April 1990. Where a legal aid certificate has been in force for more than 18 months, the conducting solicitor will be required to complete a computerised form of 'Annual Report on Case', issued by the accounts department. The information required will be:

(1) the estimated costs and disbursements to date;

(2) a certificate that the grounds on which legal aid was granted still apply and that it is reasonable for legal aid to continue; and

(3) an undertaking that the solicitor assigned has been and still is in possession of a practising certificate.

In appropriate cases the Board will ask for more detailed information.

6 Revocation and discharge of certificates

The Area Director may terminate a certificate by revoking or discharging it under Pt X of the General Regulations 1989. Where a certificate is revoked, the assisted person is deemed never to have been legally aided, save for the provisions of s 18 of the Act relating to orders for costs against him and the Board. The effect of the certificate being discharged is that the assisted person ceases to be an assisted person only from the date of the discharge (reg 74).

(a) Obligatory discharge

A certificate must be discharged where:

(1) the Assessment Officer assesses the assisted person as:

   (a) having a disposable income which makes him ineligible for legal aid, or (*b*) having disposable capital which makes him ineligible for legal aid and the probable cost of continuing the proceedings would not exceed the contribution payable; or

(reg 76)

(2) the Area Director considers that:

(*a*) there are no longer reasonable grounds for taking, defending or being a party to proceedings or continuing to do so, or

(*b*) the assisted person has required the proceedings to be conducted unreasonably so as to incur unjustifiable expense to the fund, or

(*c*) it is unreasonable in the particular circumstances that the assisted person should continue to receive legal aid

(reg 77).

(b) Discretionary discharge

The Area Director may discharge a certificate from such date as he considers appropriate:

(1) with the consent of the assisted person; or

(2) where payment in respect of a contribution is more than twenty-one days in arrear: or

(3) on being satisfied that:

(*a*) the assisted person has died, or

(*b*) the assisted person has had a bankruptcy order made against him, or

(*c*) the proceedings to which the certificate relates have been disposed of, or

(*d*) the work authorised by the certificate has been completed (reg 80).

(c) Discretionary discharge or revocation

The Area Director may revoke or discharge a certificate where it appears to him that the assisted person has:

(1) made untrue statements or failed to disclose any material fact concerning his financial resources, unless the assisted person can prove that he used due care and diligence to avoid such misstatement or failure: or

(2) intentionally failed to comply with the General Regulations 1989 by not furnishing the Area Director, or his solicitor, with material information, other than information as to his financial resources; or

(3) knowingly made an untrue statement in furnishing such information (reg 78); or
(4) failed to attend for interview or to provide information or documents when required so to do (reg 79).

(d) Appeal against revocation or discharge

Before a certificate can be discharged for reasons of merit under reg 77, discharged or revoked for abuse under reg 78, for failing to provide information or documents under reg 79 or on the grounds of bankruptcy, notice must be served on the assisted person informing him of the Area Director's decision, and he must have been given an opportunity to show cause why his certificate should not be revoked or discharged (reg 81(1)).

Where the certificate is discharged or revoked after such notice, there is a right of appeal to the Area Committee, whose decision is final. Notice of the decision of the Area Committee must be given to the assisted person and his solicitor. Where applicable the provisions of regs 36 to 39 apply to such appeals (reg 81).

(e) Notice of revocation or discharge

Two copies of a notice of revocation or discharge must be issued to the solicitor and a further copy to the assisted person unless he is dead. If the costs have already been determined, the notice is not sent. A solicitor who receives a notice of discharge or revocation, or a notice of dismissal of an appeal must:
(1) serve notice thereof on any other parties to the proceedings; and
(2) inform counsel; and
(3) if proceedings have been commenced, send a copy of the notice by post to the court office or registry (reg 82).

The effect of revocation or discharge is that upon receipt of the notice, the retainer of the assisted person's solicitor and counsel is determined forthwith, or, if proceedings have been commenced, when the notices required by reg 82 have been filed and served (reg 83). As soon as is reasonably practicable after the termination of the retainer, costs must be taxed or assessed. The liability of the fund for payment of such costs remains (reg 84). If the assisted person continues to take, defend or be a party to the proceedings after the revocation or discharge of his certificate, the statutory charge under s 16(6) of the Act applies to any property which is recovered or preserved as a result of him so doing. This also applies where the proceedings are continued by his personal representative, trustee in bankruptcy or official receiver, following discharge on the grounds of death or bankruptcy (reg 85). The Board has the right where the certificate has been revoked to recover from the assisted person the costs paid or payable, less the amount of any contribution. The solicitor also has the right to recover the difference between the costs paid to him by the Board and the full amount of his solicitor and own client costs (reg 86(1) and (2)).

Discharge of a certificate does not affect the liability of the assisted person to pay his assessed contribution up to the amount of the costs paid by the Board (reg 86(3)).

Chapter 16

Legal Aid in Divorce and Other Family Cases

1 Availability of civil legal aid

Civil legal aid, advice and assistance and ABWOR are available as follows, subject to financial eligibility, for divorce and judicial separation proceedings and for other family cases:

(1) the Green Form Scheme is used for undefended divorce and judicial separation proceedings (see undefended divorces page 31);

(2) ABWOR is available for the matrimonial and family cases set out in the Schedule to the Scope Regs 1989 (see ABWOR approved by the Board page 49);

(3) where ABWOR is not available, a summary jurisdiction certificate can be applied for in respect of the proceedings specified in Sched 2 Pt I para 2, Legal Aid Act 1988 (see Specified Proceedings page 125 and Civil legal aid in the Magistrates' Court page 131).

(4) a civil legal aid certificate is available for proceedings in the High Court or county court, subject to the limitations imposed in the case of matrimonial proceedings by Sched 2 Pt II para 5(*a*) Legal Aid Act 1988 (see Specified Proceedings page 125).

(a) Maintenance proceedings in the magistrates' court

Before approving ABWOR or an application for a summary jurisdiction certificate for proceedings for a matrimonial order in the magistrates' court, the Area Director will have to satisfy himself on the following points:

(1) whether it is in the best interests of the client to obtain such a matrimonial order rather than some other form of relief;

   (2) whether the magistrates are likely to make an order in favour of the client;

   (3) whether an order is likely to be enforceable having regard to the finances of the proposed defendant; and

   (4) whether the advantage of the order to the client or to the client's children is likely to be more than trivial.

The Board takes the view that the fact that a spouse is receiving income support does not prejudice her right to take maintenance proceedings, but she must prove that she will obtain some personal benefit from the proceedings. Thus if a wife is unlikely to obtain a maintenance order for more than the amount of income support she receives, the Board may refuse legal aid because she will not receive any personal benefit. A factor which the Board will regard as relevant is whether the wife is looking for employment which would end her entitlement to income support. If there are children, issues of custody and access may make proceedings necessary, and it is economical from a cost point of view to deal with the wife's maintenance at the same time.

The Department of Social Security (DSS) will also, in the end, be likely to threaten to withdraw benefit payable to a wife who fails to try and obtain maintenance against a husband who can afford it. In those circumstances, she should be granted approval by the Board, because even if it is only the DSS which benefits from the maintenance to be paid, the preservation of the wife's entitlement to income support is a benefit which she will obtain personally by commencing proceedings (Note for Guidance 28(*a*), 1989 edition and see also *Barnes* v *Barnes* (post.).

(b) Maintenance applications in divorce proceedings

A party to divorce proceedings who wishes to apply for maintenance is expected to be able to satisfy the Area Director that the other party to the proceedings has sufficient means to pay and that the applicant has reasonable grounds for seeking the order. Where a wife is in receipt of income support, examples of facts which the Board will regard as justification for seeking an order are:

   (1) that the respondent:

      (*a*) can and ought to pay maintenance for the children;

      (*b*) should not be allowed to throw onto Social Security a burden which he himself ought to bear (*Barnes* v *Barnes* [1972] 3 All ER 872); and

(2) that the applicant is advised to make the application at that time because she then has a nil contribution. She is entitled to apply at the time which is most advantageous to her.

It is to the benefit of the legal aid fund for all the proceedings to be concluded in as short a time as possible, and the cost of preparation is reduced if it is carried out at the same time as instructions are obtained in respect of the other matrimonial proceedings, rather than starting afresh, perhaps many months later (Note for Guidance 28(*b*), 1989 edition).

(c) Scope of certificates 'to prosecute or defend a suite for divorce'

Guidelines have been agreed between the Board and the Senior Registrar of the Family Division as to what is and what is not within the scope of a certificate which is issued 'to prosecute or defend a suite for divorce'. It covers all steps normally necessary to prosecute or defend such a suite, but unless amended, it does not cover any steps after decree, other than applications for ancillary relief, custody or access, which are made promptly after the decree. If the cause becomes undefended the certificate will not cover any further steps in the decree proceedings.

The agreed note provides that the following matters are to be regarded as being within the scope of the usual form of certificate (Note for Guidance 12A, 1990 edition):

(*a*) A certificate covering the prosecution or defence of proceedings for a decree of divorce is regarded as covering:
    (i) filing supplemental pleadings;
    (ii) raising or opposing an issue as to domicile;
    (iii) making or opposing an application for maintenance pending suit;
    (iv) satisfying the judge as to the arrangements to be made for a child of the family;
    (v) an application to remove a child of the family from the jurisdiction of the court, provided it is made before the final decree;
    (vi) an application for an injunction of one of the following types, provided it is made any time up to the final decree:
        (*a*) to prevent molestation of one spouse by the other,
        (*b*) to prevent the removal of a child of the family from the jurisdiction of the court,
        (*c*) to require a spouse to leave the matrimonial home,

(*d*) to require the return of a child of the family to the person from whom it has been taken;

(vii) an application for custody of, or access to, a child provided it is made before, on or promptly after the final decree;

(viii) an issue as to the status of a child provided it is raised at any time up to the making of an order for ancillary relief in respect of that child which is made before, on or promptly after the final decree;

(ix) an application for an injunction to restrain the other spouse from dealing with property to defeat an order for ancillary relief, provided it is made at any time up to the making of an order for ancillary relief, in respect of a party or a child of the family, which is made before, on or promptly after the final decree;

(x) an application for rescission of a decree nisi consequent upon the reconciliation of the parties;

(xi) making or opposing an application to expedite the making absolute of a decree nisi;

(xii) making or opposing an application before or promptly after the final decree, for:
  (*a*) a periodical payments order,
  (*b*) a secured periodical payments order,
  (*c*) a lump sum order,
  (*d*) a transfer of property order,
  (*e*) a settlement of property order,
  (*f*) a variation of settlement order,
  in respect of a party or a child of the family, excluding the trial by a judge of an issue as to conduct;

(xiii) an application made before the final decree for a variation order;

(xiv) making or opposing an application for a periodical payments order or a lump sum order in respect of a party or a child of the family when the applicant has been unsuccessful in the main suit;

(xv) the registration in a magistrates' court of an order for ancillary relief provided that the application is made not later than six months from the date of the order or the date of the final decree, whichever shall be the later;

(xvi) steps by a petitioner in connection with an application by the respondent under s 10(2) of the Matrimonial Causes Act 1973;

(xvii) an application under Section 7 of the Matrimonial Causes Act 1973;

(xviii) attendance before a Registrar on a summons for directions or pre-trial review.

Matters regarded as outside the scope of the usual form of certificate
The legal aid regulations deal with the instances when it is necessary

to obtain specific authority from the Area Director to obtain an amendment to the certificate in order to take certain steps in the proceedings. Unless such specific authority or amendment has been obtained, then, having regard to the principles enumerated in paragraph (1) above, a certificate to prosecute or (as a respondent spouse) to defend a suit for divorce will not cover the initiation or opposing, as appropriate, of the following steps in such proceedings:

   (i) On the part of the petitioner:
      (*a*) filing an answer to a separate cross-petition by the respondent;
      (*b*) filing a second petition;
   (ii) on the part of the respondent spouse:
      (*a*) making cross-charges in an answer, followed by a prayer for divorce or some alternative matrimonial relief,
      (*b*) filing a separate cross-petition;

(the cover afforded by such a certificate will be taken to extend to proceedings under a second petition or separate cross-petition which have taken place after an order for consolidation with the previous proceedings, but not otherwise)

   (iii) an application for a variation order after the final decree;
   (iv) the enforcement of an order for ancillary relief or costs;
   (v) an application for alteration of a maintenance agreement;
   (vi) an application for provision to be made out of the estate of a deceased former spouse;
   (vii) an application for an avoidance of disposition order;
   (viii) protracted negotiations subsequent to, and to give effect to, an order for access to a child;
   (ix) an application by the unsuccessful party for the decree nisi to be made absolute;
   (x) proceedings under section 17 of the Married Women's Property Act 1882;
   (xi) opposing an intervention by the Queen's Proctor to show cause against the decree nisi being made absolute;
   (xii) resisting the respondent's application under section 10(1) of the Matrimonial Causes Act 1973 for rescission of the decree;
   (xiii) an application for committal for breach of an injunction.

(It is emphasised that the above list is not exhaustive).

(4) Limitations and conditions

Where a legal aid certificate has been granted to continue to prosecute or to defend a defended suit for divorce, it will provide that the certificate covers the decree proceedings so long as the cause remains defended.

The certificate will also contain the following limitations.

Whilst the cause remains defended the certificate is limited to:—
   (i) all steps up to and including discovery of documents, and, thereafter,

(ii) the obtaining of counsel's opinion on the merits of the cause continuing as a contested cause.

Despite this limitation, attendance before the Registrar on a summons for directions or a pretrial review is within the scope of the certificate, (see (2)(xviii)).

Without amendment or prior authority from the Area Director, the following steps are not within the scope of a certificate to prosecute or defend a suite for divorce.

(i) On the part of the petitioner: —
    (a) filing an answer to a separate cross-petition by the respondent;
    (b) filing a second petition;

(ii) on the part of the respondent spouse: —
    (a) making cross-charges in an answer, followed by a prayer for divorce or some alternative matrimonial relief,
    (b) filing a separate cross-petition;

(the cover afforded by such a certificate will be taken to extend to proceedings under a second petition or separate cross-petition which have taken place after an order for consolidation with the previous proceedings, but not otherwise)

(iii) an application for a variation order after the final decree;

(iv) the enforcement of an order for ancillary relief or costs;

(v) an application for alteration of a maintenance agreement;

(vi) an application for provision to be made out of the estate of a deceased former spouse;

(vii) an application for an avoidance of disposition order;

(viii) protracted negotiations subsequent to, and to give effect to, an order for access to a child;

(ix) an application by the unsuccessful party for the decree nisi to be made absolute;

(x) proceedings under section 17 of the Married Women's Property Act 1882;

(xi) opposing an intervention by the Queen's Proctor to show cause against the decree nisi being made absolute;

(xii) resisting the respondent's application under section 10(1) of the Matrimonial Causes Act 1973 for rescission of the decree;

(xiii) an application for committal for breach of an injunction.

(It is emphasised that the above list is not exhaustive.)

Limitations and conditions

Where a legal aid certificate has been granted to continue to prosecute or to defend a defended suit for divorce, it will provide that the certificate covers the decree proceedings so long as the cause remains defended.

The certificate will also contain the following limitations.

Whilst the cause remains defended the certificate is limited to: —

(i) all steps up to and including discovery of documents, and, there-after,

(ii) the obtaining of counsel's opinion on the merits of the cause continuing as a contested cause.

Despite this limitation, attendance before the Registrar on a summons for directions or a pre-trial review is within the scope of the certificate, (see (2)(xviii), ante).

(Note for Guidance 12A, 1990 edition).

(d) Legal aid certificates for ancillary relief

All legal aid certificates issued for ancillary relief in matri-monial proceedings are limited to the obtaining of one substan-tive order. Any further hearings are outside the scope of the certificate unless the certificate is amended. Legal aid certificates for access and custody applications can only be granted if there is reason to believe that the application will be opposed (Legal Aid (Matrimonial Proceedings) Regulations 1989, reg 2).

Where a certificate is issued to enforce an order for ancillary relief or costs, it will normally specify the process of enforcement which has to be used. Maintenance orders providing for payment of maintenance directly to a child can only be enforced by that child acting by its next friend or guardian ad litem, and the parents' legal aid certificate cannot therefore be amended to include such enforcement proceedings. Registration of a mainten-ance order in a magistrates' court is part of the process of obtain-ing the original order and is not regarded as enforcement of the order. Registration is therefore within the scope of a certificate to prosecute a suite for divorce, but it is not within the scope of any other form of certificate unless specifically mentioned in the certificate or an amendment thereto. If an application is made for legal aid to enforce or vary such an order, the Area Director will in order to reduce costs, have to be satisfied that there is good reason for not bringing such proceedings in a magistrates' court following registration of the order. (Note for Guidance 26(c).)

(e) The choice of court

The Board accepts that the court in which matrimonial pro-ceedings shall be brought is a matter for the client and the solicitor to decide, but the Area Director will take the following matters into account where an application for legal aid is made in respect of such proceedings:

(1) Multiplicity of proceedings should be avoided where possible (the Board's view is that it could be unreasonable to bring maintenance proceedings or an application for a protection order in the magistrates' court prior to divorce proceedings, where the client wants a divorce and the marriage has irretrievably broken down);

(2) The Divorce Court is the correct forum where that court's wider powers are needed to deal with injunction applications or applications relating to property matters or for lump sum orders in excess of £500;

(3) Because of the comparative speed and cheapness, application should be made in the magistrates' court for protection orders or orders in relation of ancillary matters where:

(a) the lump sum is not likely to exceed £500,

(b) maintenance payments will be classed as small maintenance payments, or

(c) no property settlement is sought.

Chapter 17

Legal Aid in Emergencies

Immediate advice and assistance is available under the Green Form Scheme to those who are financially eligible and irrespective of means to those who require advice and assistance at police stations in connection with criminal matters. Suspects at police stations can obtain advice and assistance either under a twenty-four hour duty solicitor scheme or from a solicitor of their own choice.

The immediate availability of representation in proceedings is more limited. Representation is available at hearings of applications for warrants of further detention, and the magistrates' court or county court has power to authorise representation under the Green Form Scheme, but only to those who are financially eligible and only within the strict confines of the 'within the precincts of the court' rule. Representation is also available in those magistrates' courts where a court duty solicitor scheme operates. This is free of charge to the client and provided without reference to the client's means, but its scope is somewhat limited.

1 Emergency certificates

Where Legal Aid is required as a matter of urgency for civil proceedings, application is made to the Area Director for an emergency certificate (Legal Aid (General) Regulations 1989, reg 19). The application is normally made on the pink form CLA3 which must be accompanied by the application form for a full certificate CLA1 or 2 and the Statement of Means CLA4 unless these have already been submitted to the area office. An emergency certificate cannot be granted in respect of authorised summary proceedings, ie proceedings in a magistrates' court for which Legal Aid is available under Pt I for Sched II, Legal Aid Act 1989.

In order to make the emergency procedure even more immediately available, the Area Director has power to accept an application for an Emergency Certificate in such other manner as he may direct (LAA 1989, s 19). With the approval of the area office, application can be made by telephone, but the Board indicates that this is only acceptable in cases of extreme urgency and only on the solicitor giving an undertaking to forward a completed application form for an emergency certificate, accompanied by an application for a full certificate and any necessary accompanying papers.

The area office will not accept telephone applications for emergency certificates, if the telephone call is made late in the day and there has been ample time during the day to submit the application form duly signed by the client (Practice Note Number 8).

Until such time as area offices are served by fax, this requirement ignores the practical realities of submitting applications from areas which may be many miles from the nearest area office. The cost incurred in personal delivery must be an unnecessary and added financial burden on the cost of the Legal Aid Scheme. There also appears to be wide divergence between area offices as to the application and interpretation of the Board's advice relating to telephone applications.

The Area Director must satisfy himself before granting an emergency certificate that the applicant is likely to fulfil the conditions for the grant of a full Legal Aid Certificate. If it appears that the applicant is not financially eligible for a full certificate, this rule can be used to refuse him an emergency certificate, although the Area Director has power to issue an emergency certificate without reference to the Assessment Officer and would normally do so. Secondly, the Area Director must be satisfied that it is in the interests of justice for Legal Aid to be granted as a matter of urgency (Legal Aid (General) Regulations, reg 19(3) 1989).

If there is a valid reason why the applicant cannot furnish all the information which the Area Director is entitled to require, the Area Director may still issue an emergency certificate, but make it subject to conditions as to the applicant furnishing any such further information.

(a) Criteria for the grant of an emergency certificate

There are only three grounds on which an application can be refused:

(1) on one of the grounds specified in reg 34 for refusal of a full certificate, ie basically for lack of legal merit or reasonableness; or

(2) the applicant is unlikely to fulfil the conditions under which legal aid may be granted; or

(3) it is not in the interests of justice that legal aid should be granted as a matter of urgency.

(reg 20 of the General Regulations 1989.)

In assessing the criteria for the issue of an emergency certificate, the Area Director should take into account the likelihood of a miscarriage of justice, the imposition of an unreasonable degree of hardship on the applicant or the creation of exceptional problems in the handling of a case and which should be avoided. The fact that it is inconvenient to be without an emergency certificate is irrelevant. An emergency certificate will not be granted purely because there are steps to be taken in proceedings, where those steps can be postponed.

The purpose of an emergency certificate is to protect the immediate interests of the applicant, and it will usually be limited to the steps necessary to afford that protection.

Appeals, applications for injunctions and matrimonial protection orders are all cases for which the emergency application is justified. If a client wishes to defend proceedings instituted against him, the proper course is not to apply for an emergency certificate because the proceedings have already commenced, but to ask the plaintiff to agree not to take any further steps in the proceedings and to grant the defendant any necessary extension of time, pending determination of the defendant's full legal aid application. An emergency certificate will not be granted where this request has not been made.

If an application for a Protection Order can be made in the magistrates' court, an application for an emergency certificate to seek similar relief in the county court will not be granted, because it is not reasonable to incur the additional cost of county court proceedings where the magistrates can grant a satisfactory remedy.

Interpretation by Area Directors of what is and what is not in the interests of justice appears to vary considerably. It is not unknown for an application by a partner who has been subjected to domestic violence over a period of time, but who at last summons up enough courage to seek the protection of the courts, to be refused an emergency certificate on the grounds that there is no urgency—she has been beaten up regularly for many months and can easily wait, in the Board's view, for a few more weeks and the grant of a full certificate. Such decisions may outrage, because they deprive a disadvantaged person of the only immediate remedy to which, by law, they are entitled. On the other hand, if a woman becomes the victim of domestic violence and decides to do something about it immediately, the Board can then do a complete about turn and refuse an Emergency Certificate because there has been no previous history of domestic violence.

Such decisions are of course appealable, but this is of little value to a client who has to return home to even more beatings. It may well be that more guidance should be issued to Area Directors in an attempt to obviate problems of this nature.

(b) Effect of a certificate

An emergency certificate has the same effect in all respects as a full certificate (Legal Aid (General) Regulations 1989, reg 21) and remains in force until it is revoked or discharged, merges in a substantive certificate or expires at the end of the period allowed for its duration (reg 22).

The substantive certificate in which an emergency certificate merges, takes effect from the date of issue of the emergency certificate. The substantive certificate must state the date of issue of the emergency certificate and that the emergency certificate has been continuously in force until the date of the substantive certificate (reg 23).

The copy of the certificate marked 'for the court' must be filed at court when issued or when proceedings commence, and notice of issue of an emergency certificate must be given as with a substantive certificate.

The duration of an emergency certificate may be extended by the Area Director where the holder has either failed to signify his acceptance of an offer of a substantive certificate, or has appealed against the terms of that offer and provided that both certificates relate to the same proceedings. The Area Director may similarly extend the duration of an emergency certificate if there are exceptional circumstances or a substantive certificate has been refused, provided notice of appeal against such refusal has been given to the Area Committee, or the time for making such an appeal has not expired (reg 24).

If the extension is granted where the assisted person has failed to accept an offer of a full certificate, appealed against the terms of that offer or been refused a full certificate, no further work can be carried out and no further steps taken under the emergency certificate (reg 24(2) of the General Regulations).

The extensions are not automatic and have to be applied for. If granted, notice of extension must be sent to the solicitor and to the assisted person. The solicitor must file a copy of the extension by post at court, serve notice of the extension on any other party to the proceedings and must also forthwith notify counsel of the extension (reg 25(3) of the General Regulations 1989).

(c) Revocation and discharge of emergency certificates

There are two grounds on which the Area Director must revoke an emergency certificate and a further two grounds on which he has discretion either to revoke or discharge it. The certificate must be revoked where the assisted person's disposable income is assessed as rendering him financially ineligible for legal aid. If the assisted person's disposable income does not make him ineligible but his disposable capital does, the certificate must be revoked if the Area Director considers that the probable cost of the proceedings would not exceed the contribution which the assisted person would have to pay. On neither of these grounds is there power to discharge a certificate (reg 75(1) and (2) of the General Regulations 1989).

The Area Director has discretion to revoke or discharge an emergency certificate if the assisted person fails to co-operate with the Board's requirements as to attending for interview, providing information or documents or if he fails to accept an offer of a substantive certificate. The certificate cannot be revoked on these grounds until notice has been served on the assisted person and on his solicitor, and the assisted person has been given opportunity to show cause why it should not be revoked (reg 75(5) of the Legal Aid (General) Regulations 1989). Such notice does not have to be served prior to a certificate being discharged on the same grounds.

The certificate may also be revoked or discharged when the

period for which it was granted and any extension, has expired (reg 75(4) of the General Regulations 1989).

The distinction between revocation and discharge of an emergency certificate is important. If it is revoked the person to whom it was issued is deemed never to have been an assisted person, save that the court's powers under s 18 of the Legal Aid Act 1989 to make an order for costs in favour of a successful unassisted person remain unaffected. A discharge on the other hand is not retrospective and the assisted person purely ceases to be so only from the date of such discharge. Generally the effects of revocation and discharge are the same with an Emergency Certificate as with a full certificate.

(d) Pre-certificate work

If work is carried out immediately before the issue of an emergency certificate and at a time when an emergency application could not be made because the area office was closed, it is deemed to be work carried out under the certificate, provided that the application is made at the first available opportunity and is granted (reg 103 of the Legal Aid (General) Regulations 1989). The important part of this regulation is the proviso that the work must be done when the area office is closed, and this generally will mean when the solicitor's office is also closed. If the work could be done during office hours, then it would in any event be possible to make a telephone call to apply to the Area Director for an emergency certificate.

The solicitor can provide some protection for himself in respect of pre-certificate costs by giving notice of his lien to the Board in respect of them, if and when any monies are recovered for the assisted person.

Chapter 18

The Contribution

1 The mechanics of the contribution

As with advice and assistance, the contribution payable by a legally aided person (an assisted person) is one of the ways in which the Board is funded. The contribution is created by s 16(1) of the Act, which authorises the making of regulations to determine the financial resources of an applicant. The current regulations are the Civil Legal Aid (Assessment of Resources) Regulations 1989, the main purpose of which is to determine which of the applicant's financial resources, both as to capital and income, are to be either taken into, or left out of account in assessing disposable capital and disposable income.

Once the assessment has been made by the Assessment Officer, the Board ascertains what the contribution shall be and how it shall be paid. The Act requires, if it is to be made by periodical payments (which in the case of a contribution based on disposable income it must be) that it be payable by reference to the period during which the applicant is represented or a shorter period (s 16(3)). Contribution of a capital sum may be paid by instalments. This appears to conflict with reg 43(1)(*a*) of the General Regulations under which the Area Director must require that any sums generally payable out of capital, be paid forthwith.

Unlike the contribution for advice and assistance which is collected by the solicitor, the contribution towards the cost of a civil legal aid certificate under Pt IV of the Act is paid directly to the Board.

When the eventual net liability of the Board under the certificate has been ascertained, it must repay to the assisted person, such part of the contribution which has actually been paid as exceeds that net liability. The net liability of the Board is the

168

amount which it has paid in costs for the case and for advice and assistance under Pt III of the Act, after taking into account its receipts in the form of any costs actually recovered under an order or agreement for costs (s 16(9) Legal Aid Act 1988).

Any sums remaining unpaid in respect of a contribution, are included in the total for which the Board has the right to its statutory charge under s 16(6) of the Act.

(a) Determining the contribution

The contribution is further governed by reg 31 of the General Regulations 1989, which make it the duty of the Area Director to determine the amount payable on account of the applicant's contribution, and in so doing to have regard to the probable cost of the proceedings. If the probable cost of the proceedings is likely to exceed any maximum contribution which has been assessed, then that maximum contribution must be the contribution payable (reg 31(2) of the General Regulations).

Legal Aid is available to a person whose disposable income does not exceed £6,350 per year. A person may be refused legal aid where his disposable capital exceeds £6,310 and it appears to the Area Director that he could afford to proceed without legal aid (reg 4(2) of the Assessment Regulations 1989, as amended).

If a person's disposable income does not exceed £2,645 per annum, legal aid is available completely free without a contribution having to be paid, provided that disposable capital does not exceed £3,000. If disposable income does exceed £2,645 per annum, the contribution payable must not be greater than one quarter of the excess. Where disposable capital exceeds £3,000 the contribution must be not greater than the excess (reg 4(1) Civil Legal Aid (Assessment of Resources) (Amendment) Regulations 1990 amending regs 4(2) and (4) of the Assessment Regulations 1989).

Where a contribution is payable, legal aid will only be granted on condition that the applicant pays or agrees to pay the contribution. In practice the usual period for payment of the contribution from income is twelve months, and the applicant is told how much the instalments are and how they are payable, when he receives the offer of legal aid. Contributions from capital are paid in one instalment on acceptance of the offer.

(b) Personal injury claims

If the subject matter of the dispute in respect of which legal aid is applied for, includes a claim in respect of personal injuries, the disposable income limit is £7,000 per annum instead of £6,350 and the disposable capital limit is £8,000 instead of £6,310 (reg 4(3) of the Assessment Regulations 1989 as amended by reg 4(1) of the Civil Legal Aid (Assessment of Resources) (Amendment) Regulations 1990. If capital exceeds £8,000 legal aid may be refused if it appears to the Area Director that the applicant could afford to proceed without legal aid.

2 Assessment of resources

(a) The subject matter of the dispute

Any money or the value of any property which is the subject matter of the dispute in respect of which legal aid has been applied for, cannot be taken into account in assessing either disposable capital or disposable income (reg 5(1) of the Assessment Regulations 1989), save that periodical maintenance payments are taken into account whether they are voluntary or not, in assessing disposable income (reg 5(2) of the Assessment Regulations 1989).

If it later turns out, even at the end of the case, that any money or property left out of account as being the subject matter of the dispute, has never actually been in dispute, a re-assessment may be made under reg 12(1) on the grounds that there has been a change in financial circumstances.

A reduction in capital (eg by spending it), cannot lead to a re-assessment.

(b) The person whose means are assessed

For the purpose of the Assessment Regulations 1989, the person whose means are assessed is 'the person concerned', and this includes not only the applicant, but any person whose means are to be treated under the regulations as the 'resources of another person' (reg 3(1) of the Assessment Regulations 1989).

(c) Spouses and cohabitees

The resources of the spouse of the person concerned, have for these purposes long been regarded as the resources of the applicant, and therefore to be taken into account in assessing the applicant's means, although this does not apply where the spouse has a contrary interest in the dispute in respect of which legal aid application is made, nor if the spouse and the person concerned are living separate and apart (reg 7(1) and (2)). These regulations apply equally to a man and woman living with each other in the same household as husband and wife, as they apply to the parties to a marriage (reg 7(3) of the Assessment Regulations 1989).

(d) Children

A 'child' is a person whose age is under the upper limit of compulsory school education, or over that age but receiving full time instruction at an educational establishment or undergoing training for a trade profession or vocation (reg 3(1) of the Assessment Regulations 1989).

Until 9 April 1990 the resources of any person who is responsible in law for maintaining the child and with whom the child is living or will normally live, are to be assessed and taken into account in addition to the child's resources (reg 8(1)), except where that other person has a contrary interest in the dispute or there are exceptional circumstances. Despite the definition of a child in reg 3(1), the provisions of reg 8(1) of the Assessment Regulations 1989, only apply to a child under the upper limit of compulsory school age, and not to a child who is over that age. The resources of the child include any sum payable to any person for the maintenance of that child (reg 8(3)).

The whole of reg 8 has been repealed in respect of applications submitted after 9 April 1990 with the effect that as from that date only the resources of the child are to be taken into account in making the assessment (reg 4(2) Civil Legal Aid (Assessment of Resources) (Amendment) Regulations 1990).

(e) Representatives, fiduciaries and officials

If the applicant is only concerned in the proceedings in a representative, fiduciary or official capacity, the personal resources of that person are not to be taken into account in assessing his disposable income and capital. The Area Director may request the Assessment Officer to take into account the value of any property, estate or fund, out of which that person is entitled to be indemnified, as well as the disposable income, capital and maximum contribution of any person who might benefit from the outcome of the proceedings (reg 6 of the Assessment Regulations 1989).

(f) Deprivation of resources

If the person concerned, directly or indirectly, has deprived himself of any resources, or converted any part of his resources into resources which either have to be disregarded wholly or partly or in respect of which nothing is to be included in the assessment, then those resources must be treated as the resources of the person concerned (reg 9 of the Assessment Regulations 1989).

For the purposes of that regulation, the repayment of money borrowed on the security of a dwelling is included in resources which are to be wholly or partly disregarded. The affect of the final part of reg 9 is that it is not possible for a person concerned to reduce his assessable assets by paying off the mortgage on the family home and thereby reducing a capital sum which had been invested elsewhere.

In order to fall within reg 9, the deprivation or conversion must, prior to 9 April 1990, have been done with intent to reduce the disposable income or disposable capital of the person concerned. If a transaction which reduced resources was a genuine one, carried out in good faith for other reasons, it was irrelevant that a side effect of the reduction in resources or deprivation affected the applicant's disposable income or capital and thereby his eligibility to legal aid (*R v Legal Aid Assessment Officer, ex parte Saunders* (1989) *The Independent* 6 November).

This situation has now been changed by reg 4 of the Civil Legal Aid (Assessment of Resources) (Amendment) Regulations 1990 so that from 9 April 1990 it is irrelevant whether or not the deprivation or conversion was done for the purposes of making a person financially eligible for legal aid.

(g) Re-assessing and amending the assessment

There is no appeal to the Area Committee or to anybody else against the Assessment Officer's assessment, but he does have power to amend an assessment, and if he does so, the amended assessment takes effect as if it were the original assessment (reg 14 of the Assessment Regulations 1989). An amendment can be made where there has been an error or mistake in assessing a person's disposable income, disposable capital or maximum contribution, or in any computation or estimate on which that assessment was made. The amendment can only be made if it is just and equitable so to do (reg 14 of the Assessment Regulations 1989).

The power to make amendments is not, in the absence of a right of appeal, satisfactory. There can be many cases where there is a genuine dispute as to the basis of the assessment. Such disputes can be over whether there has been a deprivation of resources, whether there is a contrary interest between parents and children, or between spouses or cohabitees, or as to whether 'cohabitees' are in fact cohabitees and living with each other in the same household. These are complicated matters both of law and fact, and an officer of the DSS is not the best person to have the only and final say in their determination. The regulations do not give the person concerned even a right to make representations about any error, mistake or dispute, although presumably the Assessment Officer would be always prepared to receive these. An Appeal Committee of the DSS similar to those hearing appeals in respect of welfare benefits, and with a legally qualified chairman would be an ideal solution, where as at present the only remedy is the expensive one of seeking judicial review. Whilst legal aid is available for judicial review, that in practice would be of little use to a person who had already been assessed as being financially ineligible for legal aid, unless the income or capital, the assessment of which was in dispute, were treated by the Assessment Officer as being property in dispute under reg 5.

A person concerned has a duty to notify the Assessment Officer of any change in his financial circumstances which has occurred since the re-assessment was made, and which he has reason to believe might affect the terms on which the certificate was offered or its continuation (reg 11 of the Assessment Regulations 1989). The Assessment Officer must make a re-assessment where disposable income has increased by more than £750 or decreased by more than £300 and where disposable capital has increased by more than £750. A re-assessment must also be made where new information has come to light which is relevant to the assessment. If it appears that there will be no significant change in the liability to make a contribution, then a re-assessment need not be made (reg 12 of the Assessment Regulations 1989), although the person concerned is not relieved from the obligation to notify the changes to the Assessment Officer.

Where a re-assessment is necessitated by the acquisition of a capital resource after the date of the legal aid application, the value of that resource, is its value at the date when it was received (reg 12(2) of the Assessment Regulations 1989).

The Area Director can also request with a view to discharging the certificate, a re-assessment, where it is still in force after expiry of the computation period, and he considers that the current financial circumstances of the person concerned are such that he can proceed without legal aid (reg 13(1) of the Assessment Regulations 1989). The Assessment Officer must then re-assess disposable capital and disposable income (reg 13(2)).

(h) Estimated assessment

The Assessment Officer can make an estimate of the disposable income, disposable capital and of the maximum contribution where he is informed by the Area Director that the applicant requires a certificate as a matter of urgency, and the Assessment Officer is not satisfied that he can make an assessment and communicate it to the Area Director in the time requested by the Area Director. The estimate is based on the information then available, and until the making of the full estimate, it has the same effect for all purposes of the regulations as a normal assessment. When the Assessment Officer has received the additional information which he requires, he must then make his assessment and notify it in writing to the Area Director. The assessment then replaces the estimate (reg 15).

(i) Making the assessment

It is the Assessment Officer's duty to assess the disposable income, disposable capital and maximum contribution of the person concerned, and to notify them in writing to the Area Director (reg 10). The DSS will also supply the applicant or his solicitor with a copy of the calculations where it is felt that they should be checked.

3 Computation of income and capital

(a) Income

The computation of income is carried out in accordance with the provisions of the Second Schedule to the Assessment Regulations 1989 as amended by the Civil Legal Aid (Assessment of Resources) (Amendment) Regulations 1990. The income of the person concerned is that which he may reasonably expect to receive, whether in cash or kind, from any source, during the computation period, which is normally the preceding twelve months. The value of any emolument, benefit or privilege received otherwise than in cash is estimated at such sum as is just and equitable.

For persons other than those who are employed at a wage or salary, their income is deemed to be the profit from their trade, business or gainful occupation, which has or will accrue in respect of the computation period. The Assessment Officer can have regard to the last accounting period for which accounts have been prepared in computing that profit. All sums 'necessarily expended' to earn the profit must be deducted, except for living expenses of the person concerned and any member of his family or household, unless those living expenses form part of such person's remuneration.

Income tax payable and calculated as if the computing period were a fiscal year must also be deducted from actual income in assessing disposable income. Income tax is estimated after making the necessary allowances and reliefs by reference to the rates of tax and allowances for the fiscal year in which the application is made.

For any period during which the person concerned or his spouse is in receipt of income support, his disposable income for that period shall be deemed not to exceed the figure at which a contribution becomes payable.

Attendance, constant attendance and mobility allowances and any payment made out of the social fund under s 32 of the Social Security Act 1986 are disregarded in assessing disposable income.

Further deductions to be allowed in assessing disposable income are:

(1) in respect of a person whose income consists wholly or in part of a wage or salary from employment:
   (a) reasonable travelling expenses to and from work;
   (b) reasonable membership fees to a trade union or professional organisation;
   (c) provision for the care of a dependent child living with the person concerned, and for the period he is absent from home by reason of his employment (this would include payments to a child minder or nanny. The deduction is only allowed where it is reasonable so to do and would not be made for a period when a spouse

or cohabitee was at home available to look after any child);

(*d*) contributions to an occupational or personal pension scheme, whether voluntarily or under a legal obligation; and

(2) Social Security contributions payable by the person concerned or estimated to be payable in the twelve months following the application for a certificate; and

(3) where the person concerned is a householder, reasonable rent in respect of his main or only dwelling, which, in addition to the annual rent payable, includes:

(*a*) any domestic rates, water and sewage charges;

(*b*) reasonable expenditure on repairs and insurance;

(*c*) annual payments including both interest and capital under any mortgage charged on the house in which he resides or has an interest (any housing benefit received must be taken into account in ascertaining the net rent, as must the proceeds of any sub-letting and a reasonable notional amount in respect of a lodger or any other person residing there, apart from the spouse or a dependent of the person concerned); and

(4) reasonable cost of living accommodation where the person concerned is not a householder; and

(5) (*a*) for a spouse living with the person concerned, a sum calculated in accordance with provisions of para 1(i) Sched I of the Assessment Regulations 1989;

(*b*) for a dependent child or dependent relative who are members of the household of the person concerned, a sum calculated in accordance with the provisions of para 1(i) and (ii) Sched I of the Assessment Regulations 1989 (the income and other resources of a dependent may affect the rate of the reduction and also affect the decision as to whether they are dependent); and

(6) a reasonable amount in respect of bona fide maintenance payments made (not payable) for such period as the Assessment Officer considers adequate to:

(*a*) a spouse who is living apart;

(*b*) a former spouse;

(*c*) a child;

(*d*) a relative;

and who is not a member of the household concerned; and

(7) a reasonable amount for any other matter which the person concerned is required to or may reasonably provide; and

(8) any other income or part thereof which the Assessment Officer considers it reasonable to disregard; and

(9) any sums payable by way of personal community charge

(b) Capital

The computation of capital is carried out in accordance with the provisions of the third schedule to the Assessment Regulations 1989 as amended by the Civil Legal Aid (Assessment of Resources) (Amendment) Regulations 1990.

Every resource of a capital nature belonging to the person concerned at the date of the legal aid application is taken into account. Any substantial fluctuations in the value of a resource or substantial variation in its nature so as to affect its value, between that date and the date of the computation shall be taken into account in the assessment, as shall the fact that any resources ceased to exist or a new resource has come into the possession of the person concerned.

The value of a capital resource other than money is:

(1) the sum which it would realise if sold in the open market; or

(2) if there is only a restricted market the amount it would fetch in that market; or

(3) the value which appears to the Assessment Officer to be just and equitable.

Any money due to the person concerned, whether due immediately or otherwise and whether secured or not, is taken into account.

The person concerned can be treated as the sole owner or partner of a limited company instead of his stocks, shares, bonds or debentures in that company being valued. The Assessment Officer can take such action where the position of the person concerned in relation to the company is analogous to that of a sole owner or partner in the business of the company. In that case the valuation is the greater of:

(1) such sum or his share thereof as could be withdrawn from the assets of the business without substantially impairing its profits or normal development; or

(2) such sum as he could borrow on the security of his interest in the business without injuring its commercial credit.

Where the person concerned has any interest, whether solely, jointly or in common with any other person, whether vested or contingent in reversion or remainder on the termination of a prior estate, legal or equitable, in any real or personal property or in a trust or other fund, it shall be computed in such manner as is equitable and practicable.

For the period during which the person concerned or his spouse was and is in receipt of income support, his capital is deemed not to exceed the minimum below which no contribution is payable which at present is £3,000.

In computing capital there is to be disregarded:

(1) any payment out of the social fund under s 32 Social Security Act;

(2) the value of any interest in the main or only dwelling in which the person concerned resides (if the person resides in more than one, the Assessment Officer must decide which is the main one and then take into account any sum which might be obtained by borrowing money on the security thereof);

(3) any sum of money which the person concerned has received or is entitled to receive from a body of which he or she is a member, by way of assistance towards the cost of the proceedings for which he or she has applied for legal aid;

(4) any capital which the Assessment Officer in his discretion decides, having regard to all the circumstances of the case, to disregard; and

(5) any capital payment received from any source and made in relation to the incident giving rise to the dispute in respect of which the legal aid application is made.

No account shall be taken except in exceptional circumstances of:

(1) the household furniture and effects of the dwellinghouse occupied by the person concerned; or

(2) articles of personal clothing; or

(3) tools and equipment of a person's trade, unless they form part of the plant or equipment of a business to which para 5 of the schedule applies.

The value of any life assurance or endowment policy is the amount which the person concerned could readily borrow on the security thereof. If the person concerned has a contingent liability, or is liable to pay any sum not yet ascertained, under a bond, covenant, guarantee or other instrument, an allowance must be made for any amount which is reasonably likely to become payable within twelve months from the date of the application.

An allowance must also be made to the extent which the Assessment Officer considers reasonable in respect of any debts or part of debts which would be discharged in that period of twelve months. The person concerned must produce evidence to satisfy the Assessment Officer and the debt must not be secured on any dwelling in which the person concerned resides.

Reg 6(*b*) of the Civil Legal Aid (Assessment of Resources) (Amendment) Regulations 1990 eases the financial eligibility limits for 'pensioners' who have low income but capital which would otherwise render them ineligible. A 'pensioner' is a man aged 65 or a woman aged 60, ie of pensionable age whether or not he or she has retired. Regulation 6(*b*) sets out a table showing the amount of capital which is to be disregarded, in making the assessment, the amount being variable dependent on income. Net income derived from the capital is excluded in ascertaining the income in the left hand column.

Annual Disposable Income (excluding net income derived from capital)	Amount of Capital Disregarded
Up to £400	£25,000
£401–£900	£20,000
£901–£1,400	£15,000
£1,401–£1,900	£10,000
£1,901 and above	£5,000

Chapter 19

The Statutory Charge

The Statutory Charge has led to more litigation than any other aspect of legal aid. The all too frequent failure of the legal profession to explain the charge to legally aided clients has also been the cause of unnecessary ill feeling and friction for which the profession has only itself to blame. Counsel's all too frequent ignorance of anything to do with costs, (some will proudly boast in open court that they know nothing of the workings of costs provisions) can mean that generally they do not profess to have enough knowledge to protect the lay client properly, and ensure that orders affecting property are drawn to the best advantage of the client, with regard to the effect of the statutory charge. In order to protect themselves from negligence actions, members of the bar need to acquire a reasonable working knowledge of the effects of the statutory charge and other costs provisions.

1 The purpose of the charge

One of the underlying principles of the Legal Aid system, is that an assisted person cannot expect to win his case and also have his costs paid out of public funds. For this reason, the statutory charge has long been a major feature of the legal aid system. Often the principle will not cost the assisted person anything, for he who wins his case can normally expect that the court will also order his unsuccessful opponent to pay his costs. Not all unsuccessful defendants are however as wealthy or as responsible as insurance companies, and as many a successful litigant knows to his cost, there can be a world of difference between obtaining an order for costs and enforcing payment of those costs. The unsuccessful opponent may also be legally aided, in which case the court is unlikely to make an order for costs against him.

The statutory charge was therefore created as one of the methods by which the costs of the Legal Aid fund could be recouped in civil proceedings, on the basis that it would obviously be unjust if an assisted person recovered thousands of pounds in damages, but could still expect the fund to pay his legal costs. Similarly it would be just as unjust if all that an assisted woman recovered was maintenance at the rate of perhaps £25 per week or even less, but because the assisted person had been succesful, she was expected to reimburse her legal costs to the Board out of that maintenance.

The statutory charge is therefore an attempt to ensure that if capital sums are awarded to an assisted person, either in cash or other forms of property, the Board can recover its costs out of such capital sum. The object of litigation is not always the recovery of a sum of money, capital or otherwise, and in matrimonial cases it may well be the award of the matrimonial home or other matrimonial assets of a capital nature. For this reason the statutory charge applies not only to money which is recovered, but to property which is recovered.

The outcome of litigation is not always the recovery of property, particularly in matrimonial cases. Many such disputes are as to the share which each of the disputing spouses should have in the matrimonial assets, more often than not, the matrimonial home. It may well be that one spouse is claiming a greater share in the matrimonial assets than the other spouse is prepared to concede. If that other spouse is successful in opposing that claim, then although no property has been recovered, the opposing spouse has been successful in 'preserving' property which has been in dispute. Parliament has taken the view that for purposes of reimbursing the legal aid fund, an assisted person should not be able to preserve property, which again may be worth many thousands of pounds, and still expect public funds to finance the litigation. For that reason the statutory charge applies to property which has been preserved, as well as to property which has been recovered.

The next stage in the thinking behind the statutory charge is that there is no point in the Board having a statutory charge on property recovered or preserved, without power for the Board to enforce that charge. Enforcement provisions were therefore necessary, but these could themselves lead to hardship for an assisted person. It would be extremely unjust if a wife who recovered or preserved the matrimonial home or a share in it, so that she and the children of the family had a roof over their heads, found that the property which she had 'won' with the assistance of a Legal Aid Certificate, was then sold as a result of proceedings by the Board to enforce its statutory charge. In the 1988 Legal Aid Act the Board has therefore been given power in certain circumstances to postpone enforcement of the charge.

The aim of the provisions of the Act and of regulations relating to the statutory charge are to strike a balance between what is just for the tax payer who funds litigation, and what is just for the legally aided litigant who preserves or recovers property which has been in issue.

2 The nature of the charge

Section 16(6) of the Legal Aid Act 1988 provides:

Except so far as regulations otherwise provide:
(a) any sum remaining unpaid on account of a person's contribution in respect of the sums payable by the Board in respect of any proceedings; and
(b) a sum equal to any deficiency by reason of his total contribution being less than the net liability of the Board on his account shall be a first charge for the benefit of the Board on any property which is recovered or preserved for him in the proceedings.

The charge is a first charge for the benefit of the Board. The effect of s 16(6) is that save as regulations otherwise provide the charge covers firstly, any unpaid part of the assisted person's contribution and secondly, the difference between the total contribution and the liability of the Board for the costs of that assisted person in those proceedings. It arises not only where there have been proceedings, but also where there is a compromise which avoids or brings to an end such proceedings. The net liability of the Board includes sums payable to counsel and solicitor in respect of those proceedings for work carried out under the certificate, as well as sums paid for advice and assistance, either in connection with those proceedings or any matter to which those proceedings relate. In assessing the Board's net liability there is to be deducted the assisted person's contribution, any sums recouped by the Board under an order or agreement for costs made in favour of the assisted person, (s 16(9) of the

Legal Aid Act 1988) and any property which is exempted under reg 94 Civil Legal Aid (Gen) Regs 1989.

The Board's Note for Guidance Number 46 (1989 edition) was issued by the Board to assist the profession in understanding the statutory charge. It is couched in technical language and is not intended as a substitute for a personal explanation to the client as to the operation of the statutory charge. It has now been replaced by Note Number 5 (1990 edition). Attached to each legal aid application is a perforated page which contains a simple explanation of the charge. This must be handed to the client in all cases when the application for legal aid is completed.

The Board takes the view that the statutory charge is intended, so far as possible, to put the assisted person in the same position as the fee paying client. Furthermore, it regards the statutory charge as essential to prevent the unreasonable conduct of legally aided litigation.

If money which has been recovered or preserved is paid into court, the statutory charge attaches to it only so far as is necessary to protect the rights of the Board. It is the duty of the Area Director to notify the court in writing of the amount so attached (reg 93 of the General Regulations 1989).

The charge does not arise until the end of the case and is not affected by the discharge of a certificate.

(a) Exemptions to the charge

Exemptions to the statutory charge created by s 16(6), are set out in reg 94 of the Civil Legal Aid (General) Regs 1989 which is a further attempt to maintain a fair balance between the tax payer and the legally aided person, and which sets out a list of 'property' which is exempt from the charge even if it is recovered or preserved and has been in issue. Regulation 94 states:

94 Exemptions from the statutory charge
The charge created by section 16(6) of the Act shall not apply to—
(*a*) any interim payment made in accordance with an order made under Order 29, rule 11 or 12 of the Rules of the Supreme Court 1965(a), or Order 13, rule 12 of the County Court Rules 1981(b), or in accordance with an agreement having the same effect as such an order;
(*b*) any sum or sums ordered to be paid under section 5 of the Inheritance (Provision for Family and Dependants) Act 1975(c);
(*c*) any periodical payment of maintenance which, for this purpose, means money or money's worth paid towards the support of a spouse, former spouse, child or any other person for whose support

the payer has previously been responsible or has made payments; the first £2,500 of any money, or of the value of any property, recovered or preserved by virtue of—

   (i) an order made, or deemed to be made, under the provisions of section 23(1)(c) or (f), 23(2), 24, 27(6)(c) or (f), or 35 of the Matrimonial Causes Act 1973(d); or

  (ii) an order made, or deemed to be made, under the provisions of section 2 or 6 of the Inheritance (Provision for Family and Dependants) Act 1975 or any provision repealed by that Act; or

 (iii) an order made, or deemed to be made, after 30 September 1977, under section 17 of the Married Women's Property Act 1882(e); or

  (iv) an order made, or deemed to be made, under the provisions of section 4(2)(b) of the Affiliation Proceedings Act 1957(f); or

   (v) an order for the payment of a lump sum made, or deemed to be made, under the provisions of section 60 of the Magistrates' Courts Act 1980(g); or

  (vi) an order made, or deemed to be made, under the provisions of section 2(1)(b) or (d), 6(1) or (5), 11(2)(b) or 3(b) or 20(2) of the Domestic Proceedings and Magistrates' Courts Act 1978(h); or

 (vii) an order made, or deemed to be made, under section 9(2)(b), 10(1)(b)(ii) or 11(b)(ii) of the Guardianship of Minors Act 1971(i) or under section 11B, 11C, or 11D of that Act (j); or

(viii) an order made, or deemed to be made, under section 34(1)(c) or 35 of the Children Act 1975(k); or

  (ix) an agreement made after 1 March 1981 which has the same effect as an order made, or deemed to be made under any of the provisions specified in sub-paragraph (d)(i) to (viii); or

(e) where the certificate was issued before 3 May 1976, any money or property, of whatever amount or value, recovered or preserved by the virtue of an order made, or deemed to be made, under any of the provisions specified in subpara (d)(i) or (ii) before 1 August 1976 or which, if made on or after that date, gives effect to a settlement entered into before that date;

(f) any payment made in accordance with an order made by the Employment Appeal Tribunal, or in accordance with a settlement entered into after 1 November 1983 which has the same effect as such an order; or

(g) any sum, payment or benefit which, by virtue of any provision of, or made under, an Act of Parliament, cannot be assigned or charged.

(b) Property in issue which has been recovered or preserved

The purpose of much of the litigation over the extent and effect of the statutory charge has been to establish when property is 'recovered and preserved', rather than over the question as to what is 'property'. Perhaps much of this litigation could have been avoided if Parliamentary draftsmen had been more specific in their definition of those two words, as they were in the definition of property, and in the list of exemptions under reg 94. The basic rule is that for the purposes of the statutory charge 'recovered' and 'preserved', have the same meaning as in the Solicitor's Acts, which allow a solicitor to obtain a charging order on property which is recovered or preserved for his client.

Jessel MR in *Foxon v Gascoigne* (1984) 9 Ch Appeals P657 stated, 'it means that where the plaintiff claims property and asserts a right to the ownership of the property in some shape or other, there the property has been recovered; where a defendant's right to the ownership of the property is disputed and it has been vindicated by the proceedings, the property has been preserved'. Note for Guidance 46 points out that that decision was followed in *Till v Till* [1974] 1 All ER 1094.

It is in matrimonial cases that the statutory charge led to disputes with the Law Society which then had responsibility for administering the legal aid scheme. The original statutory provisions were not well thought out or drafted and could lead in some matrimonial cases to devastating hardship which nullified the results of the otherwise successful litigation. The 1988 Act has sought to remedy these deficiencies by extra powers which it has given to the Board, as to the administration of the charge.

In *Hanlon v Law Society* [1980] 2 All ER 199 Lord Simon of Glaisdale stated that the explanation of Jessel MR in *Foxon v Gascoigne* was too narrow for all cases under the Solicitor's Acts and continued with the following definition: 'property has been recovered or preserved if it has been in issue in the proceedings; recovered by the claimant if it has been the subject of a successful claim, preserved to the respondent if the claim fails.' Whether property has been in issue is a question of fact and not of 'theoretical risk' and can be gleaned from the pleadings, evidence, judgment and order. There was, said Lord Simon, no reason for extending the definition to property, the ownership or possession of which has never been questioned.

In that case Mrs Hanlon obtained a property adjustment order under s 24 MCA 1973, requiring Mr Hanlon to transfer the matrimonial home to her, it then being believed that there was a net equity of about £10,000. She was initially ordered to pay a lump sum of £5,000 to Mr Hanlon, but this was overturned by the Court of Appeal. Mrs Hanlon's legal aid costs amounted to £8,025 and comprised:

Divorce proceedings and injunction	£ 925.00
Custody and access	£1,150.00
Proceedings for ancillary relief	£5,950.00
	£8,025.00

The total of the mortgage on the property, legal aid costs and the statutory exemption of £2,500 in fact exceeded the value of the property. If the statutory charge was enforced, Mrs Hanlon would probably not have been able to afford another house. The husband was legally aided and no order for costs had been made against him. Mrs Hanlon had applied to the court to ascertain:

(1) whether the legal aid fund was entitled to a charge on the home, and if so, to what extent; and

(2) whether there was a discretion as to its enforcement.

What Lord Simon found crucial was that 'at the very outset in the original pleadings, each spouse was claiming the transfer of the other's interest in the house.' The husband's claim to Mrs Hanlon's interest in the house had never been withdrawn, and there had never been any evidence of agreement between the parties that Mrs Hanlon was entitled to any share in the house. The House of Lords held that the house was property which was both recovered by Mrs Hanlon (as to her husband's interest) and preserved to her (as to her own interest).

In passing, Lord Simon said that the correct approach, had the lump sum order remained, was to deduct it from the value of the house in ascertaining what property had been recovered or preserved. This rebutted the argument put forward that the payment by a spouse of a lump sum in these circumstances was to be ignored, for the purpose of assessing the extent of the property to which the charge applied.

Lord Simon concluded his judgment by observing that any tribunal exercising jurisdiction under ss 23 and 24 MCA 1973 should bear in mind the possible effect of the statutory charge, and if necessary calling in the Law Society (now the Board) for counsel. All who advise parties as to matrimonial property disputes, whether counsel or solicitor, must also bear it in mind.

Spouses are frequently still extremely bitter towards each other in the immediate post divorce period, when conflicts over matrimonial assets are raging.

Advice to a client to adopt a moderate and reasonable attitude and approach is essential if the client is to stand a proper chance of a satisfactory conclusion to the conflict. Above all, it is essential to ensure that property is not put unnecessarily into dispute in the early stages of correspondence. If there is agreement over any items of a capital nature, then this should be recorded in correspondence to the other party's solicitors as soon as possible. A spouse who refuses to agree to anything until the doors of the court are reached, may well be a fool to himself or herself. Frequently, it is at this stage when substantial changes in attitude tend to take place, and last minute agreements are reached, which could, with sense on both parts, and more importantly sensible advice from both sets of legal advisors, have been reached in the early stages of the dispute.

It is with a sense of despair that one sees so many cases where offers of a settlement are completely ignored by the other party's solicitor, the only response being the issue of proceedings, perhaps several weeks later. Similarly the issue of proceedings without any attempt being made to see if a settlement is possible, or ascertain what property is in dispute, leads to an unwarranted waste of legal aid funds and court time and frequently proves to be a disservice to the client.

Lord Scarman called in Hanlon's case for an end to what he described as the poverty trap set by the legal aid legislation, whereby a legally aided wife whose only provision for her future support was the matrimonial home, could find its value diminished catastrophically by the statutory charge which might totally destroy her one capital asset. Whilst the 1988 Act brought certain changes, their Lordships call for a radical rethink to prevent injustice was ignored. One is left with the suspicion that this was done purely on the grounds of cost. It will perhaps be many years before there is opportunity for a further legislative change. The injustice is even more blatant in cases where the lion's share of the charge is for costs incurred in a long hard fought custody and access dispute, with perhaps only minimal costs for an agreed consent order relating to matrimonial property.

The Board's rights to the statutory charge cannot be defeated by a compromise between parties to an action, designed to make it appear that a smaller sum has been recovered than is in fact the case. This is so even if the court is made aware of the purpose of the compromise and makes an order approving it. The Board is entitled to look at the reality of the compromise, not merely at its wording and legal effects (*Manley* v *Law Society* [1981] 1 All ER 401). It is irrelevant that there are no 'dirty tricks', or that the parties and their solicitors have acted with complete candour.

Dr Manley had brought an action for damages alleging breach of contract by the defendant company, in refusing to exploit his invention. He was legally aided, and it became apparent to both parties that the costs of the action would be heavy and the outcome uncertain. A compromise was negotiated whereby he would receive £40,000 in settlement of his claim. Even though his solicitors agreed to limit their costs to £17,000 the legal aid fund's charge on the £40,000 meant that there would not be sufficient left for Dr Manley to pay debts which he had incurred in developing his invention, and which were anticipated to be in the region of £40,000.

The compromise approved by the court included the payment of £40,000 into a joint account in the names of the parties' solicitors, and to be held by them as agent for the defendant. The plaintiff's solicitors were to negotiate a settlement with the plaintiff's creditors, and the debts were then to be assigned by the creditors to the plaintiff's solicitors as undisclosed agents for the defendant. Any balance of the £40,000 remaining after payment of the creditors from the monies in the joint account was then to be paid to the plaintiff's solicitors as a contribution to the plaintiff's costs. Mr Justice Bristow had held that the statutory charge attached to the plaintiff's rights to have his debts discharged and not to the £40,000. The Law Society appealed.

On appeal Lord Denning MR said that the parties cannot 'assert that black is white and expect the courts to believe it'. The court should always look at the truth of the transaction and not let itself be deceived by 'the stratagem of lawyers', nor should it allow them 'to dress up a transaction in clothes that do not belong to it'. Lord Denning held that the charge attached to the £40,000 because being paid to the plaintiff's creditors at the request of the plaintiff, it had plainly been recovered for the plaintiff. One of the main weaknesses of the plaintiff's case was that he had said to his solicitors 'you must go ahead with the action unless my creditors are paid off'. If the settlement of £40,000 was reasonable and the plaintiff refused to accept it, then his solicitor should have reported his refusal to the Area Committee.

Ormrod LJ also confirmed that the wide definition of property given by Lord Scarman in Hanlon's case was correct, and that it was sufficient if the property was recovered for the benefit of the assisted person, not necessarily for the assisted person. Regulation 91(1)(a) Civil Legal Aid (General) Regulations 1989 still employs the phrase 'for the benefit of the assisted person'. The House of Lords had already held in Hanlon's case that it is permissible to look at regulations made under the Act, as an aid to the construction of the Act.

The dangers of compromises whether to avoid proceedings or to bring them to an end was made clear by Balcombe J in *Van Hoorn* v *Law Society* [1984] 3 All ER 136 where it was held that the effect of what is now s 16(7) is to attach the charge 'to any rights of a person under a compromise or settlement'. Section 16(7) does not limit the charge to such rights only in so far as they are in property, which has been in issue. Thus where there is a compromise or settlement, the charge attaches to all property and rights recovered or preserved by the settlement, whether or not they have been in issue in the proceedings.

Balcombe J raised the question in the *Van Hoorn* case as to why the Law Society should have a wider charge if proceedings were compromised, than if they were determined by the court. He did not give a specific answer to his own question, but the only answer is because the regulations say so. Again the chance to remedy a serious anomaly was either missed or deliberately ignored in the drafting of the 1988 Legal Aid Act. To penalise compromises and settlements in this way is to encourage litigation which is supposed to be the exact opposite of the policy adopted by the Law Society and presumably now by the Board.

The note of caution, both for counsel and solicitor, is for them to ensure in appropriate cases that a judgement or order is obtained, and that it may be necessary in order to protect the client where agreement is reached before proceedings have commenced, to issue such proceedings and apply for an order or judgment by consent, incorporating the terms of the settlement. Failure to do so could be disastrous for the client and perhaps for the solicitors indemnity insurance premium. If shares in the matrimonial home have not been in dispute, but a car or a small item of family silver have, the statutory charge could attach to the share of the matrimonial home, which was recovered or preserved if the dispute is concluded purely by agreement and without a court order. If custody or access had also been in dispute, then the failure to obtain an order would have serious financial consequences for a spouse.

In *Curling* v *Law Society* (1985) 1 All ER 705 the question as to whether property was 'in issue' was defined still further. Mrs Curling's right to a half share in the matrimonial home had never been in dispute, but Mr Curling wished to remain in the house and applied for an injunction requiring his wife to vacate it. Following negotiations Mr Curling abandoned his application for an injunction, and by consent an order was made whereby he agreed to pay Mrs Curling a sum equal to her half share in the property, in return for her transferring that half share to him. Mrs Curling applied for a declaration that her share, which had never been in dispute, could not be regarded as property recovered or preserved, and on the judge refusing to make the declaration, she appealed.

In the appeal counsel for Mrs Curling argued that she had received no benefit, but had merely exchanged her half share in the house for £15,000 which was slightly less than its value. The court accepted that the ownership of the house was never in issue between the parties, but (per Neill J) 'the ownership of the house cannot be looked at in isolation'. The court held that recovery of possession of property may constitute recovery of property. Oliver J added to the arguments against Mrs Curling, but held that Hanlon's case did not decide that beneficial ownership of property being in issue was the only consideration. Mrs Curling had wanted her share to be paid out of an immediate sale, whereas Mr Curling had wished to postpone sale to provide a home for himself and the children. Mrs Curling overcame this obstacle in the consent order which she obtained, and her potential distant prospect was translated into 'immediate entitlement'. She had therefore recovered property because the property had been reduced to or restored to the possession of the owner. The *Curling* case did make it clear that neither the inclusion of a claim in a divorce petition for a property adjustment order, nor even the making of an application for a property adjustment order in respect of specified property was per se sufficient to put any property in issue without reference to what happened afterwards in the pleadings.

The test suggested by Oliver J is as to whether the assisted person has 'got in to his hands, property which he would not have had in his hands, had it not been for the proceedings'. Although Curling was decided over four years after Hanlon, Oliver J urged the desirability of reconsideration of the effects of the statutory charge in matrimonial cases. His pleas too fell on deaf ears three years later.

(c) 'In the proceedings'

The charge arises in respect of costs which have been incurred 'in the proceedings'. The question as to what proceedings are covered by the certificate is of vital importance. Regulation 46 of Civil Legal Aid (General) Regulations deals with the scope of civil legal aid certificates and provides that a certificate shall not generally relate to more than one action, cause or matter. One of the exceptions to this rule, and it is by far the most important and contentious, is matrimonial proceedings which are defined in reg 3(1). In the *Hanlon* case, Lord Scarman faced with the choice of a narrow or wide interpretation of the regulations then current held that the wider construction was the correct one, and that in divorce proceedings the charge attaches in respect of the 'totality of the proceedings, of which the proceedings to recover the property, are only part'. The costs of access and custody disputes and of maintenance applications in divorce proceedings can therefore be recovered by the Board out of any property subsequently recovered or preserved, if all those matters are covered by a single legal aid certificate.

Because s 16(9)(*b*) of the Legal Aid Act 1988 specifies that the net liability of the Board includes any sums paid or payable for advice and assistance under Pt III of the Act, the cost of a green form divorce is included in the total cost of the proceedings in respect of which the charge subsequently arises. Paragraph 17 of the Board's Note for Guidance Number 46 provides as follows:

There are not the same problems in non-matrimonial proceedings because of the provisions of reg 46 that generally only one set of proceedings can be subject of one certificate.

The note confirms that 'proceedings' also includes a compromise or settlement, even if no proceedings have been commenced.

(d) Minimising the effects of the charge

The charge cannot be avoided by the use even of skilful and honest schemes designed to defeat it, but there are legitimate ways in which the effect of the charge can be minimised. The simplest way of avoiding the charge almost in full, is to obtain and enforce an order for costs against the legally aided client's opponent, and to do so at each stage of the proceedings where such an application is possible. Provided the costs are recovered, the charge will then be limited in effect to solicitor and client costs, which will only amount to a small proportion of the total of the inter partes costs. A proper application for costs must still be made even where the opponent is also legally aided. Where it becomes necessary to take additional proceedings against a defendant, then wherever the regulations permit, application for a new legal aid certificate should be made, rather than application for an amendment to the existing certificate.

In matrimonial cases it is generally far cheaper and quicker to obtain an order for maintenance in the magistrates' court, than it is to have the same applications dealt with as part of divorce proceedings in the county court. There will always be cases where a magistrates' court application is not advisable, either because of the complex nature of the finances involved or because of their amount. Nonetheless, providing that the client has no pressing reason for wishing to institute divorce proceedings immediately, many agreed and even contested maintenance, custody and access applications can reasonably be brought before the magistrates. All that would then be left for the county court to deal with would be any lump sum and property applications and the charge would only attach to the cost of those proceedings and of the divorce itself, if under the green form scheme. An explanation to the client that bringing magistrates' court proceedings first could reduce the client's liability to the legal aid fund would generally be well received. Failure to give such advice could amount to negligence but regard should be had to the Board's views about this (see Notes for Guidance 25 and 28).

The general rule that costs are awarded to the successful party, means that there can sometimes be a race between warring spouses to be the first to file an application for ancillary relief. The use of a Calderbank letter at the earliest possible stage is an effective counter measure, and because, if successful, it can give some protection as to costs, it thereby helps to minimise the effect of the charge once any such costs have been recovered.

Care as to what property is put in issue will help to minimise the effects of the charge. If the only dispute is, for example, over maintenance, custody and access, it should be made apparent as soon as possible in correspondence, that there is agreement over the matrimonial property or in respect of part of it. This will help to limit any argument with the Board as to what property, if any, has been in issue.

Because the charge arises in respect of any property recovered or preserved in an agreement or settlement, whether or not it has been in issue, the effect of the charge can sometimes be limited by ensuring that the terms of the agreement are incorporated in a court order, so that charge is then limited to property which has been in issue.

Wherever possible a client should be advised to avoid bringing proceedings under s 30 of the Law of Property Act 1925 as neither reg 94 (exemptions) nor regs 96 and 97 (postponement provisions) apply to such proceedings.

(e) Further duties of solicitors

Any sums paid under an agreement or order for costs in favour of an assisted person must be accounted for to the Board. Solicitors who recover costs on behalf of an assisted person cannot keep the costs in payment of their fees. Costs recovered must be handed over to the Board, which will then pay the solicitor on the basis of his claim for costs and report on case. A solicitor's costs can only be paid out of the legal aid fund and not from any other source, and the Board has sole responsibility for paying both solicitor and counsel.

So that the Board can protect its rights to the statutory charge, a solicitor acting for a legally assisted person must forthwith:

(1) inform the Area Director of any property recovered or preserved (reg 90(1)(*a*));
(2) send him a copy of any order or agreement under which the property was recovered or preserved (reg 90(1)(*a*));
(3) pay to the Board all monies, including costs received under an order or agreement in favour of the assisted person, unless the Area Director directs that reg 96 applies, in which case the money must only be released in accordance with the provisions of reg 96 (reg 90(1)(*b*));
(4) inform the Area Director if:
  (*a*) property is to be used by order or agreement as a home for the assisted person or his dependents; or
  (*b*) any money is to be used by order or agreement for the purchase of such a home (reg 90).

The Area Director may direct that out of monies recovered,

the solicitor must only pay to the Board such sum as is necessary to safeguard the rights of the fund, and that the balance can then be paid to the assisted person. If the fund incurs a loss because the solicitor has failed to comply with the regulations, payment of all or part of his costs may be deferred by the Area Committee until the default has been remedied (reg 102). The solicitor must explain the effects of the charge to the client at the beginning and confirm the advice in a letter. The client should be reminded of the charge before any hearing, and both the court and counsel should be reminded of its effect. Serving notice of issue of a civil aid certificate puts the other party on notice that the client is legally aided. A solicitor acting for a client whose opponent is legally aided must ensure that money is paid to the legally aided person's solicitor, or if he is no longer represented, to the Board. The payment must never be made directly to a legally assisted person, as only his solicitor or the Board is capable of giving a good discharge for the money payable (reg 87(1) of the (General) Regulations 1989. The solicitor is under a statutory duty to inform the Board of any attempt to circumvent the provisions of reg 87. Similarly, a solicitor acting for a legally aided client is under a duty to ensure, so far as he practicably can, that he receives all money payable to the client under an order or agreement.

Use of the Board's form of undertaking with regard to costs, assists in speeding release of money to the client.

(f) Challenging the charge

Where there is a dispute about the charge which cannot be resolved with the Board, proceedings should be taken against the Board for a declaration that the charge does not arise. Legal Aid is available for the proceedings and a separate certificate should be obtained to cover them. If the proceedings are successful, a statutory charge will apply in respect of the amount of the original charge which has been successfully challenged, for that amount is property which has been recovered in the proceedings for a declaration. Hopefully the Board would satisfy any order for costs made against it, and there would be no need for the charge to be made effective.

(g) Enforcing the charge

The statutory charge vests in the Board which has power to enforce it in any manner available to a chargee in respect of a charge given inter partes (reg 95(1) and (2)). Prior to the Legal Aid Act 1988 the Law Society did not have any statutory discretion as to whether the charge should be enforced immediately or postponed.

In the *Hanlon* case, [1980] 2 All ER 214 Lord Scarman said, in referring to the charge being vested in the Law Society:

> The charge becomes its property to be managed as it thinks fit. The Law Society is of course a trustee, for the benefit of the charge vested in the Law Society is to accrue to the legal aid fund. For instance the Law Society could not properly allow the charge to be switched to a property offering less security for costs than the original property, but the Law Society is not merely the guardian of the fund. Its function is to secure that legal aid is available as required by the statute. If therefore in its judgement it is able without endangering its security to defer the enforcement of the charge, or to switch it to another property, both of which would be options open to a person owning a charge, reg 19(1) enables it to do so, provided always that the security is not thereby endangered. Nevertheless the discretion whether or not to enforce the charge or how otherwise to manage it, belongs to the Law Society. In the present case therefore, it is for the Law Society not for the court, to decide whether to allow the charge to be transferred to another property, or to require the cost deficiency to be met out of the proceeds of the existing home.

The strictures passed by the House of Lords in *Hanlon* appear to have forced the Law Society to adopt a policy of not enforcing the statutory charge over the matrimonial home, for so long as it was occupied by the assisted person as a residence. Guidelines were published showing how the discretion to transfer the charge to a substituted property would be exercised.

The *Hanlon* case was distinguished in the Court of Appeal in *R v Law Society, ex parte Sexton* [1984] 1 All ER 92 and subsequently in the House of Lords in *Simpson v Law Society* [1987] 2 All ER 481 where it was held that because different regulations applied where money was the property recovered, the Law Society did not have a discretion as to postponing the charge or in allowing it to be transferred to a home purchased with that money. Lord Bridge expressed concern about the disfigurement of the legal aid scheme, by what he referred to as 'the arbitrary and capricious' impact of the statutory charge in matrimonial cases, adding that it was grotesque that the Law Society should have a discretion where the matrimonial home was the property recovered, but not where the property recovered was money with which to buy a home.

Such judicial anger is rare, especially when directed at the establishment, but in this instance (alas, not in others) it bore fruit, and the 1989 Civil Legal Aid (General) Regulations give the Board power to postpone enforcement of the charge over money, land and substituted property, provided certain conditions are met (regs 96, 97 and 98). The power is however discretionary and there are no statutory provisions or guidelines as to any circumstances in which the Board must exercise its discretion. The cases referred to previously in this chapter are still valid, in so far as they give judicial guidance to the Board as to its duties and as to how it might wish to exercise its discretion.

3 Postponing the charge

(a) Postponement of the charge over money

If a sum of money is recovered, which by order of the court or under the terms of any agreement, is to be used for the purpose of providing a home for the assisted person or his dependents, the Board may agree to defer enforcing any charge over that sum (reg 96(2)) provided:

(1) the money is recovered in proceedings under:
   (a) the Married Woman's Property Act 1882;
   (b) the Matrimonial Causes Act 1973;
   (c) the Inheritance (Provision for Family and Dependents) Act 1975; or
(2) the assisted person wishes to purchase a home in accordance with the order or agreement; or
(3) the assisted person agrees in writing on a form approved by the Board to comply with the following provisions:
   (a) the property to be purchased shall be subject to a charge executed in favour of the Board and registered in accordance with reg 95(3); and
   (b) from the date of first registration simple interest shall accrue at 12 per cent per annum (or such other rate from time to time prescribed) on the sum in respect of which the Board has agreed to postpone its charge; or
(4) the Area Director is satisfied that the property to be purchased will provide adequate security for the sum in

respect of which the charge is to be postponed, plus interest.

Regulation 96(4) allows the assisted person's solicitor to release the money where the Board has agreed to defer enforcement of the charge, to the vendor or his representative on completion of the purchase of the property which is being purchased in accordance with the order or agreement. There is no authority in reg 96(4) to use any of the money as a deposit on exchange of contracts.

If no agreement has been reached under reg 96(2) to defer enforcement of the charge, but the Area Director has directed that the provisions of reg 96 apply to the money, the assisted person's solicitor may release the money, either to another solicitor or to a person providing conveyancing services and to whom s 22 of the Solicitor's Act 1974 does not apply. Such other solicitor or other person must first have given an undertaking to the Board on its approved form, that he will comply with all the obligations imposed by reg 96(5) of the Civil Legal Aid (General) Regulations 1989.

The assisted person's solicitor must inform the Area Director as soon as practicable, of any money released, either under paras (4) or (5) of reg 96, and provide the Area Director with enough information to enable him to register a charge on the property which has been purchased. He must also send to the Area Director a copy of any undertaking given under para 5.

If the recovered money has been retained by the assisted person's solicitor and has not been used for the purchase of a home after one year from the date of the order or agreement, it must be paid to the Board.

In assessing how much will be available to an assisted person from the proceeds of sale of a matrimonial home, the court is entitled to assume that the Board will postpone enforcement of the charge by transferring it to the new property *Scallon* v *Scallon* (1989) *The Times* 4 November.

(b) Postponement of charges over land

In any of the three types of proceedings to which reg 96 (above) applies, where property has been recovered which is to be used as a home for the assisted person or his dependents, the Area Director may direct that reg 97 shall apply to the property. The Board may then defer enforcement of the charge if:

(1) the assisted person wishes to use it as a home for himself or his dependents; or

(2) the assisted person agrees in writing on the form approved by the Board that interest shall accrue in the same terms as under reg 96(3); or

(3) the Area Director is satisfied that the property will provide adequate security for the amount of its charge plus interest.

4 Substitution of charged properties

(a) Where the charge has not been registered

If the statutory charge has not been registered against property to which reg 97 of the Civil Legal Aid (General) Regulations 1989 applies, but the assisted person wishes to purchase a different property in substitution for that property, the Board may agree to defer enforcing the charge on that property. The only condition is that the assisted person agrees in writing on the Board's form, that the substituted property shall be subject to a charge executed in favour of the Board and registered, and that simple interest shall accrue under para (4) if the charge is first registered after the 1 December, 1988.

(b) Where the charge has been registered

Regulation 98 of the Civil Legal Aid (General) Regulations 1989 allows the Board to release the charge where it has been registered under reg 96 ie against a home purchased out of money recovered, or under reg 97 ie against either the original home recovered or against another property substituted under paragraph 5 of reg 97 of the original home, before the charge had been registered against the original. This enables the assisted person, subject to the conditions set out in the regulation to sell a house against which the statutory charge has been registered, and purchase another property against which the Board registers a charge, so that its interests continue to be protected. Without this provision, the assisted person would in effect be 'frozen' into the first home against which the charge was registered. Paragraph 4 of reg 98 permits repeated substitutions.

The conditions which have to be fulfilled for the release of the charge under reg 98(1) are:

(1) the assisted person wishes to purchase a different property in substitution for that over which a charge already exists;

(2) the assisted person agrees in writing on the Board's approved form that:
  (a) the property to be purchased shall be subject to a charge in favour of the Board and registered under reg 95(3);
  (b) simple interest shall continue to accrue in respect of the sum due to the Board;
(3) the Area Director is satisfied that the property to be purchased will give the Board adequate security for the amount due to it plus interest.

The same three conditions also applied to any further release of the charge where the assisted person wishes to make a further substitution.

(c) Solicitors' duties under regulations 96 and 97

It is of the utmost importance to ensure that any court order and any agreement incorporates a provision that the property recovered, whether it be money under reg 96 or land under reg 97, is to be used for the purchase of a home for the assisted person or his dependents, or as such a home. Without such an order or agreement, the Board has no power to postpone the charge under either reg 96 or 97 and the assisted person can well be left without a home or with insufficient money to purchase one. The aim of the successful proceedings will have been defeated, and the assisted person's solicitor facing a claim for negligence. Instructions to counsel must always draw counsel's attention to the need to obtain an order, the wording of which meets the requirements of regs 96 and 97, as the case may be.

The assisted person's solicitor is required by reg 90(3)(a) and (b) to inform the Area Director forthwith of any property or money which has been recovered, and which by order of the court or by agreement is to be used for the purchase of a home for the assisted person or his dependents. If the Area Director so directs, the assisted person's solicitor is relieved of the duty to pay the recovered money to the Board under reg 90(1)(b) as is normally the case instead the money is dealt with under Regulation 96(4) to (7).

(d) Interest and capital

Where interest accrues under regs 96, 97 and 98 of the Civil Legal Aid (General) Regulations 1989 it is simple interest at the rate of 12 per cent per annum or such other rate as shall from time to time be prescribed. It is payable on the sum which the Board would have received, but for the operation of those regulations. If enforcement of the charge over land has been postponed under reg 97, interest only accrues where the charge is first registered after the 1 December, 1988. If a property is substituted under reg 97(5) before a charge has been registered against the original property to which the charge is attached, then interest only accrues if the charge is first registered against the substituted property after the 1 December, 1988.

The fact that the charge has been postponed does not mean that the assisted person cannot if he so wishes make interim payments to the Board, both on account of interest and capital, but any such interim payment must first be taken into account against any accrued interest outstanding, before there is any reduction in the capital outstanding.

(e) The board's discretion

The board's guidelines as to the exercise of its discretionary power to transfer the charge to a substituted property are (Note for Guidance Number 46, 1989 edition):

(1) possession proceedings to enforce a charge registered against a dwellinghouse, shall not be commenced by the Area Committee without the consent of the Board;

(2) unless the Area Committee gives prior authority for substitution, the sum due to the Board must be paid to the legal aid fund when a house subject to the charge is sold;

(3) the Area Committee may agree to substitution for the original charge of a charge on another property, provided:

(*a*) there is sufficient equity in the second house to cover the amount of the charge;

(*b*) the substituted property is to be occupied as the sole residence of the assisted person, together with at least one unmarried child of his/hers under eighteen years of age or undergoing full time education at the date of purchase of the substituted property or it is necessary for the assisted person or dependents to move for reasons of health, disability or employment;

(*c*) it is just and reasonable to authorise the substitution; and

(*d*) a refusal would cause hardship to the assisted person;

(4) a subsequent substitution will only be authorised in exceptional circumstances;

(5) the proceeds of sale of a property subject to the charge must be wholly utilised in purchasing the substituted property. There will be immediate enforcement against any surplus cash.

Whilst the majority of the Board's guidelines are eminently reasonable, two of them give cause for concern in that the Board may prove to be as intransigent as the Law Society was before it. Both Parliament and the Lord Chancellor were quite capable of ensuring, if they so wished, that the regulations imposed a condition that the substituted property had to be occupied as a home by the assisted person, and at least one of his unmarried children. Neither of them thought fit so to do. The only similar restriction imposed by Parliament was a condition for postponing enforcement of the charge over land where it was satisfied that the property had to be a home for the assisted person 'or his dependents' — not 'children', unmarried, dependent or otherwise. Regulations 97 and 98 contain no additional provisions such as those referred to at 3(*b*) above. The Board did therefore appear to be seeking to impose a condition never intended by Parliament to be imposed, and thereby to negative the effect which Parliament intended to create. Note for Guidance Number 46 has now been modified in the 1990 edition (Note 5(6)).

Even more alarming is the fact that the Board will only exercise its discretion in favour of second or subsequent substitution 'in the most exceptional circumstances'. Parliament has ensured that various legal aid regulations are liberally sprinkled with the phrase 'in exceptional circumstances' or similar, but it is patently absent from regs 97 and 98. The Board's policy again negates the intentions of Parliament and rejects the strictures of the judiciary delivered over a ten year period. Admittedly the courts have said that the manner in which the discretion is exercised is a matter entirely for the Board, but the Board appears to wish to ignore that its duty is to the legal aid scheme as a whole, and not just to the fund.

The Board has not thought fit to include in its guidelines the comments set out in *Hanlon* v *Law Society* [1980] 2 All ER 201. There is however a duty not merely to the fund but to the scheme as a whole, and that includes amongst other things the position of the assisted person, the purpose and results of the litigation and the intention of the court as manifested in its judgment. The Board would appear to accept the court's finding that it is for it and not the court to decide how the discretion should be exercised. Decisions by the Board based on its present Note for Guidance have not yet been challenged in the courts. In so far as they appear to attempt to negate regulations laid before Parliament, there will no doubt be opportunity for these to be tested.

Chapter 20

Costs

1 Sources from which payment can be claimed

In order to understand the position of both solicitor and counsel with regard to payment of their fees, it is necessary to consider the combined effects of s 15(6) of the Act and regs 64, 87 and 90 of the General Regulations. Section 15(6) provides that the only payment which a legally assisted person can be required to make for work carried out under a legal aid certificate is his contribution, and that it is for the Board to pay both solicitor's and counsel's fees. Regulation 64 prohibits solicitor or counsel from receiving any payment for any work done in respect of the proceedings during the currency of a certificate, except such payment as is made out of the fund. Regulation 87 ensures that only a solicitor or if he is no longer acting, the Board, can give a good discharge for monies payable to an assisted person, and reg 90 imposes a duty on the solicitor to pay all monies recovered, and this includes costs as well as damages, to the Board.

Apart from payments on account of costs and disbursements, the Board can only pay costs to a solicitor where these have either been taxed or assessed, and this procedure cannot be avoided, nor can a top-up payment in addition to that allowed out of the legal aid fund be received, either from the client or from anybody else (*Littaur* v *Steggles-Palmer* [1986] 1 All ER 780). The affect of these provisions is that for example, where a claim for damages has been settled and agreed costs have been paid to the assisted person's solicitor, these must be paid to the Board by the solicitor, and his costs must then be assessed before the Board can pay him. Normally the costs will be assessed in the amount which has been paid by agreement to the solicitor.

These provisions can lead to some difficulty where a certificate has been issued for a limited purpose or for a limited step in proceedings. In the *Littaur* case a certificate was granted to the plaintiff, to apply within the main proceedings in which he was defendant, to purge his contempt for breach of an order. He was however charged by his solicitor on a private basis for other work carried out in the main proceedings, excluding the application covered by his certificate. It was held that the defendant's solicitors were entitled to charge him privately and therefore to a lien on his papers. 'Proceedings' in this context means the proceedings for which the certificate had been applied and granted. The court rejected the argument that because the certificate had not been discharged it was 'current'. Ackner LJ commented that such an argument was as fallacious as saying that a person could not be pronounced dead until it was established that he had been buried.

Following *Littaur*, the Board has issued Note for Guidance Number 43, because a solicitor must always bear in mind the duty to advise his client as to the availability of legal aid. If a certificate is issued for a limited step, but further steps in the proceedings are contemplated, application should be made for an amendment to the certificate. If the amendment is refused, the further steps can, with the client's agreement, be undertaken on a privately paid basis, even if the certificate has not yet been discharged.

If a full certificate is not granted, eg it is limited to defending an action, reg 64 does not prevent the solicitor from acting privately in a counterclaim which is not covered by the certificate. In circumstances such as these, there are the following duties on the solicitor before he acts privately:

    (1) to ensure that an application for legal aid or for an amendment has been refused; or

    (2) to obtain the client's consent:

        (*a*) not to apply for a certificate or an amendment for those steps, or

        (*b*) to act prior to the application being determined;

    (3) to obtain the client's instructions to act privately;

    (4) to explain to the client what they will mean and that the Legal Aid Board will have to be informed; and

    (5) to notify the Area Office in writing, as soon as possible, and explaining the reasons.

(a) Payments on account of costs

Both solicitor and counsel can submit to the Board during the currency of a certificate, a claim for payment to be made on account or profit costs incurred to date (reg 100(1) and (2) of the General Regulations 1989). At intervals during the currency of a certificate, the Board issues to the solicitor a questionnaire requesting information as to progress of the case, and attached to this is a form which must be completed and returned to the financial controller, where a payment on account is desired. The new Annual Report on Case form can be used to claim payment on account of profit costs where the certificate was issued not more than 42 months before the claim.

A claim can be made for payment on account:

(1) if the certificate was issued on or after 1 October, 1986:
   (a) after eighteen months from the date of issue of the certificate,
   (b) and then at twelve monthly intervals after the date on which an interim payment could first be claimed;
(2) if the certificate was issued before 1 October, 1986:
   (a) after thirty months from the date of issue of the certificate,
   (b) and then at twelve monthly intervals after the date on which an interim payment could first be claimed.

The maximum which can be paid in any one financial year in respect of any claim for payment on account is:

1989/90	38 per cent
1990/91	46 per cent
1991/92	54 per cent
1992/93	62 per cent
1993/94	70 per cent
1994/95 and thereafter	75 per cent

Where there has been a change of solicitor acting under a legal aid certificate, the first solicitor's retainer having been determined and another solicitor is acting, the Area Committee has power to authorise the payment of a sum on account of the first solicitor's costs, where it appears unlikely that they will be taxed within six months of the date on which the retainer was determined (reg 100(6) of the General Regulations 1989).

The making of a payment on account does not in any way release the solicitor from his obligations under the regulations to submit his and counsel's fees for taxation or assessment at the end of the case. If it is then found that the payments on account have exceeded the amount allowed on taxation or assessment, the solicitor must on demand, repay the amount due to the fund (reg 100(8)). Otherwise the fund pays the balance due to the solicitor.

Counsel may also apply directly to the Area Committee for a payment on account of 75 per cent of his fees where the case is concluded, or where the solicitor is entitled to have his costs taxed, and counsel has not received any payment in respect of his fees for six months after the date of the event which gave rise to the right to taxation (reg 101(2)). This is in addition to counsel's right to apply for payment on account under reg 100.

Hardship caused by delay in taxation is a further ground on which the solicitor can apply to the Area Committee for a payment on account, either of his own fees or of counsel's fees. The conditions for such an application are that the proceedings to which the certificate relates must have continued for more than twelve months, and it must appear unlikely that an order for taxation will be made within the next twelve months (reg 101(1)). The regulations contain no definition of 'hardship', but the Area Committee is unlikely to accept impecuniosity as a ground, except perhaps in the case of newly qualified barristers.

What could give rise to hardship in a practice with a reasonable amount of legal aid work, is the funding of disbursements. Solicitors can apply for reimbursement of disbursements actually incurred or about to be incurred in connection with proceedings (reg 101). This is a valuable provision, and it means that solicitors do not have to be out of pocket until the conclusion of the case and eventual taxation and payment, but reimbursement is unlikely to be made under reg 101 if a disbursement has already been incurred without prior authority where that is needed.

(b) Pre-certificate work

If a legal aid certificate is issued after proceedings have been commenced, so that work previously carried out has been on a private basis, a solicitor may give notice to the Area Committee that he has a lien on any documents necessary for the proceedings, and has delivered them up subject to that lien (reg 103(2)). If any monies are recovered and there is sufficient to pay both the solicitor who has given notice and the solicitor who acted under the certificate. The Board must pay to the solicitor who gave notice, the cost to which he would have been entitled, following a solicitor and own client taxation. If the monies so recovered are not sufficient to pay both sets of costs, they are divided on a pro rata basis between the solicitor and the fund. If, for example, the pre-certificate costs for which notice of lien has been given amount to 30 per cent of the eventual total cost, the solicitor carrying out the pre-certificate work must receive 30 per cent of the amount which the Board has recovered (reg 103(4)).

If the costs payable under reg 103 are not taxed, the Area Committee must assess them on the basis of a solicitor and own client taxation. The inter partes costs incurred whilst the certificate was in force are assessed as if taxed on the standard basis (reg 103(5)).

For the purposes of reg 103, work done immediately prior to the issue of an emergency certificate and at a time when an application for an emergency certificate could not be made because the Area Office was closed, shall be deemed to be work done under the certificate, provided an application for an emergency certificate is made at the first available opportunity and is granted (reg 103(6)). Because notice of lien under reg 103 can only be given by a solicitor who has delivered up his papers, subject to his lien, it can not apply where the solicitor assigned under the certificate is also the solicitor who carried out the pre-certificate work. If, however, there is a subsequent change of solicitor during the currency of the certificate, notice of lien could then be given by the first solicitor in respect of his pre-certificate costs, and he would still have his rights under reg 100(6) to apply for a payment on account of costs incurred during the certificate.

(c) Deferment and re-payment of profit costs

The sanction which the Area Committee can impose on a solicitor who causes a loss to the fund by failing to comply with any of the general regulations, is to defer payment of his costs in connection with the proceedings to which the certificate relates. Deferment of the costs continues until the solicitor has complied with the provisions. The Area Committee can also retain any sum, payment of which has been deferred, if it refers the conduct of the solicitor to the Solicitor's Disciplinary Tribunal and the solicitor is disciplined (reg 102). The most likely cases in which a solicitor is likely to cause a loss to the fund is in failing to comply with the regulations relating to the statutory charge, and those imposing a duty on the solicitor to notify the Board of monies and property recovered or preserved, and to pay such monies to the Board. Regulation 102 does not give the Board any statutory power to recover any loss which it has sustained out of any costs due to the solicitor for other legal aid cases in respect of which he has submitted a claim for payment. Although the Board has a statutory duty to pay costs which have been taxed or assessed, it will in practice offset against those costs, any loss which it has suffered in a particular case where the power to defer payment cannot be exercised eg where costs have already been paid before the Board realised it had suffered a loss.

The Board accepts that it will normally only defer costs if there has been a failure to comply with any of the provisions in Part XI of the General Regulations 1989 (regs 87 to 99) and that the power to defer payment of costs under reg 102 is compensatory and not punitive. The loss to the fund may comprise:

(1) its net liability as defined in s 16(9) of the Act;
(2) any additional costs incurred by the fund, eg where it has taken its own proceedings under reg 91(1); or
(3) the amount of any costs recovered and payable to the Board under s 16(5) of the Act.

Even where the solicitor has been negligent or in breach of a statutory duty and proceedings are taken against him, counsel's fees will still be paid, but payment of disbursements may be withheld as a credit against the claim for damages (Note for Guidance Number 45).

There is a loss to the fund:

(1) where monies are recovered or preserved, and instead of being paid to the Board are paid directly to the assisted person or a third party who dissipates them;
(2) where, as the result of a solicitor failing to notify the Board forthwith that monies have been recovered under a compromise or order, the compromise or order has been rendered worthless;
(3) where monies recovered or preserved have not been dissipated but used for the purchase of a property. In this case the Board has been deprived of its right to immediate enforcement of the statutory charge. The Board may obtain some protection by registering a charge or caution against the property, and if it does, the solicitor will still

be paid his profit costs when the property is sold and the loss to the Board made good.

Where property other than money has been recovered or preserved, a loss to the Board may arise where:

(1) the solicitor fails to report forthwith, and as a result of the delay, the assisted person sells the property and dissipates the proceeds; or

(2) the property is sold and the proceeds invested in other property against which a charge or caution can be registered.

In this latter case the loss to the Board arises if:

(1) the circumstances relating to the original property were such that the Board did not have a discretion to transfer the charge to substituted property; or

(2) if it did have such a discretion, the Board would not have exercised it. If it would have done so, there has been no loss to the fund (Note for Guidance Number 45 para 7).

If a charge or caution is registered in a case where payment of the solicitor's costs have been deferred, the charge will be for a sum which includes the solicitor's deferred costs, and the Board is obliged to pay those when the loss to the fund has been made good. Generally when the charged property is sold (Note for Guidance Number 45 para 8).

A solicitor who has caused a loss to the fund by failing to comply with the regulations may be asked to make good the loss by sending to the Board, a cheque to cover counsel's fees and any payments on account which have already been made by the Board, or if all his costs have already been paid, a sum which covers the Board's net deficiency (Note for Guidance Number 45 para 9). This would appear to clash with the Board's practice of offsetting its loss in certain circumstances against other costs claimed by the solicitor.

The court has inherent jurisdiction to order a solicitor to repay to the legal aid fund, costs which have been incurred by a legally aided client as the result of either a serious dereliction of duty (*Myers* v *Elman* [1939] 4 All ER 484) or of conduct which was inexcusable and such as to merit reproof (*R & T Thew Limited* v *Reeves* [1982] 3 All ER 1086). In *Clark* v *Clark* Number 2 Fam Div (New Law Journal 16 February, 1990) Booth J applied the words of May LJ in *Davy Chiesman* v *Davy Chiesman* [1984] 1 All ER 321 to the solicitors duty of care to the Board, as well as to the client. Thus whilst a solicitor can generally rely on counsel and will be absolved in so doing, from personal liability for his action, he is not entitled to rely on counsel's opinion blindly with no mind of his own. Unless there are exceptional circumstances, the Board must apply swiftly for an order for repayment by a solicitor and must not be dilatory. In any event, the court has a discretion as to whether the solicitor should be ordered to make repayment, and the test goes beyond reasonableness or error of judgment. There must be a serious breach of duty amounting to improper conduct and leading to the loss.

The decision in *Clark* should be compared with that in *Sinclair Jones* v *Kay* [1988] 2 All ER 611 where it was held that gross misconduct being no longer a part of RSC Ord 62 r 11, it was proper to order a solicitor to pay costs personally where he had failed to give notice of issue of a civil aid certificate and had delayed in applying to set aside a judgment. In these circumstances unreasonable conduct is all that is required.

2 Assessment of costs

If before proceedings have begun, the retainer of solicitor or counsel has been determined and there has been no subsequent change of solicitor or counsel, the Area Director may assess both solicitor's costs and counsel's fees. The assessment is made on the basis of the costs which would be allowed on the taxation on a standard basis under the rules of court (reg 105(1) and (2) of the General Regulations 1989).

If proceedings have been commenced, a solicitor may apply to the Area Director for an assessment to be made of his costs and counsel's fees where:

(1) the solicitor is of the opinion that his costs and counsel's fees would on the standard basis for taxation, not exceed £500;

(2) there has been a settlement without any direction from the court as to costs, and the settlement includes an agreed amount for costs which both solicitor and counsel are willing to accept in full satisfaction;

(3) taxation will be against the interests of the assisted person, or would increase the amount payable from the fund; or

(4) after a direction or order for taxation on a standard basis, the solicitor incurs costs for the purpose of recovering monies payable to the fund (reg 105(3)).

If proceedings to which the assisted person has been party are brought to an end by judgment, decree or final order, and there has been an agreement as to the costs to be paid by the other party which solicitor and counsel are willing to accept in full satisfaction, the costs must be assessed by the Area Director, who may ask the taxing officer to carry out the assessment on the standard basis, but without taxation (reg 106). The taxing officer will then normally carry out the assessment without requiring the attendance of the solicitor and will issue a certificate of assessment (Practice Direction (Legal Aid: Agreed Costs) Number 4 *Law Society Gazette* 10 January 1990).

(a) Reviews and appeals of assessments

Where an assessment has been carried out under regs 105 or 106 and either solicitor or counsel is dissatisfied, written representations may be made to the Area Committee within twenty-one days of the decision. The Area Committee reviews the assessment and has power to confirm it, increase it or decrease it. If solicitor or counsel is dissatisfied with the review, application can be made to the Committee within twenty-one days of its decision to certify a point of principle of general importance. Where it does so certify, there is then a further twenty-one days to appeal in writing to a committee appointed by the Board. That committee may reverse, affirm or amend the decision of the Area Committee (reg 105(4)–(7)).

If counsel's fees have been reduced or disallowed on an assessment or review, the solicitor must, within seven days thereafter, notify counsel in writing.

3 Taxation of costs

The costs of proceedings to which an assisted person is a party must be taxed in accordance with any direction or order given in the proceedings (reg 107 of the General Regulations 1989). Costs must be taxed on the standard basis and (except in (3) below) a direction given to that effect, where in any proceedings to which the assisted person is a party:

(1) judgment is signed in default;

(2) the court gives judgment or makes a final decree or order; or

(3) the plaintiff accepts money paid into court (reg 107(3)).

Costs must also be taxed on the standard basis on production to the taxing officer of a notice of discharge or revocation of the certificate, where in any proceedings to which an assisted person or a former assisted person has been a party:

(1) the proceedings end without a direction for taxation on the standard basis having been given; or

(2) a judgment or order against the opposing party and including a direction for taxation has not been drawn up or entered; or

(3) notice of discharge or of revocation has been served by the Area Director on the solicitor under reg 83, thereby terminating the retainer of both solicitor and counsel (reg 107(4)).

If an assisted person has obtained an order or agreement for payment of his costs, but has failed to ask for his costs to be taxed or his certificate is discharged before taxation, the Board can authorise the making of an application for taxation on his behalf. The costs both of the application and of the taxation are costs in the proceedings to which the certificate relates (reg 108). On a taxation, any costs wasted by lack of reasonable competence or expedition must be disallowed or reduced. If the solicitor has without good reason delayed in filing his bill for taxation, the whole of the costs may be disallowed or reduced. Before any costs are so disallowed or reduced, the taxing officer must serve notice on the solicitor and if counsel's fees are in question, on counsel as well, requiring cause to be shown, orally or in writing, why those costs should not be so reduced or disallowed (reg 109).

(a) Counsel's fees

When the bill is prepared for taxation, counsel's fees must be claimed in accordance with the fee notes submitted by counsel. Counsel may prepare a memorandum to be supplied by his instructing solicitor as to any factors which affect the amount of his fees. If a solicitor feels that he cannot support the amount claimed by counsel, he should notify counsel before taxation.

Counsel's fee notes must be attached to the taxed bill when it is submitted to the Area Committee for payment.

(b) The procedure on taxation

The complicated form of a bill of costs is such that in the majority of solicitor's offices there is no longer the specialist knowledge to draw the bill properly. It is also a time consuming exercise for which little payment is received, and for economic reasons, if nothing else, it is best to employ a specialist firm of costs draftsmen for this task.

The bill of costs has to be lodged for taxation pursuant to a court order whether the assisted person was successful or unsuccessful. If successful and an order was made for costs to be made by the other party it will be a six column bill, the three inner columns being for the inter partes taxation and the outer three for any legal aid costs incurred over and above the inter partes costs. If the assisted person was unsuccessful or did not obtain an order for payment of his costs by the other party, the bill of costs is required only for legal aid taxation and is therefore a three column bill.

With the bill there must be lodged the solicitor's copy of the legal aid certificate, any written prior authorities from the Area Director, counsel's fee notes and all vouchers for any disbursements. If work was carried out or expenditure incurred without prior authority where it was needed, this will not affect an inter partes taxation, but it will affect a legal aid taxation. The allocatur or certificate issued following completion of a legal aid taxation shows the legal aid costs allowed, sub-divided into profit costs, counsel's fees and other disbursements plus VAT on the profit costs. In addition, on inter partes taxation, it will show the total costs and disbursements allowed inter partes. If the certificate or allocatur includes the costs of more than one assisted person, a copy can be obtained for forwarding to the Area Director or the solicitors involved can agree about lodging it with the Area Director.

Where a legally assisted person has an interest in the taxation of the bill, a certificate should be endorsed thereon in the following terms, by the assisted person's solicitor:

We hereby certify as follows:

(1) That our client, a legally aided person, has an interest in the taxation of this bill being liable to the Legal Aid Board's statutory charge. He has been supplied with a copy of this bill and informed of his right to apply to the court to be heard on the taxation thereof and been allowed fourteen days to do so before lodging this bill. Our client has/has not indicated a wish to be heard on taxation.

(2) That any amounts claimed in respect of travelling time and expenses of travel were wholly attributable to the business transacted.

(3) The following are the names and addresses of persons who have

a financial interest in the taxation of this bill for the purposes of
Rule 6(8) of the Matrimonial Causes (Costs) Rules 1988:
[insert name and address of client]

(c) Objections, reviews and appeals

It is the solicitor's duty to safeguard the interests of the fund
on any inter partes taxation, following an order for costs in
favour of the assisted person. In carrying out this duty, he must
take such steps as are necessary to object to the taxation under
reg 113 and to have it reviewed by a judge under reg 114. There
is also a further right of appeal under reg 115.

Before objecting under reg 113, the solicitor must apply to the
Area Committee for authority to make an objection, and he can
only carry in an objection if that authority is given. An application to the Area Committee must be made by a solicitor where:

(1) he is dissatisfied with the taxing master's decision either
on an inter partes taxation pursuant to an order for costs
in favour of the assisted person, or on a legal aid taxation;
or

(2) where the assisted person is dissatisfied with the taxing
officer's decision as to the amount:

(a) which he is entitled to recover under an order or agreement for costs in his favour, or

(b) for which he is liable under an order for costs made
against him.

'Legal aid taxation' means for the purposes of both regs 113
and 116 dealing with counsel's fees, the taxation of a solicitor's
bill to his own client where the bill is to be paid out of the fund.

If the solicitor or the assisted person is still dissatisfied with
the taxing master's decision after an objection has been made
under reg 113. The solicitor must apply to the Board for authority
to have the taxation reviewed by a judge. Only if the Board
gives such authority, may the application be made (reg 114).

A further appeal against a judge's decision on a review may
only be made with the authority of the Board (reg 115). But this
is not required where the solicitor wishes to be heard on such
an appeal brought by any other party. An appeal may be brought
even where the assisted person has no interest in the appeal or
would but for the provision of reg 118 of the General Regulations
1989 have an interest adverse to that of his solicitor. Counsel
may be instructed on any such appeal.

A solicitor must, within seven days after taxation, or after a provisional taxation, notify counsel in writing if his fees have been reduced or disallowed, and must endorse the bill of costs either with the date on which the notice was given or that no such notice was necessary. If notice is given to counsel, the taxing officer may then issue the certificate or allocatur. If notice has been given, he must wait fourteen days before doing so. This gives counsel the opportunity to request his instructing solicitor to report the matter under reg 116.

A solicitor must report to the Board or to the Area Committee any matter in respect of which counsel is dissatisfied on a legal aid taxation, unless the taxation is a provisional one, in which case he must inform the taxing officer that he wishes to be heard on and to attend on the taxation. If, having received such a report the Board or the Area Committee give authority, it is the solicitor's duty to make objection, apply to a judge for review and to appeal as if he, and not counsel, was the person dissatisfied (reg 116). The provisions of the relevant regulations (reg 113 for objections; reg 114 for review; reg 115 for appeals and reg 120) apply where the solicitor has in effect to act on behalf of counsel, under reg 116. Counsel's rights, unlike those of a solicitor, are limited to legal aid taxation.

Notice of any application made under paras 113, 114 or 116 must be given to the taxing officer and to any opposing party (reg 121(4)). In addition, the solicitor must also notify the Board of any application which he makes under reg 113 for a review by a judge and of any application made by another party to a judge, to review the inter partes taxation.

The Board must notify the Lord Chancellor of such applications and also of any authorities which it has given for a solicitor to apply to a judge for a review. A solicitor can then be appointed by the Lord Chancellor to intervene in any review by a judge. A solicitor so appointed has the right to production of all relevant documents, to appear by counsel and to be heard on the review. On the hearing of the review, the judge has power to order payment of costs to or by that intervening solicitor. Costs in his favour are paid by the Board, and any costs which he is ordered to pay are paid out of the fund, as are his own costs incurred on the intervention (reg 122).

If there is an objection or an application for review brought by him or any other party, a solicitor can still be heard, even if the assisted person himself has no interest in the taxation (reg 117). If the assisted person does not have any interest in the taxation or would but for reg 118 have an adverse interest in it, the solicitor must, in making an objection or applying for a review, ensure that all matters which it is proper to take into account are placed before the taxing master or judge. The assisted person, cannot be required to make any contribution to the fund in respect of the costs of any proceedings, under the regulations governing objections, reviews and appeals as to costs. Nor does the statutory charge apply to any increase in the net liability of the fund, arising out of the costs of such proceedings (reg 118(*b*) and (*c*)). These provisions ensure that the assisted person does not lose financially as a result of a dispute over costs.

These provisions concerning contribution and the statutory charge, also apply if the assisted person does have an interest in the taxation, but then his or her solicitor must explain the extent of that interest to the client, and the steps which can be taken to safeguard it. If requested so to do by the assisted person, he must give notice to the taxing officer that the assisted person has an interest (reg 119).

The costs of proceedings relating to objections, reviews and appeals under regs 113 to 119 are to be paid out of the fund, and are deemed to be proceedings to which the certificate relates, even if it has been discharged or revoked.

(d) Costs of applications, reports and notices

The costs of any application made under Pt XIII of the Act (regs 59 to 64) for the Board's prior authority for certain types of expenditure, and of any report made by a solicitor under Pt IX (regs 65 to 73) which includes reports relating to abuses of the scheme, progress of proceedings, changes of circumstances and completion of the case are to be taxed on the standard basis (reg 111).

Costs incurred in giving notice of extension of an emergency certificate of issue, amendment, revocation or discharge of a full certificate shall be costs in the cause, as shall costs incurred in determining the amount of an assisted person's liability under s 17 of the Act, where an order for costs has been made against him (reg 111).

(e) Time limits for issue of certificate or allocatur

Without the agreement of the parties, the certificate or allocatur cannot be signed until twenty-one days after the taxing officer's decision, or fourteen days after the date of endorsement of the bill, as to the notice due to counsel under Regulation 112. If a solicitor applies for authority to carry an objection or for a review, either of his own costs or of counsel's fees, he must do so before expiry of the time allowed by rules of court (reg 121(1)). Similarly where there is an application under reg 115 for authority to appeal, the application must be made before expiry of the time allowed for an appeal from a judge's decision (reg 115(3)), and time is extended by one month for that purpose. If the application is for an authority for an objection or for a review, time is extended by one month or such longer period as the taxing master may allow.

4 Costs against an assisted person

Assisted persons are in a privileged position with regard to costs, when compared to the privately funded litigant, in that if the assisted person succeeds, an order for costs will be made on exactly the same principles as if he were not legally aided. If he is unsuccessful he is protected by s 17 of the Act as to the amount of any costs which can be recovered from him. Section 17(1) of the Act limits an assisted person's liability for costs to an amount which it is reasonable for him to pay, having regard to all the circumstances, including the financial resources of all the parties and their conduct in connection with the dispute. Refusal to accept a payment into court where a greater sum was not eventually awarded, is relevant as to conduct for this purpose.

If the assisted person's means are such that he can afford to pay the whole or part of the costs, bearing in mind the factors set out in s 17(1) the court will order him to do so, but if they are not, then no order for costs will be made against him.

A litigant assisted or otherwise should always be properly and carefully advised, if necessary by counsel, when any payment is made into court. The result of failing to give that advice or of an assisted person failing to accept it, could be that the damages which he recovers are subject to the statutory charge for his own costs and in addition, assuming that they are sufficient, he may well have to resort to them to satisfy an order made against him for costs incurred after the payment in.

The assisted person has a further advantage over the privately funded litigant, in that his dwellinghouse, clothes, household furniture and the tools and implements of his trade cannot be taken into account in assessing his financial resources, except in so far as they can be taken into account by the assessment officer in determining his disposable income and capital, when considering his liability to costs. These items cannot be subject to execution, nor to any corresponding process to enforce an order for costs (s 17(3) of the Legal Aid Act 1988 and reg 126(*b*) of the General Regulations 1989.

A party who is not an assisted person may file an affidavit exhibiting a statement of means for the purposes of his resources being determined under s 17(1). A copy of the affidavit and exhibit must be served on the assisted person's solicitor, who must send a copy to the Area Director (reg 125). Both the assisted person and any party who has filed an affidavit of means may be required by the court to attend for an oral examination (reg 128). The court also has power to postpone and adjourn the determination and to refer it to a master, registrar or clerk of parliaments, or in a summary case or on appeal from the Crown Court to the justices clerk or the chief clerk, for an investigation of any relevant facts and with a requirement to report the findings back (reg 127).

Once the amount of the order has been determined, the court decides the manner of payment which may be by instalments or such other manner as the court thinks reasonable. It can even think it reasonable to order that no payment should be made immediately, or that the assisted person should have no liability for payment. Payment may be suspended, even indefinitely (reg 129).

The party in whose favour an order for costs is made, but not the assisted person against whom it is made, can within six years from the date on which it was made, apply for it to be varied. The grounds on which an application for variation can be made are that:

(1) material additional information is available as to the assisted person's means which could not with reasonable diligence have been obtained by that party when the order was made; or

(2) the assisted person's means have changed since the making of the order.

The court may vary the order as it thinks fit, but its decision is final and there is no right of appeal (reg 130).

The personal resources of a person acting in a representative, fiduciary or official capacity are not to be taken into account in making an order for costs against an assisted person, unless there is a reason to the contrary. Regard has to be paid, however, to the value of the property, money or estate out of which the representative etc is entitled to be indemnified (reg 131). If the assisted person is a minor, the court can take into account, for the purpose of an order for costs against him under s 17(1), the resources of any person whose resources were taken into account by the assessment officer in assessing disposable income and disposable capital (reg 132). A guardian ad litem or next friend of a minor or patient has the protection of s 17(1), but for the purposes of reg 132, his means are taken as being the means of the minor or patient.

Save for the exceptions referred to above, the Regulations do not provide for financial resources of anybody other than the assisted person to be taken into account in determining a costs order, even though there may be a person such as a spouse or cohabitee whose means have been taken into account by the assessment officer. The means of such persons may however affect the resources of the assisted person, for example by contribution to rent or mortgage payments or to general living expenses. The principles applied in *Adams and Another* v *Riley* [1988] 1 All ER 89 with regard to costs orders against the Board should be considered in this respect.

The Area Director and the unassisted party have the right to appear at any hearing or enquiry. The Area Director but not the unassisted party may make written representations which must be supported by a sworn affidavit and sent to the court and to the unassisted party, not less than seven days before the hearing or enquiry (reg 136).

5 Orders for costs against the Board

Without some sanction against the Board an unassisted litigant would be at a distinct disadvantage against a legally aided opponent who would, for all practical purposes, be backed by limitless funds provided by the state. Section 18 of the Act gives power to a court to make an order for the Board to pay the costs to an unassisted party where proceedings to which a legally assisted person is a party, are finally decided in favour of that unassisted party. From the Board's point of view this is an extremely cogent reason why it should not support the initiation or continuation of fruitless litigation, nor of litigation which the assisted person wishes to continue or to be conducted, unreasonably. It is for this reason that many certificates are limited in the first instance for the Board's own protection as well as the protection of the assisted person, to obtaining counsel's opinion. It is also one of the reasons behind the regulations which impose duties on solicitors acting for assisted persons, to provide reports and information to the Board during proceedings.

An order against the Board under s 18 can only be made:

(1) after the court has considered what order for costs should be made against the assisted person and determining his liability in respect thereof;

(2) if an order for costs would be made normally but for the provisions of the Act;

(3) if, where the costs are incurred in a court of first instance, the provisions are instituted by the assisted party and the unassisted party will suffer severe financial hardship unless the order is made; and

(4) in any case it is just and equitable in all the circumstances that provision for costs should be made out of public funds (LAA 1988, s 18(3) and (4)).

The affect of (3) above is that severe financial hardship does not have to be established where the order is sought in an Appellate Court. The Divisional Court can never in any circumstances be called a Court of first instance and it can therefore make an order for an unassisted parties costs to be paid out of the legal aid fund (*R* v *Leeds County Court ex parte Morris* [1990] 1 All ER 550).

If severe financial hardship is established by the unassisted party, he is only entitled to payment from the Board of the amount which would cause that hardship and not of the whole of his costs. The capital and income of his spouse are not to be aggregated with his means in determining whether he would suffer severe financial hardship, but they can be taken into account to the extent that they relieve him from the need to provide day to day financial support for the spouse and is therefore in a better position to pay his own costs, than is a person who had a dependent spouse (*Adams and Another* v *Riley* [1988] 1 All ER 89). If no regard at all was paid to the spouse's resources, the regulations would not have provided that they must be included in the unassisted party's affidavit of costs and resources.

There is no appeal against the making of or the refusal to make a costs order under s 18, save on a point of law.

For the purposes of s 18(1):

(1) 'costs' means party and party costs, but where a party is an assisted person for only part of the proceedings, the order can only relate to the costs of the unassisted party in that part of the proceedings (LAA 1988, s 18(6));

(2) any proceedings in respect of which a separate certificate could be issued (not 'has been' issued) shall be treated as separate proceedings (reg 134(2));

(3) proceedings are to be treated as finally decided in favour of the unassisted party:

(*a*) if no appeal lies against the decision in his favour; or

(*b*) on expiry of the time limit for application for leave to appeal, without leave having been granted; or

(*c*) if leave to appeal is granted or is not required and no appeal is brought within the time limit for an appeal (s 18(7));

(4) 'court' includes a tribunal (LAA 1988, s 18(9)).

If an appeal is brought out of time by the unassisted party, the Appeal Court can order him to repay the whole or any part of any costs paid to him by the Board pursuant to an order under s 18 (LAA 1988, s 18(7)).

The Area Director has the same right to appear as does the unassisted party, and to make written representations as on a hearing or enquiry in connection with a costs order against the assisted person (reg 136). Where an appeal does lie against a decision in favour of an unassisted party, a court other than a county court can make or refuse to make an order forthwith for costs against the Board, but an order made forthwith cannot take effect until the proceedings are finally decided in accordance with the definitions in section 18(7)(*b*) and (*c*).

(a) Procedure for orders made by the county court

A county court cannot make an order forthwith, but may in its discretion adjourn or dismiss the application or refer it to the Registrar of that court for hearing and determination (reg 138).

If a county court does adjourn the hearing of an application for costs against the Board, it may still refer it to the registrar for enquiry and report under reg 140, as opposed to hearing and determination where the application is immediately referred to the registrar under reg 183(*b*). Where a referral to the registrar is made following an adjournment for him to make an enquiry and report, the court must serve a copy of the order on the unassisted person. Within twenty-one days of the order or such longer time as the court allows, the unassisted party must file an affidavit of costs and resources together with any exhibits and a copy. The court serves a copy of the order and of the affidavit of costs on the Area Director (reg 140).

As soon as that has been done, the registrar must give not less than twenty-one days notice of the hearing date to the Area Director and to the unassisted party. The registrar who has the same power as a taxing officer under the county court rule, must give a written report to the court and send a copy to the Area Director and the unassisted party. A hearing date is then fixed by the court for determining the application and twenty-one days notice thereof is given to the Area Director and to the unassisted party (reg 141).

If a county court refers the application to the registrar for hearing and determination under regulation 138(*a*) or adjourns it without referring it to the registrar for enquiry and report, the procedure is governed by reg 142. The unassisted party must file his affidavit within twenty-one days of the adjournment and not less than twenty-one days before the adjourned hearing the court serves a copy of the affidavit and notice of the hearing date on the Area Director. At the hearing the registrar makes his determination without any report back to the court.

(b) In the Supreme Court and House of Lords

If an application for an order for costs against the Board is made in the Supreme Court, other than on appeal from a county court or in the House of Lords, an order cannot be made forthwith, and there is the same power as under reg 138 to make a referral or adjourn or dismiss the application. The referral is to a master or registrar, which in the case of the Court of Appeal means the registrar of civil appeals, and in the Employment Appeal Tribunal or restrictive practices court, the registrar of that tribunal or court.

If the court adjourns the application it can refer it to the master for enquiry and report. Within twenty-one days of the order or such longer time as the registrar allows, the unassisted party must file his affidavit of costs and resources, lodge a copy of the order, affidavit and original exhibits thereto with the master and serve copies on the Area Director. The Area Director and the unassisted person must then be given twenty-one days notice of the date and time of the enquiry. When the enquiry is completed the master makes a written report to the court and sends copies to the unassisted person and to the Area Director. It is the duty of the unassisted person to seek an appointment for the hearing to be determined in chambers and must give the Area Director not less than twenty-one days notice (reg 145 and 146).

Where the application is adjourned by the court without a referral for enquiry and report, or where it is referred for a hearing and determination under reg 143 (i) (a) the unassisted person must file his affidavit within twenty-one days of the adjournment. Not less than twenty-one days before the adjourned hearing he must serve notice of it on the Area Director, together with a copy of his affidavit (reg 147). There is a right of appeal to a judge in chambers, but only on a point of law and only where the matter has been referred by the court to a master for hearing and determination under reg 143(i)(a).

6 Costs orders and ABWOR

A person who has the benefit of assistance by way of representation is not an assisted person for the purposes of the Civil Legal Aid (General) Regulations 1989, and the provisions of those applications relating to the application for costs against an assisted person do not apply, nor do the regulations relating to applications for costs against the Board.

For the purposes of those regulations a person having the benefit of ABWOR is not in receipt of legal aid under Part IV of the Act. The award of costs against a person who has received ABWOR at a court, tribunal or statutory enquiry is dealt with separately in s 12 of the Act and reg 34 and Sched 5 of the Advice and Assistance Regulations 1989.

The award of costs against the Board where proceedings to which a person who receives ABWOR is a party, and where those proceedings are finally decided in favour of an unassisted party is governed by s 13 of the Act.

7 Costs orders and summary jurisdiction certificates

Where an assisted person has legal aid for authorised summary proceedings in a magistrates' court, ie for any of the proceedings set out in Pt I of Sched 2 to the Act, an order for costs can be made against him pursuant to s 17 of the Act and reg 124 of the General Regulations 1989. There is no requirement for the unassisted party to file an affidavit of means (reg 125(1)), and there is no power for a magistrates' court to refer the application to the clerk to the justices, although a court hearing an appeal from a magistrates' court may do so (reg 127(1)). The power of a magistrates' court is therefore limited to making the order subject to the provisions of s 17 and the relevant parts of regs 124 to 133 of the General Regulations 1989.

The Regulations relating to applications for costs against the Board do apply in respect of authorised summary proceedings, and the magistrates do have power to adjourn the hearing as well as to grant the application forthwith or dismiss it. If it is adjourned, the unassisted party must swear an affidavit of costs and resources, a copy of which must be served on the Area Director, together with notice as to the date of the adjourned hearing, not less than twenty-one days before that hearing (reg 137). The original affidavit must be produced at the hearing.

8 Contents of an affidavit of resources

The matters which have to be included in an Affidavit of costs and resources are set out in Schedule 2 to the General Regulations 1989 which is reproduced below. Schedule 2 only applies to an Affidavit required to be filed in connection with an application for costs against the Board. It does not apply to the affidavit required to be filed by an unassisted person in connection with an application for costs against an assisted person which is an affidavit of means.

SCHEDULE 2
MATTERS TO BE INCLUDED IN AN AFFIDAVIT OF COSTS AND RESOURCES

(1) An estimate of the unassisted party's inter partes costs of the proceedings in respect of which his application is made, supported by—
  (a) particulars of the estimated costs in the form of a summary bill of costs; and
  (b) all necessary documentary evidence to substantiate each item in the bill.

(2) A statement, supported by evidence, of the unassisted party's financial resources of every kind during the period beginning three years before his application is made, and of his estimated future financial resources and expectations.

(3) A declaration that to the best of his knowledge and belief the unassisted party has not, and at any relevant time has not had and will not have any financial resources or expectations not specified in the statement described in paragraph 2 above.

(4) A declaration that the unassisted party has not at any time deliberately foregone or deprived himself of any financial resources or expectations with a view to furthering his application.

(5) A statement supported by evidence of the unassisted party's reasonable financial commitments during the period covered by his statement described in paragraph 2 above, including, if desired, his estimated solicitor and own client costs of the proceedings in respect of which his application is made.

(6)—(1) If the unassisted party has, or at any relevant time has had, a spouse, his statements and declarations described in paragraphs 2 to 5 above shall also take account of and (to the best of his knowledge and belief) specify that spouse's financial resources, expectations and commitments, unless he or she had a contrary interest to the unassisted party in the proceedings in respect of which his application is made, or the unassisted party and his spouse are or at the relevant time were living separate and apart, or for some other reason it would be either inequitable or impracticable for the unassisted party to comply with the requirements of this paragraph.

(2) Paragraph (1) shall apply to a man and woman who are living with each other in the same household as husband and wife as it applies to the parties to a marriage.

(7) Full particulars of any application for legal aid made by the unassisted party in connection with the proceedings in respect of which his application is made, including the date and reference number of any such application and the Area Director to whom it was made.

Index